THE CLEAN PLATES COOKBOOK

Sustainable, Delicious, and Healthier Eating for Every Body

By Jared Koch with Jill Silverman Hough

RUNNING PRESS
PHILADELPHIA · LONDON

ISBN 978-0-7624-4647-6
Library of Congress Control Number: 2012930286

E-book ISBN 978-0-7624-4684-1

9   8   7   6   5   4   3   2   1
Digit on the right indicates the number of this printing

Edited by Kristen Green Wiewora
Typography: Scala and Neutra

Running Press Book Publishers
2300 Chestnut Street
Philadelphia, PA 19103–4371

Visit us on the web!
www.runningpresscooks.com

*To anyone and everyone working to improve our
food system by growing, transporting, preparing, eating,
writing about, or advocating for better-quality food.*

Acknowledgments

It truly amazes me how many hard working, talented people it takes to create something. I am very grateful to have had the opportunity to collaborate with so many of you on this project—and I admire, respect, and appreciate all of your contributions.

First and foremost, I want to express my deep gratitude to Jill Silverman Hough for working tirelessly in the kitchen creating amazingly fun and delicious recipes, and for consistently offering her wisdom in so many areas throughout the process. Jill and I would also like to thank her fantastic group of recipe testers, angels who generously spent their free time to help us do our work—Lori Adleman, Kate Aks, Kay Austin, Melissa Austin, Lori Bowling, Claudia Brown, John Danby, Lynn Forsey, Susi and Paul Heidenreich, the Javier Guerrero Family, Terri Hughes, Jan Kroeger, Michael and Lanniece Hall, the McIver Family, Deirdre Spero Nair, Susan Norman, Alexander Ocker, Susan Pruett, Hilary and Mike Rak, Lisa and Richard Rhoan, Keven Seaver, Charlene Small, Andrea Stupka, and Suzanne Young. Thank you so very much.

Of course, a very special thank you to the talented chefs who contributed recipes, as well as for their dedication to serving healthy and delicious food—Michael Anthony of Gramercy Tavern, Jeremy Bearman of Rouge Tomate, Ed Cotton of Plein Sud and now, Fishtail by David Burke, Marc Forgione of Marc Forgione, Ann Gentry of Real Food Daily, Daniel Holzman and Michael Chernow of The Meatball Shop, Sarma Mengalis of Pure Food and Wine and One Lucky Duck, Jamie Oliver, Joy Pierson of Candle 79 and Candle Café, Hadley Schmitt of Northern Spy, Shigefumi Tachibe and Lee Gross of M Cafe, and Bill Telepan of Telepan.

To our agent Jennifer Griffin at Miller Bowers Griffin and to Kristen Green Wiewora and the entire team at Running Press, our deepest gratitude for making this possible and for caring so much about it along the way.

A big thank you to Ashley Spivak, CNP (www.figandgruyere.com) for helping in countless ways. And to Ellen Daly for helping to shape my ideas and making me a better writer. And to Angela Starks and the late, but not forgotten, Bunny Wong for their invaluable contributions.

Thank you to Megan Murphy for facilitating the chef recipes and writing their introductions.

Thanks to Nicole Fiscella, MS, CNS, for her invaluable nutritional feedback and suggestions.

Thanks to the rest of the team at Clean Plates, including but not limited to Niles Brooks, Laura Mordas-Schenkein, and Tory Davis, for their dedication and efforts toward realizing the Clean Plates mission.

I also want to thank my nutrition and science teachers throughout my journey, including but in no way limited to Deepak Chopra, Andrew Weil, Mark Hyman, and Joshua Rosenthal, as well as my spiritual teacher Andrew Cohen and everyone at EnlightenNext. In countless and unimaginable ways, you have shaped my thinking.

Perhaps my greatest teachers of all, however, have been my clients. Through their willingness to be vulnerable and their commitment to improving their lives, they have deepened my understanding of what leads to change. My sincere thanks to each and every one of you.

Jill adds her appreciation to her husband, family, and friends for their love and support, in this and all things.

And of course, a heartfelt thanks to my dear family and friends, who fill my life with love and joy every day.

Contents

Introduction

IN MORE THAN A DECADE OF STUDYING NUTRITION, health, and meditation and my many years working as a nutritional consultant, I've discovered one key to improving my clients' well-being and enabling them to eat healthier and feel better. It's not a miracle diet, or a superfood, or a scientific breakthrough. It's simply this: *practical advice*. As a culture, we tend to be obsessed with *what* we should eat, but we rarely stop and look practically at *how* we eat. Of course, what we eat matters—a lot—but simply knowing what's good for us won't necessarily get us to change our deep-rooted habits. Most people do not hesitate to say they want to eat healthier, and many can even explain what foods they should be eating, but actually doing it, consistently, is another matter altogether. What I have discovered with my clients is that when I give them practical advice and tools for making better choices, they start to change immediately.

It all began with my restaurant list. I live and work in Manhattan—a city of over twenty-four thousand restaurants. New Yorkers like to dine out—but often they pay the price with their health. I believed that it was possible to eat healthier and still enjoy the culinary diversity of NYC. I wanted to be smart about my food choices without having to sacrifice the pleasure of eating. So I started compiling a list of what I considered to be healthy restaurants— places I could eat with no sacrifice and no guilt. As I shared this ever-growing list with my clients, they actually started implementing changes and feeling better—a fact that inspired me to turn my list into a book: *Clean Plates Manhattan*. I expanded my research, hired an amazing food critic, and set out to create a restaurant guide that told New Yorkers where they could go to find food that was healthy, sustainable, *and* delicious.

Three years later, my original guide is in its third edition, *Clean Plates Brooklyn* and *Clean Plates Los Angeles* have launched, we have a new website (www.cleanplates.com) and iPhone app, and more guides are on their way. But I also found that readers want a way to bring my practical approach to nutrition and diet into their home, their trips to the grocery store, and all the places where they make their food choices each day. That's what this book is about. I see it as a way to contribute to a growing awareness of healthy, responsible, and sustainable eating, and most important, to empower people to make better choices.

After intensively studying nutritional science and dietary theories, learning from experts in the field, observing and talking to hundreds of people at my talks and events, and coaching individual clients from all walks of life, I want to offer what I think is a reasonable assessment of the nutrition landscape. While my approach is informed by the very latest discoveries in health and nutrition, this book is intentionally light on science. It is meant to be practical. I read countless nutritional studies, and understand how they are conducted and evaluated. And this has only confirmed my belief that while studies can be very helpful, they are also limited. I can almost guarantee that for any study you find, there is another that directly contradicts it. One expert will declare, based on his extensive research, that you must eat meat to get enough essential protein. Another will insist that a raw, vegan diet is the only one that offers the nutrients you need. Who is right?

I would suggest that, in fact, this is not the most important question. Too many of us are just seeking "the answer"—the perfect diet that will allow us to finally stop worrying about what we eat. What you will learn in these pages is that there's more than one right way to eat—a theory called bio-individuality. In keeping with that principle, this book is not a diet book. It is a guide to help you navigate the vast cultural experiment that is taking place around food and nutrition, and learn how to independently make better, more informed choices for yourself. My goal is to bring a rational and practical approach to this confusing topic, free from stress, fear, and guilt. Our relationship with food is one of the most intimate relationships we have, but it is often fraught with these unhealthy emotions. I hope that this book will help you not only to figure out how to eat healthier, but also to have a healthier relationship to food.

This book is divided into three parts. In Chapters 1–8, I will share with you my approach to nutrition, and the Five Precepts that I use as guiding principles in making healthy choices, as well as a practical guide to the different kinds of foods you are likely to encounter. In Chapter 9, you will find more than 120 recipes that you can prepare at home, including contributions from some of our favorite Clean Plates chefs and restaurants, such as Jamie Oliver, *Iron Chef* winner Marc Forgione, and many more. Using ingredients that are easily available at most supermarkets, these recipes are designed to help you thoroughly enjoy and celebrate clean eating. And in Chapter 10, you will find practical resources and recommendations to support you in making the transition to a healthier lifestyle and sample menus to help guide you in planning your meals.

You will see my personal leanings sprinkled throughout this book, but my goal is not to impose them on you. Most people I meet want to know what conclusions I've come to myself and what choices I've made. I consider myself an experiment, and I hope that my example will inspire you not to simply adopt my conclusions, but to experiment with your own diet in the same way. Together, let's shatter the myth that healthier eating is a sacrifice and prove that we can do it without the guilt, inconvenience, boredom, and sheer lack of long-term success that characterize the usual diets.

Remember, the goal in life is not to have the perfect diet. The goal is to eat food that supports the body rather than depletes it, and to have a healthy relationship with food, free of guilt and full of pleasure, so you have the energy and clarity of mind and time to live life to your fullest potential.

In good health,

Jared Koch

CHAPTER 1

Clean Eating: The Practical Approach to Food

"I'VE BEEN A VEGAN ALL MY LIFE," SAID THE YOUNG woman in line ahead of me at Whole Foods, looking at me earnestly over her cart piled high with vegetables. "Did you know that the animals slaughtered for food adds up to more than nine billion per year in the United States alone? It's a genocide going on right under our noses! And did you know that it's been scientifically proven that eating animal products causes heart disease, cancer, and diabetes?" I listened sympathetically, but did not attempt to hide the pasture-raised eggs and grass-fed beef in my cart. Later that same night, at a party, I found myself talking to an athletic-looking man in his forties who told me his life had been completely transformed by adopting a diet of meat and vegetables, rejecting grains and all processed foods. "It's the way evolution designed us to eat," he told me. "It's written in our genes. Our Paleolithic ancestors ate this way. It's been scientifically proven: This is what is best for the human body." Again, I listened sympathetically, but did not reject the brown rice sushi when it came my way.

Most people reading this book have probably had moments like these.

Different people we meet will confidently give us completely contradictory advice, absolutely convinced that theirs is the only "right" answer, and backed up with seemingly credible scientific evidence. We tend to get our ideas about food from our family, our friends, and above all, the media. Every time our children sit down in front of the television, they are getting nutritional messages. Their heroes are promoting certain products, and so the message is clear: Drinking soda will make you a superstar athlete. We're conditioned to want these processed products and even to believe that they are good for us. Even the health foods industry can be misleading—promoting such terms as *organic, vegan,* or *local* as if they guarantee that a food is good for you. Just because a cupcake is vegan doesn't necessarily make it healthy. Organic sugar is still sugar. Adding to all this misinformation are the recommendations of our government via the USDA. While I was encouraged recently to hear that the USDA had changed its requirements for school cafeterias to include more vegetables, I was less than encouraged when I discovered that pizza is classified as a vegetable because the small amount of tomato paste on the pizza is enough tomato to constitute a vegetable (regardless of sugar content in that paste). Clearly, we have a long way to go.

When I started studying nutrition more than ten years ago I was immediately struck by the lack of knowledge (both my own and society's) on the subject. Even most doctors are not well educated on the subject. As a second-year internal medicine resident at UCSD told me recently, "A healthy diet is increasingly accepted as a fundamental pillar of health and yet education on healthy eating in Western medical schools and during subsequent training continues to be subpar." Nutrition is a relatively new science. There is so much waiting to be discovered. Every plant contains thousands of nutrients, and each of these has different properties and effects, and interacts with our body and with other nutrients in unique ways. Every new process we use to produce, prepare, preserve, and present our food changes its nutritional makeup. When you consider how many questions are still unanswered, it is hardly surprising that there is such an abundance of conflicting information. Adding to the confusion is the fact that many of the studies are evaluated based on particular biases and are funded by organizations with an investment in particular outcomes.

We hear about new nutritional studies every day, it seems, from the frightening ("Inflammatory Food Toxins Found in High Levels in Infants") to the ridiculous ("Chocolate Cake for Breakfast Helps You to Lose Weight"). But there is a much larger experiment going on in our culture right now—one that too few of us seem to be aware of, but that we are all part of. What effect does eating a diet of highly processed and chemically produced foods have on the human body? This experiment began back in the Industrial Age, when human beings in the more developed parts of the world discovered new ways to process foods. Rather than cooking and eating things in the forms in which they grew from the land, we outsourced food preparation to industry, which, through large-scale processing, altered the very nature of what we were used to eating. With the population shifting from the rural farmlands to the fast-growing cities, this was an essential wave of innovation, enabling more and more people to have affordable access to food at greater distances from the farms where it was grown. Centuries later, the results of this experiment are written all around us, and you don't need to be a scientist to interpret them. The incidence of all major diseases is increasing and they seem to be showing up more frequently at younger ages. Obesity is becoming an epidemic.[1] According to *CBS News*, more than 190 million Americans are overweight or obese, and obesity-related diseases cost $147 billion in medical expenses every year.[2] Childhood obesity has tripled in the last thirty years.[3] Diabetes is increasingly common, affecting 25.8 million children and adults in the United States—8.3 percent of the population.[4] Children suffer from all kinds of allergies that we have never even seen before.[5]

This is the study we should be paying most attention to: the one we are all participating in. Experts may be arguing about whether a low-fat or a low-carb diet is the way to go, or whether vegans live longer than omnivores, but they all agree on some things, whether they state it or not. For example, I've never seen a study that says vegetables will harm you. No one is arguing for the health benefits of refined sugars. And most experts agree that it would be good for most of us to eat a lot less overall. No one has "the answer," but we have a lot of information that can help us make better choices. Of course, much of that information seems to conflict, but when we have some basic guiding principles to help us navigate, we can start to take greater responsibility for our daily decisions. That's the approach this book is based on. It's a common sense and rational assessment of the nutrition landscape as far we can see it, organized in such a way as to give those who want to be healthier the practical tools and advice for making better choices in daily life, free from stress, fear, and guilt.

What Is "Clean" Eating?

One of the greatest challenges we face in navigating the maze of nutritional choices is a lack of clear criteria to base our choices on. Many of us simply choose foods because we like how they taste. Others make choices based on what they think is good for their health. And these days, an increasing number of people recognize the impact of food production on animals and the environment, and make choices based on minimizing their negative effects. I think all of these criteria are important. I don't think we should have to sacrifice taste for the sake of health. And I don't think our planet should have to sacrifice to feed us. That's how I came up with my definition of "clean" eating, and the criteria on which I base my nutritional advice and the restaurant reviews in my Clean Plates guides.

Clean eating, as I define it, is eating that's good for your health, good for the planet, and good tasting. In other words: *healthy, sustainable, and delicious.* For many, the idea of healthy eating often evokes images of bland vegetarian food. For me, clean eating transcends the issue of whether you are a vegan or a vegetarian or an omnivore. It means eating high-quality real food as often as possible, based on what is right for your body and what stimulates your taste buds. Over the years, I have boiled down my advice for how to achieve this into Five Precepts, which I'll be explaining in depth, and with plenty of practical tools and advice, in the chapters that follow:

1. There's more than one right way to eat.
2. The overwhelming majority of your diet should consist of real, high-quality, and whole foods.
3. Everyone would be better off if a larger percentage of their diet consisted of plants—mostly vegetables (in particular, leafy greens), and some nuts, seeds, and fruits.
4. If you choose to eat animal products, consume only (a) high-quality and sustainably raised animals (ideally pasture-raised and grass-fed, but at least hormone- and antibiotic-free); and do so (b) in moderation—meaning smaller portions with less frequency, and (c) cooked using the most healthful methods.
5. To feel better immediately, simply reduce your intake of artificial, chemical-laden processed foods—especially poor-quality oils and refined sugars.

If this sounds like a lot to take in, don't worry. I'll be walking through each of these precepts slowly and practically. But first, take the time to think about why you would want to embark on this journey. It might be for personal reasons, such as improving your own health or looking better. It might be for the sake of your family. Or it might be for altruistic or ethical reasons, such as saving the environment or not supporting the factory farming of animals. Whatever your motivation is, make sure it is powerful enough to inspire you. Let's take a quick look at just a few of the reasons you might want to embrace this way of eating.

Clean Eating Is Good for Your Health

Financial columnists like to point out that ordering a $3 latte every day adds up to $1,000 a year that otherwise could have been accruing interest in a CD. Our daily food choices operate according to similar principles; instead of just building up our financial assets, however, we need to build our health resources.

To illustrate: You wake up, yawn, get dressed, and (A) start the day with a cup of herbal tea or glass of water with lemon to accompany your bowl of oatmeal and fruit; or (B) purchase a coffee with sugar on your way to work, skipping breakfast. Later the same day, you and your co-workers order in (A) wild salmon with vegetables and brown rice; or (B) fast-food hamburgers and fries. You get the picture: Going for option A adds multiple nutrients to your health resources, whereas option B is taxing your already depleted nutrient resource bank.

Our health may be affected more by the foods we eat than by any other factor. I think that's great news, as it means we can do something about it. Of course, exercise, sleep, and genetics—not to mention our relationships, career, and spirituality—count, too. But the reason "You are what you eat" has endured as a phrase is because what we consume literally builds, fuels, cleanses, or—unfortunately—pollutes our cells.

Clean Eating Is Good for the Environment

Whether you choose to be vegetarian or not, there's no question that eating fewer animal products—poultry, beef, fish, dairy, and eggs— is a powerful way to help the Earth. Precious resources in the form of water, land, and energy are consumed in the process of producing animal foods. For example, it takes about 600 gallons of water to produce the meat for just one hamburger.[6] That's more water than the average hot tub holds. And it takes ten times more fossil fuels to produce a meat-based diet than a plant-based one—a statistic that led the United Nations to declare, "Raising animals for food generates more greenhouse gases than all the cars and trucks in the world combined." And then there's the waste . . . just imagine the amount of sewage generated by farm animals, which outnumber the planet's humans three times over.

Going organic is another way to positively change the environmental impact of your food choices. More toxic than ever before, pesticides and herbicides contaminate the soil, water, and air, which in turn poison both humans and wildlife.

Choosing locally grown foods when possible reduces the need for packaging, the production of which wreaks its own havoc on the environment, plus it avoids the pollution created by the long-distance treks that much of our food takes. Barbara Kingsolver's *Animal, Vegetable, Miracle* puts it this way, "If every U.S. citizen ate just one meal a week composed of locally and organically raised meats and produce, we would reduce our country's oil consumption by over 1.1 million barrels of oil every week."

Steering clear of genetically modified organisms, a.k.a. GMOs, can alleviate some environmental concern. These artificially altered crops cross-contaminate other crops and harm wildlife. The majority of soy (as in tofu), corn, and canola crops are now GMO plants. If these items are staples in your diet, you can tread more gently on the Earth (and your body) by buying organic versions, which are not genetically modified.

In addition, clean eating can have a powerful impact on the economic environment that affects all of us. For example, economists from Cornell and Lehigh universities have estimated that obesity is now responsible for 17 percent of America's annual medical costs, which amounts to about $160 billion per year. Reducing the waste and health costs associated with food production and poor dietary habits is the kind of economic stimulus I'll vote for.

A WORD OF CAUTION

Just because locally grown and organic foods are better for the environment doesn't mean they're always healthier for our body. Locally grown organic sugarcane? Sorry, still sugar to your body.

Clean Eating Is Good for Your Taste Buds

Our taste buds have been desensitized by a lifetime of eating over-salted, oversweetened, chemically enhanced foods. Artificial sweeteners such as Splenda are up to six hundred times sweeter than sugar—is it any wonder that we find it hard to enjoy the simple sweetness of a plum? As you begin to change your eating habits, you will slowly become more sensitive to the subtlety of flavors that are found in real foods. You will come to appreciate the fragrance of fresh herbs, crave the crispness of vegetables, and relish the piquancy of spices. Eventually, chemically enhanced foods will start to lose their appeal.

The pleasure we derive from eating is one of the great joys in life. Many of us associate healthy eating with the loss of that pleasure—seeing it as a sacrifice to be made for the sake of health or beauty. I don't believe this has to be the case. Eating is something we all do every day, and we want it to be a positive experience. If our relationship to food is defined by guilt, self-deprivation, or sacrifice, we create a negative state of mind, which has been proven to exacerbate some unhealthy patterns. For example, stress triggers the release of cortisol, a hormone that has been linked to higher blood pressure, weakened immune system functioning, and weight gain. Joy, on the other hand, creates a different hormonal balance in the body.

Think of your journey to clean eating not as a sacrifice, but as a re-education. Imagine that all the chemicals, oils, salts, and sugars have left a thick coating over your taste buds, numbing them to the subtleties of more natural flavors. Clean eating metaphorically cleans your taste buds of this coating, making them more sensitive and receptive to a whole new world of flavorful nuances. Instead of thinking about what you'll have to give up, think of all the undiscovered pleasures that await you. Before you know it, you'll be craving vegetables!

These benefits are just a few of the reasons you might decide to eat clean. Other factors could be financial (lower health-care bills) or professional (more energy and better health will improve your performance at work *and* release your creativity). It doesn't matter what your motivations are, as long as they are compelling *to you*.

1. Source: http://www.cbsnews.com/stories/2010/01/07/eveningnews/main6069163.shtml.
2. Source: RTI International, the Agency for Healthcare Research and Quality, and the U.S. Centers for Disease Control & Prevention, http://www.rti.org/news.cfm?objectid=329246AF-5056-B172-B829FC032B70D8DE.
3. Source: *F as in Fat: How Obesity Policies Are Failing in America 2009*, a report released by the Trust for America's Health (TFAH) and the Robert Wood Johnson Foundation (RWJF): http://healthyamericans.org/reports/obesity2009/.
4. Source: American Diabetes Association, 2011 National Diabetes fact sheet: http://www.diabetes.org/diabetes-basics/diabetes-statistics/.
5. According to the Centers for Disease Control, in 2007, about 3 million children under age 18 years of age (3.9 percent) were reported to have a food or digestive allergy.
6. Source: http://www.cnbc.com/id/39156898/there_s_how_much_water_in_my_hamburger?slide=4

CHAPTER 2

Bio-Individuality: Know Your Body

A FEW YEARS AGO, IN MY PRACTICE AS A NUTRITIONAL consultant, I was approached by a couple who were each close to weighing 300 pounds. They had committed to losing weight together and supporting each other in the process. For this reason, as well as financial considerations, they asked to do their sessions together, and while this is not normally how I work, I agreed. Some weeks later, after diligently following my recommendations, the wife was making good progress, but her husband was struggling. When I sat down one-on-one with him, it became clear that he did not share certain digestive issues and sensitivities to foods that his wife suffered from. My recommendations to cut out gluten and dairy were making her feel great, but for him they were too extreme, triggering counterproductive cravings. When I modified his diet to allow moderate portions of these foods, his cravings lessened, he was able to be more consistent, and he started seeing results quite quickly.

As a result of many cases like this, I've come to the conclusion that there *is* a dream diet for everyone—it's just not the same for each person. That brings me to the first, and most foundational, of my Five Precepts:

The First Precept: There's more than one right way to eat.

As nutrition pioneer Roger Williams writes in his groundbreaking 1950s book *Biochemical Individuality*, "If we continue to try to solve problems on the basis of the average man, we will be continually in a muddle. Such a man does not exist."

The old saying, "One man's meat is another man's poison," is not just metaphorical. When it comes to our dietary needs, we are not the same. We are all biochemically—genetically, hormonally, and so on—different. This simple fact might seem obvious, but it has been shockingly absent from the conversation around diet and nutrition until fairly recently. The United States Department of Agriculture's (USDA) "MyPlate," its predecessor, the food pyramid, and those recommended daily allowances (RDAs) you find on food labels are all created with the "average" person in mind. The $59.7-billion diet industry thrives on our craving for the perfect one-size-fits-all answer. The idea that a more individualized approach should guide our eating habits has only recently begun to excite the leading-edge medical and nutrition community. Experts are finally beginning to talk about the benefits of personalizing our diet rather than giving advice based on a nonexistent ideal—an approach known as biochemical individuality (or bio-individuality).

When was the last time you listened to what your body was telling you over and above the messages in the TV ads featuring a celebrity model with a completely different lifestyle, body type, and genetic background than yours? When it comes to almost any other arena of life, we accept, and even celebrate, our differences. Let's bring that same attitude to our approach to food. Let's honor and embrace the diversity of our bodies, our lifestyles, and our life cycles.

How We Differ

The principle of bio-individuality doesn't just mean that you are different from other people you know. Yes, if you sit at a computer all day, have a history of heart disease in your family, and are entering middle age, you have different dietary needs than does your twenty-something neighbor who owns a landscape design business and runs marathons. But there's more to it than that. It also means that you yourself have different needs in different circumstances. Bio-individuality manifests itself not only between individuals, but also between your different selves—your tired self, your active self, your stressed self, and your relaxed self. The key is to pay attention to how your body reacts to various foods and to what it's telling you at any given moment. Here are just a few of the factors that need to be considered:

- **Genetic makeup:** To a large extent, the anatomy and body chemistry that you inherited from your ancestors determine your nutritional needs and ability to benefit from particular foods. For example, a few recent studies have shown that some people possess the genetic ability to metabolize caffeine more efficiently than do others. Research has also revealed that specific groups of people have the genetic makeup to benefit from certain foods—for example, to absorb vitamin B_{12} with ease, or to benefit from broccoli's cancer-fighting nutrients—whereas others lack those genes.

- **Culture and background:** Your ethnicity and upbringing influence your genetics. For instance, some Americans have inherited a genetic ability to digest milk products, which was likely influenced by the fact that generations of their families have lived a traditional agricultural lifestyle, with plenty of dairy products on the menu.[1] Many Asians, however, are lactose intolerant, probably due to the fact that they were raised in cultures where milk is rarely part of the average family's diet, and has not been for generations. So it's helpful to consider which foods are part of your culture and background, and incorporate the appropriate ones into your diet.

- **Lifestyle:** A woman training for a triathlon requires different foods than does a person who does an hour of yoga each week. A construction worker, whose job involves strenuous physical activity, has different dietary needs than does a writer who sits at a desk for forty or fifty hours a week. The high-octane lifestyle of a globally mobile business executive demands different nutritional support than does the settled routine of a family. Sleep, stress, and emotional states, all a result of your lifestyle, can also play a significant role.

- **Day-to-day physical health:** Pay attention to your physical health symptoms to figure out what foods you need from one day to the next. Feeling under the weather? Miso soup may be just the thing. Sneezing constantly? Avoid dairy and sugar; the former causes the body to produce mucus and the latter weakens the immune system. Experiencing dramatic fluctuations in your energy and attention span? Make sure you are eating regularly, and avoid sweet foods—keeping your blood sugar levels steady could make all the difference.

- **Gender:** Whether you're a man or a woman affects your dietary needs. For example, menstruating women require more iron than do men, but men need more zinc than do their female counterparts to nourish their reproductive system.

- **Age:** A growing, active teen will be ravenous at dinnertime; the same person, sixty years later, will likely find that his or her appetite is waning. Children have different dietary needs at different stages in their development, as do adults. Don't assume you can just continue eating as you did in your twenties, when you are in your forties.

- **Seasons and climate:** Even the weather affects what's best for you to eat. When it's hot outside, the body will likely crave cooling foods such as salads; on a cold winter day, hot soup is more appealing. Some people, particularly advocates of the local foods movement, also like to pay attention to what foods are in season—although you can buy blueberries all year round, for example, eating them in December is not really what nature intended if you live in a cooler climate. Seasonal eating also results in food that is more flavorful, and leaves a smaller carbon footprint.

Eating as a Bio-Individual

The philosophy that no single way of eating is right for everyone isn't new. Both traditional Chinese medicine and India's ayurvedic system revolve around prescribing the most appropriate diet for specific categories of body types and constitutions.

More recent incarnations of these ancient approaches include the blood-type diet and metabolic typing. The blood-type diet was made famous a decade ago by naturopath Peter D'Adamo, who theorized (to put it very simply) that people with blood type O do best eating meat, but type As thrive as vegetarians, while type Bs do well with dairy products, and type ABs are generally more flexible. The thinking behind the discovery? Your blood type indicates which part of the world and which era in history your ancestors came from. Type Os descended from ancient hunters, whereas type As came from agricultural civilizations. Type Bs evolved later, in cultures that relied heavily on dairy products, and type ABs, as the most recently evolved blood group, are more adaptable. The idea behind metabolic typing (again, to put it simply) is that your metabolism dictates the appropriate percentage of proteins or carbohydrates in your diet; those who metabolize proteins well require extra animal foods, whereas others do better with more carbs.

Not everyone agrees with an individualized approach, especially when it comes to whether we should eat meat. Proponents of *The China Study*, a 2005 book by two nutritional biochemists who conducted a twenty-year survey of Chinese diets, argue that animal consumption is the leading cause of human disease; whereas followers of Weston A. Price, a dentist who carried out extensive health research in many countries, rely on culturally based studies to back up their claim that animal proteins and organ meats have benefits. Ultimately, the jury is still out (and probably always will be) on whether we have evolved to be omnivores or vegetarians. Although I do believe in the importance of our culture moving more toward a more plant-based diet, I have also observed that, whereas some people thrive on a vegetarian or vegan diet, others do not. Some people require (high-quality) animal protein to function optimally. Once again, we're not all the same, and if the experts can't agree on the merits of meat, it makes sense to listen to your own body.

I've come to espouse this approach through careful experimentation—on myself and in partnership with my clients. I grew up eating a typical standard American diet, and my food choices were guided simply by what I felt like in the moment. I suffered from quite an extreme case of irritable bowel syndrome (IBS) and was plagued by constant digestive issues as a child, but I never really connected the dots between my food choices and my health problems. It was only when I began to study nutrition that the connection became obvious to me. I began to experiment with my diet, and over time, completely healed myself of IBS.

During this process, I tried a raw food diet, experimented with macrobiotics, and went sugar-free, gluten-free, and dairy-free. I was vegetarian and vegan for approximately three years, but that never felt quite right. I liked the idea of being vegan, and felt that it aligned with my values and my environmental concerns, but my body seemed to be telling me that it wasn't enough. So in keeping with the concept of bio-individuality, I kept experimenting. When I started adding high-quality (grass-fed and pasture-raised) meat into my diet, I felt a lot better. Today, I am very happy with the way I eat, both in terms of health and enjoyment. And I satisfy my ethical and environmental concerns by paying close attention to how and where my meat is produced. I eat a lot of vegetables and fruits and a moderate amount of well-sourced animal foods. I use a lot of herbs and spices when I cook, and in general I limit my intake of dairy and grains. I eat very little processed food and consume almost no refined sugar, though I use some natural sweeteners. I'm not saying this diet would be right for everyone. But I am confident that you can find a way to eat that feels just as good for your body—a diet that keeps you healthy and makes you look forward to meal times.

What's Right for You?

When people hear the concept of bio-individuality, it usually makes intuitive sense right away. So much sense that people quickly want to know: How do I figure out what my body needs? How do I find the optimal diet for my unique set of circumstances? Is there a test I can take?

The answer I usually give is that yes, certainly diagnostic tests can help you. In fact, these are one of the great gifts of modern medicine. You can take blood tests for various nutrient levels, you can check for food sensitivities or allergies, you can analyze certain symptoms you may be experiencing, and you can undergo metabolic type testing. You may even want to take a DNA test to understand your particular ability to metabolize certain nutrients. All of these can provide helpful information. If you're dealing with more serious issues, I suggest seeking out a physician trained in functional medicine, a newer paradigm that takes into account the whole system, offers detailed diagnostic testing, and emphasizes nutrition and supplements over medicine (see Resources, page 284, for more information).

But to my mind, even more helpful, especially in the long run, is simply training yourself to pay attention. The most important thing I encourage all of my clients, and now you, to do is to listen to your body, experiment, and become ever more conscious of how you respond to different foods.

Here's an example of a simple experiment you can try. Breakfast, some people say, is the most important meal you eat, because it gives you the energy to start your day. So what you eat for breakfast is one of the key food choices you make. As a way of tuning into your body and learning to listen to its messages, try eating different breakfasts during the week. Write down what you eat, how you feel right after eating, and how many hours it takes until you are hungry again. Note how your energy level, moods, and physical symptoms are affected by your food choices.

Try each of these different breakfast categories for two to three days:

High Protein
Ideas: eggs or omelet with veggies; organic tempeh with veggies; organic plain yogurt or kefir

High Carb
Ideas: oatmeal with fruit

Mixed Protein/Carb
Ideas: oatmeal with nut butter and fruit; organic plain yogurt or kefir with fruit

Upon completion of this exercise, you will have insight into what the best choices are for you to start your day off well. You should get a clear sense of which kind of breakfast keeps you going longer and gives you the energy to do what you need to do. And perhaps even more important, you are training yourself to pay more attention to the impact of food on your body. Developing this mind-set is essential to transforming your relationship to food. Keep in mind that your needs and your physical responses may change over time or through lifestyle changes, so always pay attention to how you feel.

Once you've begun this process, you may want to experiment with some more dramatic dietary shifts. Recognizing that we all have different needs doesn't mean we have to invent diets from scratch. Established dietary theories can be great starting points. You don't have to adopt them wholesale (and typically shouldn't), but it's worth knowing what they recommend so you can consider which parts of each work for you.

For instance, if you're energetic, enjoy a challenge, and possess a strong digestive system, you might be a good candidate for a raw food diet. This is a relatively new diet based on ancient principles in which vegetables, fruits, nuts, and seeds are served uncooked—or heated to a maximum of 118°F so as to maintain nutrients and enzymes. Fit the description but balking at consuming only uncooked foods? Maybe partial raw foodism is right for you (say, 50 percent raw and 50 percent cooked). Or perhaps you're eager to transition away from junk food or dairy, and are very disciplined and love meat to boot; in that case, a Paleo diet may be the right starting point for you—a route that heavily emphasizes nondairy animal foods and vegetables. And for many people, considering vegetarianism makes sense. If you do decide to experiment with not eating meat, be sure to avoid the pitfalls that many vegans and vegetarians accidentally step into—namely, eating too many processed foods, refined carbohydrates, dairy (for vegetarians), and sugar, as well as consuming too much soy or seitan (wheat gluten) in the form of fake-meat products.

On the other hand, maybe, like me, you've tried being a vegetarian or vegan and don't feel quite right. If you sense that you need to add some animal products to your diet, do so carefully, one step at a time, and pay attention to the results. Adding a little organically farm-raised or wild cold-water fish, such as salmon, mackerel, cod, or sardines, may give your diet the extra boost you are seeking, while also ensuring you get plenty of heart-healthy omega-3 fatty acids. Or you may want to go a step further and add chicken, or even red meat. The key is to be methodical and pay attention to the results. Your body will tell you what's right for you. And in keeping with the Clean Plates philosophy, pay attention to what you enjoy at the same time, and make sure it is responsibly sourced.

Still confused? Think of it as designing your own diet using bits and pieces of good, but different, approaches. The point is that you don't need to adhere to any particular theory (they all have their pros and cons, and none is right for everyone). Find out what works for you! You don't dress exactly the same as your friends—you've developed your own personal style over your lifetime, inspired by different trends and influences, but also suited to your shape, lifestyle, coloring, budget, and so on. Think of bio-individuality as your food style. Tailor what you eat to your biology, body, blood type, hormones, tastes, lifestyle, and way of looking at the world.

Accept What Your Body Is Telling You

One of the challenges of bio-individuality is that we often don't like what our body is telling us. Perhaps you have a particular symptom that you suspect is connected with eating certain foods. In fact, if you're honest with yourself, it's pretty obvious. Every time you eat dairy products, you end up with a migraine. But you love cheeses, and so you resist making the connection too conscious. Or perhaps you find that while eating that wonderful, crusty fresh bread from the local bakery feels so good in the moment, it leaves you bloated and lethargic. You may be gluten intolerant. Often, we know much more than we want to admit about which foods work for us and which would be better for us to avoid. But we keep making the same choices. Denial seems to be part of human nature, particularly when we are attached or even addicted to certain things.

When you find that you are deeply attached to certain foods, ask yourself why there is such an attachment. Maybe it is simply the pleasure they give you. But as we have discussed, there can be emotional and psychological reasons why we cling to things that are in fact causing us to suffer. Feeling guilty or frustrated with yourself won't help. Resenting the fact that your significant other can eat those same foods without any negative effects won't help, either. Look objectively at the situation—face the consequences of continuing to make choices that your body is telling you are not health promoting. At moments like this, you need to come to a deep acceptance of the facts.

The good news is that your dietary needs are not set in stone. Food sensitivities are not permanent or irreversible. When I began experimenting with my own diet, I completely cut out dairy, gluten, and sugar. I came to terms with the connection between my IBS and these foods that I loved to eat, and so I made a choice to put them aside for the sake of healing my body. These days, however, I find that I can occasionally eat those foods that I was once so sensitive to, without much negative impact, so long as I do so in moderation. Because my overall diet is clean and healthy, my body has developed an ability to process them. But you may need to begin by simply accepting that certain foods are not serving your body. It's not that they are inherently "bad"—they are just not a fit with your needs. If you cultivate a deeper respect and appreciation for your body, a gratitude for the fact that you have this extraordinary vehicle through which to live in and serve the world, it makes these choices easier.

Embracing Our Differences

This chapter has focused on our differences. But we shouldn't allow our differences to divide us. Our food choices too often become another source of separation. Especially when there are moral underpinnings to our choices, such as veganism, for example, it's tempting to think, "My way is the only right way to eat," or to judge others for making different choices from our own.

Being different should bring us together. Realizing that other people have needs distinct from ours can expand the circle of our empathy and temper our critical inclinations. Some types love to begin their day with a shot of wheatgrass—but perhaps the thought makes you turn green. And while your friends can't imagine living without an occasional hamburger or slice of pizza, you might thrive on hearty salads and raw foods. And we all know that irritating person who can gobble up everything in sight and remain slim—a profile that many of us don't have. Hopefully being aware of these distinctions will lead us to be less critical of others—and less likely to feel guilty about our own choices. Judgment and guilt, after all, are bad for your health and bad for your relationships. At the very least, they really mess with your digestion.

What I like most about bio-individuality is the focus on how our physical selves can achieve their fullest potential. In my opinion, when that happens—when we're able to thrive physically—we've created an unshakable foundation for living to our fullest potential and for making a meaningful contribution to our collective well-being as a species and a planet.

---

1. Even though eating dairy products is traditional in the ancestry of many Americans, a huge portion of the U.S. population is lactose intolerant. Thirty to 50 million U.S. residents (adults and children) are lactose intolerant. Seventy-five percent of all African-American, Jewish, Mexican-American, and Native American adults are lactose intolerant. Ninety percent of Asian-American adults are lactose intolerant. Lactose intolerance is least common among people with a northern European heritage. Source: http://medicalcenter.osu.edu/patientcare/healthcare_services/digestive_disorders/lactose_intolerance/Pages/index.aspx and http://www.ploscompbiol.org/article/info%3Adoi%2F10.1371%2Fjournal.pcbi.1000491.

CHAPTER 3

Quality over Quantity: Don't Count Your Food, Make Your Food Count

◦∕∼∘

THE LATEST RANGE OF DIET SODAS PROCLAIM "ZERO calories." One-hundred-calorie packs are becoming common in the snack aisle of the supermarket. Certain states require restaurants to give calorie counts next to their menu items. As a culture, we've become obsessed with calorie reduction.

I'm not saying that calories don't matter—far from it. Most scientific studies agree that a reduced-calorie diet would be good for many of us, increasing our longevity. When we eat a lot, we cause our body to work harder. Even if we are eating healthy food, overeating taxes our body. So calories do matter, but they are only one part of the equation. I firmly believe that the quality of the foods we eat is much more important than the quantity—even when it comes to losing weight.

Think of food as fuel. Does a car run best on poor-quality fuel? Of course not. Our body is the same: It needs optimal fuel. Ask yourself: What's better for my body—1,800 calories of junk food and candy bars, or 2,000 calories of vegetables and fruits?

Which brings me to the second of the Five Precepts:

The Second Precept: The overwhelming majority of your diet should consist of real, high-quality, and whole foods.

Our body was designed to eat this way, regardless of our lifestyle variations, genetic makeup, and so on.

So what, exactly, is "real" food? It's a question I often hear from my clients. Once upon a time, it had an obvious answer, but, over the past hundred years, food has become increasingly unlike itself: processed, altered with chemicals, genetically modified, dyed unnatural colors, and flavored with suspect ingredients.

These kinds of changes generally result in more toxins and fewer nutrients. In my opinion, the success of diets such as macrobiotics and raw foods in claiming to help heal diabetes and even cancer (according to some studies) is due in large part to the fact that such diets call for increasing your intake of real, high-quality, whole foods, while reducing consumption of artificial and chemical-laden dishes. Similarly, the weight-loss impact of low-fat or low-carb diets may have more to do with the fact that dieters often cut out processed foods, than the particulars of the diet they choose.

As you make food choices, consider the impact of what you are putting into your body. What is it used for? Is your body metabolizing it efficiently? Is what you are consuming having an overall positive, negative, or neutral effect? A lot of things we eat have a negative effect because they contain toxins, chemicals that the body doesn't know how to deal with. Even if you just think in terms of energy, you can see that often the body is expending extra energy—more than it is getting from the food—to process the toxins.

The quality of the food you eat can also affect your appetite. If you are simply reducing calories and not eating a healthy, nutrient-dense diet, your body will be always in a state of depletion, and therefore always craving more food because it's not getting the nutrients it needs to function. No one wants to live in this state. Yes, you might lose weight for a couple of months, but sooner or later, as we know, it's all too easy to fall back into old habits. Calorie counting alone is rarely a sustainable healthy lifestyle—at best, it is a short-term weight-loss solution. Interestingly, even Weight Watchers has recently changed its longstanding method in ways that suggest a recognition of this truth—reducing the "points" value of most fruits and vegetables to zero.

Is Your Food Real?

Knowing what's real is largely a matter of intuition and common sense. You'll become a pro at identifying the real thing more quickly if you ask yourself a couple of questions the next time you eat. These questions include: What would I eat if I lived in the wild? What has the earth and nature provided for humans to eat? What have I, as a human, evolved to eat? To keep it simple, focus on what grows out of the ground, on a tree, or in the ocean. In addition, think vegetables, fruits, nuts, seeds, beans, grains, herbs, and animal-based foods.

AN EASY WAY TO FIGURE OUT WHETHER IT'S REAL FOOD

Next time you're considering a purchase in the grocery store, just ask yourself this question: Was it made in nature or in a factory? Visualize where the item began its life. Perhaps you'll see it hanging on a bush, growing on a tree, sprouting up from the earth, or grazing in a field. If it's fizzing to life in a test tube or making its way down the conveyor belt of an assembly line, move on.

Questions of Quality

A peach from the grocery store is a real-food item—it was made in nature and wasn't flavored in a factory—but that doesn't mean it's the best quality. Ask yourself the following questions to assess the quality of your real food:

Is it organic? If so, it has fewer chemicals and more nutrients and likely more flavor than its nonorganic counterpart.

Is it locally grown? If so, it will have required less artificial ripening and storage and lost fewer nutrients and less flavor en route from farm to plate.

Is it irradiated? Radiation destroys nutrients and changes an item's chemical structure.

Is it genetically modified? Genetic modification is an unnatural process if there ever was one, and at this point, we don't know the consequences—but I doubt they are positive.

Is it fresh? Canned fruit, for example, often contains preservatives, not to mention extra sugar.

Were additives, flavorings, colorings, or preservatives used? It's not always obvious, but it's worth considering. Canned peaches may not naturally be that wonderful golden yellow.

WHAT'S MORE IMPORTANT: LOCALLY GROWN OR ORGANIC?

Organic but nonlocal produce is free of pesticides harmful to our body and the soil, but requires extra energy to travel from farm to table and loses nutrients along the way. *Locally grown* but nonorganic goods retain most of their nutrients because of the speed at which they get to our plates, but they may be sprayed with chemicals, which are damaging to our body, the soil, and the atmosphere. *The answer:* Unfortunately, if you can't get an item that is both organic and locally grown, there is no easy answer. It is a matter of personal choice and if you choose one or the other you are doing pretty well.

What Is a Whole Food?

The term *whole foods* **was first used in the sixties, and today has** shed its back-to-the-land hippie roots and become a household name thanks to the fast-growing supermarket chain Whole Foods Market. Technically, the term refers to processing and refining methods. To put it simply, the fewer things done to a food, the better. Think a whole potato as opposed to potato chips, brown rice rather than white rice, an apple in lieu of a glass of apple juice, or whole oats instead of a box of cereal.

When examining the wholeness of a meal, you should consider:

- The simplicity of the ingredients, such as a bowl of berries (good) versus fruit juice with sugar (not as good).
- The number of steps or processes used to make the food, such as a bowl of oatmeal made from whole oats (good) versus cereal made into flakes using high pressure, heat, and additives (not as good).
- The cooking methods used. Err on the side of undercooking, as prolonged exposure to high heat destroys nutrients, enzymes, and water content.

Raw vs. Cooked

Raw foods (that is, uncooked foods) are in their natural state with their nutrients intact. Some foods are best consumed in this form to get their full health benefits, whereas for others (tomatoes, for example), cooking makes some of their nutrients more bioavailable. Cooking is often considered the first step in the digestive process. Why? Because it breaks down the food's cell walls and fiber, making it easier to absorb the nutrients. Again, there is not a one-size-fits-all answer to the raw vs. cooked debate, and I think it's important to consider it on the basis of specific foods as well as personal digestion and tastes. I don't think it is necessary or even healthy to embrace a 100 percent raw-food diet, but I do believe that we should aim to eat a significant amount of raw foods as well as some cooked foods. If you are someone who finds raw foods challenging to digest, salads and smoothies can be an easy way to get a quick, nutrient-rich raw boost.

Strengthen Your Food Radar

Real. High quality. Whole. These might seem like a lot of ideas to consider, but I like to think of these ideas as practice exercises for your "food radar"—a muscle of sorts that will grow stronger with use. The more you check for the differences between real and processed, whole and less wholesome, high quality and run-of-the-mill, the more automatic eating real, whole, and high-quality foods will become.

As your food radar becomes more sensitive, you will learn how to ask the right questions, whether eating out in a restaurant, reading a label, or talking to a salesperson in a grocery store. Ask the server in your favorite restaurant whether brown rice can be substituted for white. (Brown rice is a whole food, whereas white rice has had its husk, bran, and germ removed, all of which contain important nutrients.) Inquire as to whether the vegetables on your plate have just been cooked in-house or whether the only kitchen tool required was a can opener. Peas from a can, for instance, often come with added salt. The same goes for fruit, only the added ingredient is sugar. Ask the salesperson at the deli counter whether the cheese is raw or pasteurized. (Pasteurization is a process of heating then cooling milk to destroy harmful bacteria and extend its shelf life, but it also alters the nature of the food, removing beneficial bacteria and enzymes.) Ask whether salmon is artificially colored or is the genuine wild-harvested article, and whether beef comes from a grass-fed cow or one fattened with grains, antibiotics, and growth hormones.

Again, it's important to recognize that there is much we still don't know about the benefits and pitfalls of different foods and food-processing techniques. Confusion and controversy surround many types of food, and sometimes there are no easy answers. To help you skillfully navigate the choices you need to make every day, and to give you the tools to design your own diet, my next three precepts offer both general guiding principles and specific information about various foods and food categories, from vegetables and fruits to meat and dairy products to sweeteners, oils, beverages, and so forth. I don't have all the answers—no one does—but I am confident that what you learn in these pages will enable you to make smart dietary choices that have an immediate, noticeable impact on your health and well-being.

CHAPTER 4

Plant-Based Foods: The Foundation of a Healthy Diet

MY THIRD PRECEPT MIGHT BE DIFFICULT TO absorb—not because you've never heard it before, but because you have heard it, in some form, thousands of times. My goal in this chapter is to make it stick.

The Third Precept: Everyone would be better off if a larger proportion of his or her diet consisted of plants—mostly vegetables (in particular, leafy greens), along with some nuts, seeds, and fruits.

To get this message to sink in, I encourage clients to think about it in big, overarching terms. I like to point out that eating plants is a way of taking in the energy of the sun. As a life force, the sun contributes enormously to our health and sense of well-being. Without it there would be no life on earth. Want more life-energy? Eat more plants. They're a more direct source of "sun food" than meat is. It's worth taking a few moments to think about the fact that when you choose to eat animals, you are indirectly consuming what they themselves already ate—whether it be grass, or grains, or hormones, or worse. The same is true when you eat plants— but all that plants eat is sun and soil. If this concept is a bit too esoteric, consider it from a scientific point of view. What gives green plants their color? It's chlorophyll, the pigment in leaves that enables them to absorb the sun's rays, using a process called photosynthesis. Many nutritionists believe that when we eat green leaves, we take in that stored solar energy. Chlorophyll enriches blood, kills germs, detoxifies the bloodstream and liver, reduces bodily odors, and controls the appetite. Still snoozing off when you hear "eat more plants"? Maybe telling yourself, "I'll have more energy," will provide the necessary motivation.

When I recommend a "plant-based diet" I am not saying you have to become vegetarian or vegan. I am suggesting, however, that the basis of your diet should come from plants. Need convincing? There are plenty of studies that have proven the benefits of eating more vegetables. The China-Oxford-Cornell Diet and Health Project, more commonly known as the China Study, is one of the best known and most comprehensive, analyzing the connection between diet and lifestyle factors and disease mortality over a twenty-year period in sixty-five rural Chinese counties. T. Collin Campbell, one of the study's directors, writes, "People who ate the most animal-based foods got the most chronic disease . . . People who ate the most plant-based foods were the healthiest and tended to avoid chronic disease." Citing more than eight thousand statistically significant cases, "These results could not be ignored," claims Dr. Campbell. And while I hesitate to draw the sweeping conclusion that the findings of these studies apply unilaterally, I do think they support the case for a reduction in animal products and an increase in plant-based foods.

CROWD OUT THE BAD STUFF

The concept is simple: The more vegetables we eat, the less room we'll have for junk foods and the like. One extra helping of veggies a day crowds out one helping of unhealthy food. So, instead of trying to avoid bad foods, focus on eating more vegetables. You'll actually start craving them, while the junk will slowly become less appealing.

Think about it this way: Have you ever seen a study that concludes that eating more plants is damaging to your health? To me, it's just common sense to shift the balance of your food intake toward those real foods that have been shown to have only positive benefits. I understand that many people feel threatened by the idea of a plant-based diet, considering it an extreme step to take. And once again, I'm not personally advocating that everyone should give up meat altogether, though for some, that may be a smart option. If you are one of those people who have a strong reaction to the very idea, it may be wise to ask if your perspective really is rational. As Dr. Dean Ornish, a pioneering cardiologist, writes: "I don't understand why asking people to eat a well-balanced vegetarian diet is considered drastic, while it is medically conservative to cut people open and put them on cholesterol-lowering drugs for the rest of their lives."

To help you navigate among different types of plants, the majority of this chapter is devoted to information about vegetables and fruits, as well as grains, seeds, and nuts. It's not wrong to eat meat—in fact, I believe it can be healthy for certain people, myself included—but eat lots of plants, and you'll start to feel better right away and improve your health.

Vegetables

Pity the unappreciated vegetable. Perpetually shunted to the side— as a garnish, appetizer, side dish—it rarely gets to give all that it has to offer. What does it offer? you may ask. An enormous amount of nutrients and health-boosting properties in the form of vitamins, minerals, fiber, phytochemicals, and antioxidants. Vegetables should form the bulk of your diet. Because they are nutrient-dense foods, you'll also find that you fill up more quickly, and therefore eating more veggies can be a great weight-loss strategy. The more you eat, the more you will start to crave them. To get the point across, I sometimes tell my clients that it doesn't even matter if you have to douse your veggies in ketchup, so long as you start adding them! Of course, that's not a long-term strategy for success, but if it's what it takes to get those vegetables on your plate, it's better than not eating them. If you're a vegetarian, aim to increase the proportion of veggies that you consume relative to the amount of grains, beans, dairy, sugar, and tofu in your diet. Similarly, omnivores should be mindful of the meat-to-vegetable ratio in each meal. A good general guideline is that half of your plate should consist of vegetables, one-quarter protein, and one-quarter whole-grain carbohydrates. Strive for at least some meals to be all-vegetarian, with beans as the protein source.

And I'd like to take a moment to remind you about my Second Precept—eat high-quality, real, and whole vegetables. For one thing, they taste noticeably better. In addition, local, organic vegetables are richer in nutrients because they were grown in organic soils, and suffer less nutrient and flavor loss during transportation than their long-distance counterparts.

SELF-RELIANT ORGANIC VEGETABLES: DID YOU KNOW?

Raised without pesticides, organic vegetables must develop their own immune system in the form of nutrients and phytochemicals. That's excellent news for your body because it benefits from these über-nutrients in myriad ways—a major immune-system boost, for instance.

In addition, these do-it-all veggies possess a characteristic that's important for good health: They're alkalizing. In contrast, most foods in the standard American diet—especially meats, sugar, and white flour—are acid-forming. Without getting into the nitty-gritty science of it, I'd like to point out that most diseases within the body thrive in an acidic environment. Foods that support alkalinity are healthier.

WHY PH MATTERS

You may remember the term *pH* from your high school chemistry class, but it's relevant to your food choices as well. Our body is meant to be slightly alkaline, but if we eat too many acidic foods, such as animal products and processed foods, our pH can shift. An acidic environment decreases the body's ability to absorb certain minerals and nutrients, inhibits the repair of damaged cells, causes inflammation, and hinders detoxification. It is important to note that some foods we may think of as acidic, such as lemons, actually have an alkalizing effect once ingested. See page 288 for resources on which foods are alkalizing and which are acidic.

Here's a roundup of the types of vegetables you're likely to encounter in your local grocery store—and how they affect your body:

Leafy greens should be a priority in any diet because they are one of the most nutrient-dense foods. Chock-full of chlorophyll, they also boast a calcium-to-magnesium ratio that makes them great bone builders and encourages relaxation and appropriate nerve-and-muscle responsiveness, ensuring the body's smooth functioning. And as well as being a good way to obtain iron, vitamin C, and folic acid, leafy greens contain essential amino acids, meaning they're an excellent source of protein—one that potentially rivals the kind we get from eating animals. Let's take a look at some of the more common leafy greens.

Kale, chard, collards, and spinach are readily available. If possible, eat them lightly steamed or even served raw, both options that retain more nutrients than a long cook. A quick sauté with garlic is another delicious and healthy alternative. Spinach enjoys an impressive reputation (think Popeye) but contains oxalic acid, an antinutrient that prevents the absorption and use of calcium and may contribute to kidney stones and gout. While some nutritional experts insist that thorough cooking neutralizes the acid, others report that overcooking makes it toxic (the latter group suggests eating it raw). Until there's a definitive answer, I recommend enjoying spinach without overdoing it, and opting instead for kale, chard, or collard greens when possible. Mustard, dandelion, beet, and turnip greens are also great options.

Lettuce, mixed greens, watercress, and arugula often appear in salads, meaning they're raw and still contain all their nutrients and enzymes (watercress in particular is rich in B vitamins). Skip iceberg lettuce. Although it is the most common salad green in the United States, iceberg lettuce has few nutrients and tends to be heavily sprayed with pesticides.

Drinking the juice of any type of green is a speedy way to get a nutrient infusion without your teeth or digestive system having to work at breaking down the plants' cell walls. Nevertheless, don't stop eating whole greens, because they provide fiber as well as some nutrients that may be lost or oxidized in the juicing process.

Cruciferous vegetables are plants in the cabbage family, a category that includes broccoli, cauliflower, Brussels sprouts, kale, bok choy, and all cabbages (yep, there's some overlap with the "leafy greens" group). High in vitamin C and soluble fiber, these foods also are crammed with nutrients boasting potent anticancer properties, including diindolylmethane (DIM). And only cruciferous vegetables contain isothiocyanates, a nutrient that has been associated with a decrease in lung cancer.

Root vegetables include carrots, beets, potatoes, parsnips, yams, turnips, and radishes, each with a unique nutritional profile. Carrots, for instance, contain the antioxidant known as beta-carotene; beets, crammed with iron, enrich the blood. White potatoes, however, have more sugar and fewer nutrients than do yams or sweet potatoes or even purple potatoes. When possible, consider substituting one of these in potato-based dishes.

Squash typically recall autumnal images of leaf piles and Halloween, but these vegetables are a hearty and satisfying way to get your fill of antioxidants all year long. Try sweeter varieties, such as pumpkin and kabocha, to satisfy a sweet tooth; and heartier varieties, such as butternut and acorn squash, to make a nice soup. Zucchini and yellow summer squash are a great addition to any dish especially crudités, as they can be enjoyed raw, and spaghetti squash is a flour-free alternative to pasta. I recommend saving the seeds of your squash to add to a salad or to enjoy plain as a snack.

Mushrooms probably generate the most controversy of all vegetables, at least as far as their health claims go. Some nutritionists advise steering clear because they are, after all, fungus, and are therefore potentially infectious. They're also hard to digest. Other experts, however, particularly those who study Asian cultures, vaunt the medicinal properties of mushrooms. Personally, I like to stick to Asian varieties like the shiitake and maitake (hen of the woods) because of their cancer-fighting and immune-boosting properties. However, recent studies have suggested that even button mushrooms contain several immune-boosting properties, too, so I have been adding more varieties of mushrooms to my diet.

Kimchi and **sauerkraut** come in what is possibly the best form in which to consume your veggies—raw and fermented. Literally alive, they teem with nutrients, enzymes, and probiotics, which aid digestion. As central to Korean culture as pasta is to Italy, kimchi may contain any type of vegetable but often includes cabbage and carrots, which are typically spiced up with garlic, ginger, or cayenne. Because of its spiciness, kimchi makes not only a great snack, but also a delicious condiment. A German staple, sauerkraut is made from cultured cabbage. Both are naturally fermented treats that you can buy in your local health food store and are becoming popular in all types of restaurants as a side dish, in sandwiches, or as part of a main course. (You can also easily make your own—see page 187 for a recipe for Home-Fermented Sauerkraut.) Look for unpasteurized forms, as the pasteurization process destroys some of the nutrients that make these fermented products so healthful.

FIX YOUR GUT, FIX YOUR BRAIN

Recent studies show that the gut actually sends more information to the brain than the brain sends to the gut.[1] This means that just as nervousness can manifest in our stomach (think "butterflies"), problems in the gut can also manifest in the brain. The trillions of bacteria living inside of our intestines act like a second nervous system. Some of these are friendly bacteria and some aren't. The idea is to build up the good bacteria so that a defense system is in place against the bad bacteria, allowing for a healthy gut flora and therefore a healthy brain. Probiotics help to do just that. Eating naturally fermented foods, such as raw apple cider vinegar, cultured yogurt and kefir, kimchi, sauerkraut, and other pickled foods, will supply your daily dose of probiotics.

Seaweeds, which I like to think of as vegetables from the sea, include nori (used to wrap sushi), *hijiki, arame,* wakame, dulse, and many others. Extremely dense in minerals, they add a salty taste to dishes. You may have only encountered these in Asian restaurants, but they are easy to use at home and can be a good salt substitute.

THE RAINBOW RULE

It can be difficult to make sure you're getting the right balance of nutrients. Here's a good rule to follow: Eat as many different colors of vegetables each day as possible. Each pigment correlates to specific phytochemicals, all of which boost your immunity and act as health insurance against a range of nutrient deficiencies and diseases.

Fresh Herbs

Fresh green herbs, which are widely available these days in grocery stores, have a lot of medicinal properties and are a great source of additional nutrients as well as a wonderful way to flavor your vegetables. You've probably encountered basil with fresh tomatoes, or cilantro in fresh salsa. Parsley is a wonderful source of iron and great as an addition to salads or as a garnish. For some different flavors, try adding fresh tarragon to a salad, roasting root vegetables with fresh rosemary, sautéing zucchini with fresh mint, or enhancing a soup with fresh thyme. You can also include bunches of herbs, stalks and all, in vegetable juices, or chop them for a smoothie, or use them in a delicious pesto or chimichurri sauce.

Fruits

Think of them as clean treats: Fruits are good sources of fiber, antioxidants, phytochemicals, and vitamins, and provide energy via their easily digestible sugars.

Due to their fructose sugar content, however, they should comprise a small percentage of your overall plant intake—eaten raw, or in juices, smoothies, or desserts.

Concerned about fruits creating huge spikes in blood sugar? Don't worry. It's generally not an issue if you are eating the whole fruit because fruits contain fiber and other cofactors. However, people with diabetes or who are prone to candida or yeast infections should go easy on sugary fruits, such as bananas or grapes, or avoid fruits altogether until their health problem is resolved.

QUICK DEFINITION: COFACTOR

A cofactor is a nutrient that helps another work better.

Here are details about fruits you're likely to find in your local grocery store:

Nonsweet fruits, such as peppers, tomatoes, and cucumbers, rank low on the glycemic index and therefore barely disrupt our blood sugar balance. People with candida or diabetes can eat them safely. During the summer, I recommend checking out the many delicious varieties of locally grown heirloom tomatoes on offer.

Fatty fruits, such as avocados and olives, are arguably the best source of fats you can eat, because they are whole and come from plants (in contrast to many processed oils). Eaten raw, as they always should be, avocados contain a fat-digesting enzyme, lipase, which makes them easy for our body to process. Olives, which are cured or brined, have similar benefits.

Berries are my favorite sweet fruits, both from a culinary perspective and nutritionally speaking. On the glycemic index, they rank lowest of all the sweet fruits, and individually, each berry is touted for a specific attribute. Blueberries offer the highest number of antioxidants of all berries; while raspberries, especially the leaves made into a tea, help to nourish the female reproductive system. In addition, several berries—especially goji berries, a tart, bitter Tibetan variety, and açai, the fruit of Amazonian palm trees—constitute a relatively new category of foods called superfruits because they are so rich in nutrients.

QUICK DEFINITION: ANTIOXIDANTS

Their name says it all: They counteract oxidation—and the free radicals believed to speed up aging and disease. A variety of elements cause our body to produce excess free radicals; ranging from the bad, such as toxic air and the chemicals to which we're exposed, to the everyday, such as exercise and the normal process of metabolizing food for energy. Fortunately, you can combat these excess free radicals by eating more vegetables (as well as fruits, nuts, and seeds), which are abundant in antioxidants.

Citrus fruits include oranges, lemons, limes, and grapefruits. They tend to be high in immune-boosting vitamin C and in bioflavonoids—a type of antioxidant known for its anti-cancer properties, as well as its role in keeping blood capillaries healthy. Although citrus fruits taste acidic, they are, in fact, alkalizing and help to counteract the acidity of the meat, grains, and beans that typically form the bulk of many meals.

Orchard fruits include apples, pears, and peaches. Best eaten raw and with the skin intact for their enzymes, soluble fiber, and nutrients, these fruits are great ingredients for fruit salads and smoothies. Apples and pears also mix well in green salads—or try slicing them and spreading with almond butter for a nutritious and satisfying snack.

Tropical fruits, such as papayas, mangoes, and pineapples, are especially rich in the kinds of enzymes that are not only powerful aids to digestion, but also may help to break down scar tissue and waste materials in the body. Of course, being tropical, they're not local to most of us. Nevertheless, they offer a tasty alternative to refined sugar for someone craving a sweet snack.

Nuts and Seeds

Nuts and seeds, as well as nut and seed butters, are an important component of a plant-based diet, adding healthy fats and a satisfying crunch to salads or snacks. Almonds, cashews, walnuts, pecans, and hazelnuts are just a few that are available in most grocery stores. Opt for raw nuts over roasted as much as possible, and check for and avoid added salt or sugar. In general, I suggest opting for almonds over peanuts and cashews as the latter two can be more acidic in the body.

Sunflower seeds, sesame seeds, and pumpkin seeds are also easy to come by, and make great additions to salads. Hemp seeds and flaxseeds are valued for their essential fatty acids. Flax contains omega-3 fatty acids and is commonly thought to be a good alternative to fish oils for vegetarians; but the form of omega-3 in flax needs to be converted into a form usable by the human body, and it's unclear whether we are able to efficiently convert. Therefore, I suggest it's best to get your omega-3 fatty acids from a fish source if possible. Flaxseeds and flax oil have other benefits, such as cancer fighting lignans, so they are still good to include in your diet.

Grains and Bread

What comes to mind when you think of grains? A fresh-baked loaf of bread? Pasta with tomatoes and garlic? Fragrant jasmine rice? These are foods that many of us love and yet often see as a bit of an indulgence— something we should aim to allow ourselves to eat occasionally, but not to be devoured constantly. I agree with that general approach, but I should emphasize that not all grains are created equal, whether whole or refined. If your body tolerates them well, grains can add fiber, protein, other nutrients, and enjoyment to your diet, as long as they're properly prepared, eaten in moderation, mostly in their whole form (I'll explain shortly), and organic (many grains are heavily sprayed and genetically modified).

This is not to say there aren't drawbacks to eating grains—especially in those forms that tend to be most appealing, such as bread and pasta. In fact, I specifically advise my clients, when eating out, to avoid the complimentary bread basket served before most meals. Why? The body treats grains—especially in the form of flour—as sugar, upsetting your blood sugar balance and contributing to weight gain and insulin resistance. In addition, even if they're whole grains, unless grains are soaked or sprouted, their bran layer will contain phytic acid, which reduces mineral absorption, as well as enzyme inhibitors, which interfere with digestion. And, overall, grains cause the body to form mucus and are acidic; this last point means that the positive, alkaline effects of eating vegetables are partially neutralized when you eat grains.

HOW TO EAT GRAINS

So what is the best way to eat grains? Overall, I recommend eating fully intact grains, such as brown rice and quinoa. Grains that have been processed into flours—for use in breads, cakes, and pastas—and white rice, which is refined, are not whole foods. Brown rice is whole, but pasta made from brown rice flour isn't—although it's preferable to wheat pasta (even whole wheat), which has a high gluten content.

Preparation techniques make a big difference; certain methods yield more nutritious, easier-to-digest dishes. Soaking grains in water, as mentioned above, can make them more digestible, and soaking them until they sprout may even be better. Toasting some grains, such as buckwheat, before cooking can lessen their acid-producing effects, making them more alkaline.

TIP: AL DENTE PASTA

The Italians use the phrase *al dente*, meaning "to the tooth," to indicate the optimum texture of cooked pasta. Al dente pasta should have a slight resistance in the center when chewed. And besides being more enjoyable to eat than overcooked pasta, al dente is the best option for nutritional reasons as well. It only mildly affects your blood sugar balance, whereas overcooked pasta causes a rapid spike in blood sugar.

A host of reasons underpin these recommendations, mostly related to the negative effects of consuming refined grains. Flour causes a big, unhealthy spike in blood sugar (because the fiber, which has been removed, isn't there to slow down the release of carbs, which upset the body's blood sugar balance when they're released too quickly). And refined grains, such as white rice and white wheat flour, contain plenty of calories but little nutrition.

Used in a whopping 90 percent of baked goods, white wheat flour is one of the worst of the refined grains. In addition to having few nutrients and containing gluten, which is a problem for some people, it's usually tainted with bleaching agents and other chemicals to enhance its baking performance. Fortunately, there are some alternatives, in addition to the whole grains just discussed. The healthiest kind of bread you can buy is sprouted-grain bread, made from presoaked grains that are baked at low temperatures. Sourdough bread, even though made with white flour, can be another smart choice, since it's naturally leavened with a traditional fermentation technique that neutralizes its phytic acid, increases its nutrients' availability, and creates lactobacillus-friendly gut bacteria that aid digestion (although some of these may be killed in the baking process.) My favorite choices for breads made directly from flour are spelt and whole rye. In fact, you'll notice that most of the recipes in this book that use flour call for spelt flour.

To summarize my overall recommendations regarding grains: Say yes to moderation, traditional preparation methods, and whole grains—and no to refined, milled, and nonorganic versions. An overview of a selection of key grains follows. Although they can all contain traces of gluten, I have divided them into naturally glutinous grains and naturally gluten-free grains for people who are sensitive. Even if you aren't, cutting down on gluten is likely better for your health.

QUICK DEFINITION: GLUTEN

The name of this substance comes from the Latin for "glue," and, indeed, gluten is responsible for the elastic-like, stretchy quality of dough. It's a mixture of two proteins found in wheat and several other grains, and it's a common cause of allergies, nutritional deficiencies, and serious digestive complaints.

GRAINS WITH GLUTEN

Wheat is the highest in gluten of all the grains, which is why it's the universal choice for bread making—gluten helps bread rise and helps give breads and baked goods their familiar textures. It's also the main ingredient in most pastas, pizza crusts, pastries, crackers, cakes, and cookies, and is even used as a thickener in sauces.

Given its ubiquity, wheat is not easy to avoid. I suggest making an effort to steer clear—or at least reduce your intake—in part because wheat's high gluten level frequently disrupts the digestive system, even if you're not allergic. Reduce the percentage of wheat in your diet, and I suspect you'll be pleasantly surprised at how much better you feel day to day. (Incidentally, seitan—a popular meat substitute for vegetarians and vegans—is essentially wheat gluten with the texture of meat, so I recommend going easy on it as well. Try tempeh instead.)

Bulgur and **couscous** are actually wheat-based, but not whole grains in their own right. Bulgur is cracked pieces of wheat, and is used like rice. It's a staple in Middle Eastern cuisine and is best known as the main ingredient in tabbouleh. Couscous is typically found in North African or Moroccan cuisine and is often heavily processed—closer to a pasta than a grain. Look for the whole wheat version.

Wheat berry is the mother grain from which wheat flour, pasta, and bread are made. This is the most whole form of wheat: germ, bran, and endosperm all still intact. Packed with fiber, protein, iron, magnesium, and vitamin E, wheat berries can be eaten whole, or ground into graham flour, and are the best way to consume wheat. Graham flour is a whole flour similar to whole wheat flour, only the endosperm, bran, and germ are ground a bit differently.

Kamut, **farro**, and **spelt** are nonhybridized, more ancient varieties of wheat. They're lower in gluten than wheat—and higher in fiber and protein—and so make good substitutes. In fact, you may do well on spelt even if you're sensitive to gluten, because the grain contains a different form of it. Fortunately, it's fairly easy to find both spelt berries and spelt flour in health food stores and health-conscious restaurants—and spelt flour is becoming increasingly popular as an ingredient in breads, baked goods, and pizza crusts. Kamut and farro are delicious, chewy grains that can be added to salads or soups, or substituted for rice in many popular dishes. Try using farro to make a wonderful satisfying risotto. Soaking overnight can make these grains quicker to cook and easier to digest.

Rye, rich in a variety of nutrients, is used in place of wheat in such items as rye bread and German pumpernickel. People who are mildly sensitive to gluten tend to tolerate it in moderation. When buying rye bread, make sure it is whole rye, and not blended with wheat.

Barley is one of the most ancient cultivated grains. Although it's supposedly soothing to the intestines, it is also very acid-forming in the body. When buying barley, hulled barley or hulless barley are your best choices as they are the least processed and still contain all of the bran and germ. While pearl barley is the most common (typically used to make risotto), it is also the most refined. This being said, because the fiber in barley is distributed throughout the kernel and not just in the outer bran layer, even pearl barley is a decent choice. You can also purchase barley flakes and barley grits, both of which can originate from either hulled or pearled barley.

Oats stabilize blood sugar, reduce cholesterol, and soothe the intestines and nervous system. They're most commonly served for breakfast as oatmeal or as a major component of granola and muesli. You can buy oats in a number of forms. Oat groats and steel-cut oats are the best option, because they still contain the oat bran. Rolled oats, old-fashioned oats, and quick-cooking rolled oats all have the bran removed, reducing the high nutrient composition naturally found in oats. Although instant oats won't give you the full benefit of this grain, they can be a good option if you need to make a quick breakfast. Avoid the flavored kinds, which contain sugar and other artificial additives—use the plain variety and throw in a handful of nuts and fruit instead. Similarly, if you choose to eat granola or muesli, opt for ones that are not overly sweetened or flavored.

NATURALLY GLUTEN-FREE GRAINS

Quinoa (pronounced key-nwa) is not part of the grass family, and therefore not technically a grain. While many tend to think of it as a grain, it is actually the seed of a chenopod, which makes it closely related to spinach and beets. However, we tend to eat it as a grain and it makes a great alternative to rice, couscous, or oatmeal, and is a good choice for those who are gluten intolerant. A staple for the Inca of South America, quinoa is a relative newcomer to the North American diet; its mild taste and fluffy texture has made it enormously popular in recent years. Because it has a quick cooking time and is rich in high-quality protein, it has become a favorite among vegetarians. If you're not familiar with quinoa, try it served cold, mixed with raw veggies, fresh herbs, and avocado as a wonderful summer salad. It's also great as a breakfast cereal year-round, simply served with milk, fresh fruit, and a little cinnamon (see the recipe on page 129).

Rice is the richest in B vitamins of all the grains. It comes in numerous varieties. Short-grain brown rice is perhaps the most nutritious form. White rice (especially the aromatic basmati) is more common than brown in Indian and Asian cuisine. Why choose brown over white? Because 70 percent of the nutrients and all of the fiber in rice are lost in the refining process that makes it white.

Corn is commonly available on the cob or as kernels, but it also comes processed into cornmeal, grits, and polenta. (Grits and polenta are close relatives, but grits comes from white corn, while both polenta and cornmeal are derived from yellow.) Because corn can cause a relatively high spike in blood sugar, I suggest consuming it in moderation. Also, corn often comes from genetically modified crops, so make sure you buy organic.

Buckwheat—usually in the form of the Russian staple kasha or in Japanese soba noodles—is one of a few commercial crops not routinely sprayed with pesticides, because it has its own natural resistance to pests. With the longest gut-transit of all the grains, it is the most filling and stabilizing for blood sugar. Roasting before cooking transforms buckwheat into one of the few alkalizing grains; kasha is essentially preroasted buckwheat. Buckwheat flour is also available, often used to make soba noodles (be sure to choose a brand that is 100 percent buckwheat, rather than one that is mixed with wheat).

Amaranth is also becoming increasingly popular. It's very nutritious and contains a good amount of many amino acids, such as lysine, which tends to be low in most other grains. Use it like oatmeal for a healthy and satisfying start to the day.

Millet is a cereal grass sometimes used in the United States as birdseed, but common in all kinds of dishes in Asia and Africa. It is one of the only alkalizing grains, is easily digested, and is very nutritious, with a high silica content for healthy skin and bones. Check out the Millet-Stuffed Acorn Squash recipe on page 218.

Legumes

They may be the punch line of bad jokes, but beans—as well as peas and lentils—offer many health benefits. Known as legumes, or pulses, they lower cholesterol, control blood sugar imbalances, and regulate bowel function. Low in fat (with the exception of soybeans), they're a good source of protein (which makes them especially important for vegetarians and vegans), fiber, and B vitamins. From a culinary perspective, herbs and spices marry well with the mild taste of legumes, which absorb the flavor of sauces and have a pleasant texture that adds bulk to any meal. For a few susceptible individuals, abdominal gas and bloating may result from eating beans, no matter how carefully they are prepared, but most of us need not avoid beans for fear of their antisocial effects. Beans are available fresh, dried, and canned. Dried beans should be presoaked, rinsed, and thoroughly cooked to break down their indigestible sugars and destroy their enzyme inhibitors. If you choose canned beans, make sure they are in a BPA-free can, and contain as little added salt as possible. Here's the dish on beans:

Chickpeas, black beans, kidney beans, adzuki beans, and lentils are among the legumes that crop up in numerous cultures, having nourished humankind for millennia. For instance, chickpeas, also called garbanzo beans, are used to make the hummus and falafel in Middle Eastern cuisine, and are also popular in Indian curries; black beans are popular in Mexican cuisine; kidney beans show up in various cultures, from the red kidney beans in the south to the white kidney beans, or cannellini, of the Mediterranean; the adzuki bean is popular in macrobiotic cooking; and lentils often form the basis of dal, an easily digested Indian puree.

Soybeans merit a lengthier discussion because they're eaten so frequently and used in so many ways—and associated with numerous health claims and controversies.

Asians have been including soy foods in their diet for thousands of years, a fact that's often touted as the main reason for Asians' longevity and low rates of certain cancers and other Western diseases. However, this may have more to do with the paucity of dairy and meat in the Asian diet, as well as the emphasis on vegetables and various lifestyle factors. The truth is that soy has never been eaten in large quantities in Asia. Next time you order Chinese vegetables with soybean curd, observe how the vegetables and rice predominate. This marginal role for soy stands in stark contrast to the modern soy burger at the center of the vegetarian entrée in many restaurants these days.

Over the past few decades, vegetarians and vegans in particular have become overreliant on soy because it is a balanced protein. Restaurants dutifully offer soy, often in the form of tofu, as the vegetarian option for protein, and coffee shops offer soy milk as an alternative to dairy.

However, studies detailing soy's high nutrient content and positive effects have recently been contested by additional research. Soy is known to block the absorption of some nutrients and is thought to increase the likelihood of ovarian and breast cancer. For more information, check out *The Whole Soy Story: The Dark Side of America's Favorite Health Food* by Dr. Kaayla Daniel; the book investigates the health problems linked to the overconsumption of soy.

One solution is simply to cut back. But another is to be mindful of the kinds of soy products you consume. Those healthy Asian populations? Their soy products tend to be less processed, and mostly fermented. With that in mind, look for organic versions, which will be non-GMO, as well as such soy products as miso, soy yogurt, natto, and tempeh. They all undergo a fermentation process in which otherwise nonviable nutrients are partly predigested—and phytates and enzyme inhibitors that cause gastric distress are neutralized. In addition, soy, in these forms, is endowed with probiotics. Tofu, perhaps the most ubiquitous form of soy, provides some nutrition but should be eaten in moderation as it hasn't undergone the all-important fermentation process. As for edamame, the green soybeans often served in the pod as an appetizer in Japanese restaurants, it's a whole food but not easy to digest—good for you, but not in excess.

QUICK DEFINITION: GOOD GERMS AND ENZYMES

We hear it constantly: Such-and-such food boasts enzymes and probiotics. But what do those funny-sounding things do? *Enzymes* control the rate of every chemical reaction in your system, which means that you need them to digest food. So what happens when we don't get our enzymes, which are potentially destroyed by overcooking? Bad digestion. *Probiotics* are healthy bacteria in the gut that rid your intestines of bad stuff; you're healthier when you have them in your system.

Soy milk, soy ice cream, and soy cheese, however, are highly processed and not fermented—best consumed only on occasion. They usually come with additives of one kind or another, in an attempt to mimic the flavor and texture of the real thing. Desserts and dairy alternatives made from hemp, almonds, coconut, or rice are better choices. A soy product that should be completely avoided whenever possible is textured vegetable (or soy) protein, or TVP, which in similar forms goes by the names protein soy isolate or hydrolyzed plant (or soy) protein. Made from soybean meal after the oil has been processed out with chemicals and intense pressure, TVP is used in veggie burgers and fake meats. TVP, soy isolate, and hydrolyzed soy bear a close chemical resemblance to plastic and may contain residues from processing, including petroleum solvents, sulfuric acids, hydrochloric acid, and caustic soda. Those are just a few good reasons to bypass that fake turkey sandwich and make yourself a tempeh Reuben instead.

1. Source: http://articles.mercola.com/sites/articles/archive/2012/05/03/probiotics-impact-brain-performance.aspx.

CHAPTER 5

Animal Foods: Mindfulness and Moderation

MEAT STILL ENJOYS A REPUTATION AS ALL-AMERICAN as the Wild West and cowboy boots. But self-improvement is also an all-American quality, and one that would require us to act responsibly when it comes to animal products, including fish, meat, poultry, dairy, and eggs. As you increase your intake of plant foods, you should naturally find that there is less space on your plate and in your stomach for animal products. I'm not saying that you have to become vegetarian or vegan, though; each individual should do what's best for his or her body.

The Fourth Precept: If you choose to eat animal products, consume only (a) high-quality and sustainably raised animals (ideally pasture-raised and grass-fed, but at least hormone- and antibiotic-free); and do so (b) in moderation (meaning smaller portions with less frequency) and (c) using the right cooking methods.

Proponents of the China Study (see page 41) argue that meat-eating is a leading cause of cancer, whereas advocates of a "traditional foods" or

"Paleo" diet insist it can be beneficial. That's not the only area of contention regarding animal products. Another is the argument over whether animal fats cause heart disease. Most experts conclude that eating animal foods high in cholesterol and saturated fats cause an increase in the human body's cholesterol levels. An increasingly vocal minority of researchers claim that the cholesterol myth is just that—a myth. They believe that oxidized cholesterol (from cooking food in highly processed vegetable oils) and hydrogenated fats are more artery-clogging and lead to more heart trouble than lard. Of course, adherents of veganism and vegetarianism eschew animal products for a variety of reasons, both health related and ethical, whereas others believe that animal-free diets are lacking in some essential nutrients, such as vitamins B_{12} and D.

Different people will side with different research; your genetic makeup or lifestyle may mean that eating meat is necessary for your body to function smoothly. To figure it out, I advocate experimenting and also thinking about how certain foods and dietary principles make you feel.

If you choose to consume animal products, I urge you to do so in moderation. Why? Well, for one thing, large portions of animal products are higher in protein than is necessary for human health,[1] creating more acidity than the body can process and leading to such problems as fatigue and osteoporosis. In addition, there's substantial evidence that the practice of raising animals for human consumption—especially in conventional corporate feedlots—is unsustainable and environmentally problematic. And for many, the inhumane conditions under which most food animals live and die make it a moral issue. Easy ways to lower the percentage of animal products in your diet include thinking of meat as a side dish rather than a main course, as well as eating smaller portions and less frequently.

In addition, I urge you to indulge in animal products mindfully. Make sure your beef, dairy, eggs, chicken, and so on come from high-quality, organic, and pasture-fed animals. It's not about meditating on your food—it's about reading the labels. If you carefully pay attention to where your meat comes from, your body will thank you. As well as lacking in essential fiber, conventionally raised animal products are a concentrated source of the medications, stress, hormones, and environmental toxins from the animal's environment. That's a powerful argument for choosing an organic, pasture-fed animal that won't have been subjected to stressful conditions or injected with hormones and antibiotics. Instead, it will have been raised similarly to the way it would have been in the wild: A pasture-raised cow, for instance, grazes on grass, gets exercise, and is exposed to the sun, all of which results in a healthy cow—and extra benefits for us, such as extra vitamin E and selenium.

TIP: ORGANIC CERTIFICATION ISN'T EVERYTHING

Small farmers who raise animals without the use of hormones or antibiotics often can't afford to obtain the accreditation "certified organic." It's best while at your local farmers' market to ask your local farmer about how the meat was raised. See page 285 for farmers' markets near you.

By making those tweaks to your eating habits, you ensure that high-quality meat, fish, poultry, dairy, and eggs can become a healthy part of a balanced diet rather than a risk factor. In the following pages, I round up the different kinds of animal foods you are likely to encounter.

Meat

Not all meats are created equal. Some are organic, some not; some are high in fat whereas others are lean; some tend to be served grilled, whereas others are fried. Part of the purpose of this section is to further clarify and help you choose the healthiest options. For instance, grilled or roasted meats are better for you than are deep-fried dishes. Be aware, though, that meats smoked or barbecued on charcoal grills can develop a carcinogen called polycyclic aromatic hydrocarbons. Like most other foods, meat is best for your body when it has been cooked briefly and gently. Prolonged high heat reduces the amount of vitamins and minerals in meat and denatures its protein. Worse, it increases the toxicity of contaminants already there, such as nitrates and pesticides. Of course, with the disease-causing pathogens showing up in animal products, it may not be such a bad idea to avoid rare or raw meat (which otherwise would be the healthiest way to consume high-quality, properly raised animal products). If you have ensured that you are using products from animals that have been raised well, you shouldn't have to worry about food safety. So when possible, avoid overcooking your meat; medium-rare is a good option. (See page 252 for more about cooking grass-fed meats.)

Beef is a source of iron and vitamin B_{12}, as well as essential fats. Cows raised in pastures—where they're exposed to the sun and eat grass—provide the healthiest meat; in fact, an essential fat and anticancer nutrient called conjugated linoleic acid (CLA) occurs only in grass-fed animals. Grass-fed animals also tend to be lower in fat in general and higher in vitamin E.[2]

One rung down from grass-fed cows is organic beef, which means that the animal has been raised without hormones and antibiotics, but has been fed grains, corn, or organic vegetarian feed. Often this is to affect the taste of the meat, but sometimes these animals are overfed in an attempt to fatten them up, a practice that makes them more prone to disease. Because grass is the natural diet for cows, animals that eat grains or corn—even if it's high-quality and organic—are not as healthy as their grass-fed counterparts, and therefore not as healthy for human consumption.

As far as factory-farmed beef goes, I advise avoiding it altogether because of the health, environmental, and moral issues involved. Injected with hormones, excessive antibiotics, and who knows what else, the cows raised in such farms are usually very sick—part of the reason they're injected with excess antibiotics. Grain-fed cattle have also been shown to be more likely infected by *E. coli*.

It may be more pricey to eat the highest quality beef, but think of that as a motivator for you to eat less meat overall.

FACTORY-FARMED COWS AND OBESITY

To make more money, growth hormones are injected into factory-farmed animals. So each animal's cells contain these hormones. When we consume meat, we are eating the cells of the animal and the growth hormones contained therein. Many people see a connection between this and the obesity epidemic, as well as the phenomenon of children entering puberty at younger and younger ages.

Chicken, **lamb**, and **pork** are all sources of protein and can be good for you, like beef, if you choose an organic, naturally raised animal and eat it in moderation.

FOOD COMBINING

The idea behind food combining is that some foods are more easily digested when consumed in tandem with other foods. Other combinations can have the opposite result: consumed together, they're harder to digest. For example, protein causes the body to produce specific enzymes and hydrochloric acid, which increases the stomach's acidity, whereas starches need an alkaline environment for digestion. Which means eating a lot of meat with starches can cause gas and indigestion. A food-combining solution: Pair meat with vegetables, such as leafy greens, instead.

Game animals, such as boar, bison, and venison, are among the healthiest kinds of meats. These animals are leaner than beef or chicken and boast a higher proportion of omega-3 fatty acids. In addition, they're less likely to be contaminated or diseased. It is becoming easier to find boar and venison in trendy restaurants, as well as in establishments emphasizing organic dishes, although, for some, venison's gamey flavor is an acquired taste. Bison is one of the most easily available game meats to buy for cooking at home. Nowadays, it is becoming more popular to farm-raise game animals, so opt for wild and free-range whenever possible.

Cured meats, such as sausages and bacon, can be okay to eat in moderation; it all comes down to how the animals were raised and how the products were made. I recommend cutting out luncheon meats altogether—nearly all of them contain carcinogenic preservatives such as nitrates. If you can't stay away from, say, bologna, at least get a package labeled "nitrate-free." Two requirements should be met before you purchase bacon or sausage: (1) The meat should have come from a good-quality animal, one that was naturally raised and fed (hormone- and antibiotic-free); and (2) the way the meat was made should be as natural as possible. Sausage without casings or fillers, produced locally, for instance, gets my thumbs-up—as long as you eat it in moderation.

ORGAN MEATS

A few nutritionally minded types, including followers of Weston A. Price, believe that the organs—particularly livers—are the most vitamin-dense parts of an animal (provided that that animal was raised sustainably and humanely). When we consume meat, we tend to eat steak, which is a muscle. If it doesn't gross you out, I suggest adding some of these off-cuts to your diet.

Fish

According to Seafood Watch, nearly 75 percent of the world's fisheries are currently overfished or are in danger of becoming so. Due to an increasing world population reliant on seafood, poor fishery management, high mercury content, and natural disasters such as the oil spill in the Gulf of Mexico, it is increasingly more important to be mindful of the seafood we are consuming. Here are some general guidelines to eating sustainably and healthfully.

Think about which species are naturally abundant versus species that are naturally sparse. Usually, species lower on the food chain require less resources than the larger, predatory species, so they are a more sustainable choice. Also remember to take into account fishing methods. Is the fish wild? Organically farmed? Factory farmed? To be sure you are choosing responsibly, remember to check labels—there are now rating systems that highlight the quality of the product. Don't be afraid to ask your local fish market/farmers' market where they source their fish from and check out pages 285 and 288 in the resource section for handy apps and websites that make it easy for you to shop and eat seafood healthfully.

Cold-water fish, such salmon, mackerel, cod, and sardines, are chock-full of heart-healthy omega-3 fatty acids as well as fat-soluble vitamins and minerals, including iodine. Unfortunately, these goodies are meaningless if the fish is conventionally farm-raised, a technique that results in more PCBs, mercury, and disease—and fewer omega-3s.[3] Plus, the feed for farmed salmon usually contains dye to give the flesh a pink color. To reap the full benefits of organically farm-raised or wild cold-water fish (salmon being the most common), eat it regularly. Most nutritious in its raw form (for instance, as sushi), it's also healthy when steamed or baked.

Scavenger fish include tuna, swordfish, carp, and catfish. They eat almost anything they find in the sea, including dead fish, which is why their tissues are likely to contain toxins such as PCBs and mercury. It's also why scavenger fish are considered no-no's for women who are pregnant or breast-feeding. If you like fish, I suggest sticking mostly to the cold-water kind.

Shellfish include scallops, clams, mussels, oysters, shrimp, crabs, and lobsters. They should be eaten in moderation and always while very fresh and in season. For a number of reasons, I am not a huge fan. They can be nutritious, but shellfish spoil easily, are prone to contamination, and are a common cause of food poisoning. Be sure yours are sourced from clean waters.

Dairy

Cheese and milk are comforting foods many of us have grown up with. However, dairy products have varying effects on your health, depending on who you are, how much you eat, and the quality of what you consume. Frankly, I'm not the biggest advocate of consuming a lot of dairy products, but I try to stay open-minded.

Dairy products' big selling point is that they are a source of calcium.[4] Yet milk creates an acidic environment in the body that may cause calcium to be leached from bones and may lead to osteoporosis.[5] In addition, its low magnesium content in relation to its calcium content means that the calcium may not get completely absorbed, as a balance of the two is required for proper utilization.

All in all, I think calcium is better obtained from vegetables, seeds, and nuts. Dairy products also have a tendency, for some people, to create mucus in the body, resulting in anything from a runny nose to a clogged-up digestive system.

As only around a quarter of the world's population possesses the genetic mutation required for the proper digestion of dairy, most people are lactose intolerant. People of Asian and African ethnicities tend to be more prone to lactose-intolerance, as dairy products are not traditionally prominent in their cultures' cuisines, which is why you're not likely to find many dairy products in Asian recipes or on the menu at an Asian restaurant. That doesn't mean dairy is the devil, at least not for people who digest it well—as long as you get it from grass-fed cows, or at a minimum, opt for an organic version. I recommend avoiding products containing recombinant bovine growth hormone, also known as rBGH, a genetically engineered drug associated with growth abnormalities and malignant tumors. Another reason to go organic: Conventional dairy cows are fed unnatural diets, forced to produce excessive quantities of milk, confined to small stalls or kept in unhygienic conditions, and often suffer from infected udders. This infection, called mastitis, causes the sick cows to release pus into their milk.

THE RAW MILK DEBATE

Most milk products are pasteurized and homogenized. Pasteurization is the process of applying very high heat to destroy all bacteria and most enzyme activity in the milk, while homogenization applies great pressure (so much pressure that the heat created causes a second pasteurization) to break up fat globules for a more uniform look. The dairy industry insists these processes are necessary for consumer safety, but they cause diminished vitamin and beneficial bacteria content, denatured milk proteins, and the promotion of pathogens. Plus, although no cases of illnesses have been linked definitively to raw milk from a grass-fed, organic source, there have been tons of allergies, sensitivities, and illness linked to pasteurized and homogenized milk. Raw milk from a grass-fed organic source has been shown to provide more EFAs (essential fatty acids that must be ingested because the body can't synthesize them) and CLA (conjugated linoleic acid, a beneficial fatty acid that contains cancer fighting properties) than pasteurized milk, as well as more beta-carotene, vitamin E, and vitamin A. Although it may spoil more quickly, because all nutrients are still intact, and most raw milk is sold in smaller batches, you get more bang for your buck. See page 285 to find where raw milk can be purchased near you.

Here is a roundup of dairy products you may encounter and some ways to choose responsibly:

Milk is often consumed at breakfast, with cereal, and also used in sauces, smoothies, and added to tea and coffee. Be aware that too much cow's milk contains more protein than we need and can cause weight gain. These days, there are many preferable alternatives, such as rice, almond, coconut, and hemp milk (note that I didn't include soy; see page 61), which can be found even in conventional markets and grocery stores. Be careful when buying these to opt for the unsweetened varieties.

Cheese is often a concentrated form of milk, best eaten in moderation. Some of my clients who want to reduce their cheese consumption find it extremely hard to do so; cheese is considered one of the most difficult foods to stop eating (in addition to sugar) because of its casein, a protein with addictive qualities.

One partial solution is to eat better types of cheese, such as raw (unpasteurized) versions, which retain more enzymes and nutrients, and boast an arguably better taste than their pasteurized counterparts. Although they're not yet available in quantities comparable to that of pasteurized cheeses in the United States, with demand, their availability is increasing, particularly in stores that stress organic or specialty foods.

Sheep and goat's milk cheeses are another smart alternative. Easier to digest than cheese made from cow's milk, these cheeses are increasingly popular as salad toppings and sandwich fillings.

And it should come as no surprise that I recommend avoiding processed cheese, a staple in some sandwiches and fast-food entrées. They usually contain additives, such as emulsifiers, extenders, phosphates, and hydrogenated oils. You'll likely find them easy to give up, considering their bland taste and plastic texture.

Cultured dairy products are easier to digest than other dairy items because their lactose and casein are already partially broken down; the most common products are **sour cream** and **buttermilk**.

Yogurt and kefir are typically the most digestible forms of dairy, as their live cultures help to break down the lactose. In fact, even those who are lactose intolerant are oftentimes able to digest yogurt and kefir without a problem. When purchasing yogurt, always look for organic, and when possible, from grass-fed cows. Plain is the best way to go, as most flavored yogurts are loaded with sugar and other additives and preservatives. Goat's milk yogurt is another great option as it is also easy to digest. Greek yogurt, though more difficult to find in an organic form, contains almost double the protein of regular yogurt, as most of the liquid whey, lactose, and sugars have been removed. Kefir is a liquid fermented yogurt traditionally created from camel's milk, although versions available today use cow's milk. Kefir contains more probiotics than yogurt does. Plus, the amino acids have been predigested, making it even easier to digest and absorb the nutrients. Kefir can be found in organic and grass-fed varieties. Most store-bought yogurt and kefir are pasteurized at high heats, killing both the good and bad bacteria, so try making it at home or buying from a local, small-operation source that uses live active cultures.

Butter has gotten a bad reputation over the years, perhaps undeservedly so. It's definitely not something you want to overeat, but unless you have a dairy allergy, a moderate amount of organic butter offers some benefits, including easily digestible good fats and vitamins A and D. **Ghee** is clarified butter with the milk solids removed, and therefore has a higher smoke point, making it a decent fat to use for high-temperature cooking. (See page 77 for an explanation of the importance of "smoke point.") Also, some people with lactose sensitivity find ghee easier to digest than other dairy products.

Ice cream should only be eaten in moderation. If you're a fan of these treats, try some of the naturally sweetened nut-based ice creams (often made from cashews or coconut milk) available in specialty food stores and raw-food restaurants. At the very least, opt for versions using dairy from grass-fed and/or organically raised cows.

Eggs

Eggs are often classified with dairy products (especially by veget-arians) because, like milk and cheese, they come from animals but the animals don't have to be killed to obtain the food. Rich in vitamins, minerals, and protein, eggs can be quite a nourishing and healthy complete food, especially if they are good quality and well prepared.

The cholesterol content of eggs causes debate; however, studies have recently shown that eating whole eggs actually increases your good cholesterol. The real problem arises when eggs are overcooked. The cholesterol becomes oxidized, transforming it from a useful nutrient into a potentially harmful chemical. For that reason, avoid powdered eggs, which have been through a heating and drying process and likely contain oxidized cholesterol. To avoid oxidation in your eggs, choose lightly poached or sunny-side-up eggs rather than scrambled or fried; similarly, soft-boiled trumps hard-boiled. Raw eggs are even more beneficial than the lightly cooked kind. However, people susceptible to salmonella, such as the elderly, the infirm, and pregnant women, should avoid raw eggs.

OXIDATION

Cut open an apple and watch it turn brown—that's oxidation in action. Oxidation is a naturally occurring chemical reaction that happens during normal activities such as exercise and digestion. When we eat poor-quality foods and are exposed to environmental toxins, oxidation reactions increase and can cause damage on a cellular level. This cellular damage produces free radicals, or unstable cells. Antioxidants can protect against the harsh effects of oxidation.

EAT THE WHOLE EGG

Most of the nutritional value of the egg comes in the yolk. It is high in choline, which has multiple anti-inflammatory properties, is higher in protein than the egg white, contains more absorbable lutein than spinach, and the cholesterol content in the yolk can actually prevent an unhealthy LDL/HDL ratio. Eat the whole she-bang, yolk and whites. Your body will thank you.

As with dairy and meat, your choice of egg supplier has implications for both nutritional quality and taste, as well as ethical concerns. Battery-caged hens may produce salmonella-infested eggs with few nutrients and a bland or fishy taste—and the cruelty of crowding hens together is another reason to skip buying such eggs. Free-range, pasture-raised hens, on the other hand, produce distinctive eggs; as with heirloom vegetables, the result is a richer flavor and increased nutrient content. At the very least, stick with hormone-and antibiotic-free eggs taken from cage-free hens.

1. For recommended protein intakes and advice for how to achieve them, see: http://www.ajcn.org/content/84/6/1456.abstract; http://www.cdc.gov/nutrition/everyone/basics/protein.html.

2. Source: *Journal of Agricultural and Food Chemistry*: http://pubs.acs.org/doi/abs/10.1021/jf8001813?prevSearch=%2522grass%2Bfed%2Bbeef%2522&search-HistoryKey=.

3. According to the Environmental Working Group, results from tests of store-bought farmed salmon showed seven of ten fish were so contaminated with PCBs that they raised cancer risk: http://www.ewg.org/reports/farmedpcbs.

4. A study by the official journal of the American Academy of Pediatrics concluded that "Scant evidence supports nutrition guidelines focused specifically on increasing milk or other dairy product intake for promoting child and adolescent bone mineralization." http://pediatrics.aappublications.org/content/115/3/736.abstract.

5. Source: *American Journal of Clinical Nutrition*: htttp://www.ajcn.org/content/59/6/1356.full.pdf+html.

CHAPTER 6
Popular Foods: Intelligent Choices

MANY OF US LONG FOR A "QUICK-FIX"—A MAGICAL answer that will take away all the confusion and challenges associated with food and allow us not to have to think about our diet anymore. Of course, as I've emphasized throughout this book, it's not that simple. There is no quick fix. I'm advocating that you think more about your diet, not less—that you learn to make informed, conscious choices every day. But if you're looking for an immediate result, I can give you one piece of advice that will make you feel better right away. It's my Fifth Precept—and if you've read this far, it won't be new to you, but I would like to highlight it once again.

The Fifth Precept: To feel better immediately, simply reduce your intake of artificial, chemical-laden processed foods, especially poor-quality oils and refined sugars.

In the following chapter, I discuss the kinds of things that make your mouth water—sweeteners, seasonings, fats and oils, and beverages. These more subtle foods may be potentially harmful, but they don't have to be, as long as you approach them the right way. Remember, I'm not one of those people whose definition of healthy eating means bland, flavorless food. Taste is central to my definition of clean eating. But there are ways to make your food delicious without damaging your health or the environment. That's what you'll find in this chapter.

As you read through the categories listed below, keep the Fifth Precept in mind. It can guide you in making the right choices for your health, and it really will have an immediately noticeable impact. It's less difficult to follow than you might think: Stick to the natural flavorings, not the substances created in a test tube. Do those long, chemical, hard-to-pronounce names even sound that tasty? Not really, right? Educating yourself about all of the tasty *and* natural substances out there (raw honey, anyone?) is the perfect insurance against being lured away by processed foods.

Fats and Oils

They've got a less-than-savory rep, but don't be afraid of fats and oils. They play an important role in the human diet, slowly releasing sugar from other foods, creating a feeling of satisfaction, giving us a source of energy, and allowing us to absorb fat-soluble vitamins, including A, D, E, and K, by carrying them across the gut wall. In addition, our body uses fats as building materials, incorporating them into the cell membranes to create the right balance between firmness and flexibility. We all know the negative side—weight gain, heart disease, and so on. Truth is, it can get kind of complicated, so let's simplify. The list of different fatty foods, fats, and oils is a long one, so here's what you need to know about the ones you are most likely to encounter in your daily food choices.

FATTY FOODS

Avocados, **raw nuts and seeds**, **coconuts**, and **olives** should form the bulk of your fat intake and are excellent sources of essential fatty acids, fiber, and other cofactors (but note that when these whole foods are processed into oils, some of these goodies are eliminated). These plant fats should not cause weight gain as part of a balanced diet, nor should they contribute to heart disease.

OILS

When cooking with fats and oils, it's important to be aware that a lot of oils are not stable enough to withstand high temperatures, and become damaged in ways that can be harmful.

Trans fats or **hydrogenated oils**, made by injecting hydrogen into liquid vegetable oils to make them more solid, should be completely avoided, as they are probably the most harmful ingredient in our food supply. They are usually found in the form of vegetable shortening and hydrogenated margarine. In fact, some cities, such as New York City, have banned the use of trans fats in restaurants.

Cooking oils: The best options for cooking are grapeseed oil, coconut oil, and olive oil in moderation.

Olive oil is a monounsaturated fat. Even though it has negligible amounts of essential fatty acids, it's better than many other oils and doesn't contain a high amount of omega-6. One form in which we tend to consume it—as salad dressing—is particularly good, as it has more benefits when raw, especially if it's extra-virgin, organic, and cold-pressed. Like most oils, though, high-quality olive oil has a low smoke point and is therefore damaged by high heat. For this reason, I suggest using it in moderation as a cooking oil.

SMOKE POINT

Most high-quality oils have a low smoke point. The smoke point is the temperature at which a cooking oil or fat begins to break down, marking the decline of both flavor and nutritional benefits. Typically, the more refined and processed the oil or fat, the higher the smoke point.

Coconut oil is a very stable oil when exposed to high temperatures and therefore is a good choice for high-heat cooking. Although it does contain saturated fats, coconut oil is unique in that it is made of medium-chained fatty acids. This type of fatty acid is burned for energy instead of stored as fat. In addition, coconut oil contains lauric acid, which is recognized for its antibacterial, antiviral, and antimicrobial properties. The only downside is that coconut oil has a distinct flavor, so be sure it jives with your dish. Coconut oil can also be consumed raw in smoothies and can be used to replace eggs or butter in vegan recipes.

Grapeseed oil is made by pressing the seeds of the grapes usually used for winemaking. It offers a more neutral flavor for cooking, and is a good replacement for the commonly used canola oil, which is best avoided due to the genetic modification of most canola crops. It's my preferred oil for everyday cooking due to its high smoke point, fairly neutral flavor, and nutritional benefits. It's rich in antioxidants and has been shown to stabilize blood sugar as well as be beneficial for heart disease and cancer.

Canola oil, also known as **rapeseed oil**, is becoming more and more widely available due to its low cost, low saturated fat content, and neutral flavor. In spite of these benefits, canola oil is a common genetically modified crop and it tends to be highly refined. Choose organic and expeller-pressed if you do choose to use it, and note that when buying any oil in this high-quality variety, it will tend to have a low smoke point.

Macadamia nut oil also has a high smoke point and it can be safely used for light sautéing, although its nutty flavor may not be suitable for some foods.

Noncooking oils such as flax, hemp, sesame, walnut, and pumpkin, are a great way to add taste and variety to dressings, soups, and sauces, though their low smoke point make them inappropriate for cooking. Opt for high-quality, cold-pressed versions of these oils when possible—though pricey, a little goes a long way.

Salt and Seasonings

My friends like to tease that I have a "salt tooth" in contrast to most people's "sweet tooth," but I've learned to treat salt as I would sugar—with fondness but also caution. Salt provides sodium, an important mineral involved in many bodily processes. However, it's unhealthy when you're getting a lot of sodium but hardly any potassium, a mineral found mainly in fresh fruits and vegetables. Sodium and potassium work together as intimate partners. It is essential that they remain in proper balance for the smooth functioning of the muscles, lungs, heart, and nervous system, as well as for the water balance within our bodies. In particular, many people suffer from raised blood pressure, muscle cramps, and water retention when they consume too much salt.

Most people get *way* more than enough salt whether they try to or not, just because salt, and therefore sodium, is overabundant in our modern, processed meals. Potassium, however, is lacking, because we don't eat enough vegetables. We need less than half a teaspoon of sodium per day, but many of us are consuming *seven* times that amount. If you want to reduce your sodium intake, the easiest and most effective thing to do is to reduce your intake of processed foods. Once you've reached a bare minimum on that front, then look to reducing the salt that you add to your food.

Experiment with preparing your meals using less salt. (To that end, you'll see that the recipes in this book typically don't use a specific amount of salt—instead they recommend you add salt to taste.) And try using more herbs and spices to make your meals more flavorful. You'll be amazed at how quickly you lose the desire for excess salt and start to find too much unappealing—I certainly have, despite my "salt tooth."

GOOD SALT SUBSTITUTES

One clever and healthful way to reduce your sodium intake is to use extra herbs and spices, increasing the flavor of your meal while adding some health benefits. Some of the best additions are garlic, a natural antibiotic; ginger, an anti-inflammatory and digestive aid; cayenne, a circulation enhancer; turmeric, an antioxidant and anti-inflammatory; dulse, a sea vegetable containing lots of minerals and iron; and green herbs, such as parsley or cilantro, a good source of vitamins and chlorophyll.

Refined table salt tends to be processed and altered with chemicals—it's sodium chloride with no nutritional benefits. I recommend deleting it from your diet, as it contributes to the sodium-potassium imbalance and usually contains aluminum to boot.

Kosher salt is a coarse salt with no additives; its thick crystal grains are used in the koshering process, thus its name. Foodies like this salt for its texture and taste; and perhaps because it appears in gourmet foods, it's sometimes thought to be healthier than table salt. That's not the case, however; there's no nutritional difference between kosher and table salt. Kosher salt may be marginally more healthful because it doesn't have additives.

Sea salt or **Himalayan crystal salt**, which are grayish or pink in color in their purest form, are both increasingly available and fine to eat in moderation, and are my recommendation for use in your cooking and on the table. Natural and unprocessed, they contain minerals from the ocean and have a better flavor than table salt.

Bragg's Liquid Aminos is a low-sodium alternative to soy sauce (also made from soybeans) that can be found in many health food stores. It adds a strong, savory flavor to foods and is better than table salt, but I recommend limiting its use. Despite its name, the amount of amino acids (i.e., protein) that it provides is negligible. And like soy sauce, it has been found to contain some naturally occurring monosodium glutamate (MSG), a flavor enhancer that has been associated with various health problems.

Shoyu and **tamari**, both commonly referred to as soy sauce, are fermented soy condiments, with the only difference being that tamari is wheat-free. Asian cuisine uses shoyu and tamari as a condiment, and also as an ingredient for stir-frying. Naturally brewed and low-sodium versions are preferable to highly processed and additive-laden cheaper imitations. However, I find soy sauce a questionable substitute for table salt because of the soy, wheat, and the inevitable processing that goes into it. Use it sparingly.

Sweeteners

"You're sweet." "How sweet it is." "That's sweet." The English language is peppered with reminders of how, well, *sweet* sweetness is. So it's understandable that when I talk about sugary foods, I tend to encounter the most resistance and guilt in my clients.

It's not exactly a news flash that refined white sugar and the more insidious high-fructose corn syrup are bad for us. But it's still hard, tortuous even, to give them up. That's because sugar is addictive. Stop eating it and you'll experience withdrawal symptoms. Eat some and you will crave more.

Then there's the emotional aspect of sugar cravings. Consider how children are offered sweets if they're "good" or if they "behave." To make matters worse, it seems that we have been biologically programmed to seek out sweetness as a way to avoid poison, which tends to be bitter. But I bet evolution intended for us to eat fruits and not, say, doughnuts.

Even though you know that sweets are bad for you, it's worth pointing out the many ways they're bad. Sugar is an antinutrient, not only giving the body zero nutrition, but actually robbing us of goodies. Plus, it's probably the major contributor to weight gain: The body puts excess sugar into storage to quickly remove it from the blood, where it would otherwise create havoc and at a certain point of saturation, the body converts it to fat. After all, there is only so much sugar that we can use as energy. Sugar has been linked to a variety of other ailments, from lowered immunity and poor gut flora to cancer and diabetes.

Yet, according to the USDA, we are eating increasingly more sugar. The average American consumes over a cup a day of the stuff—an increase of 23 percent between 1985 and 1999. So what should we do? Well, we have to be really smart about our approach. Something I have noticed with my clients is that once they begin to take better care of themselves in other areas of their lives and eat better-quality foods, their cravings for sweets tend to lessen. Sometimes exercise helps, as does eating a little more protein and drinking more water. I always suggest a switch to more natural, gentler forms of sweeteners. Take these steps and over time you will gradually experience refined sugar as being too sweet and tasting fake. True, it may take a while, but I've found that this approach has worked, not only for me but for many former sugar addicts with whom I've worked.

Let's take a look at some of the common sweeteners you will encounter. And remember—while some of those listed below are far better for your health than others, none of them are health foods and even the best of them should only be eaten in moderation.

Granulated white sugar, **high-fructose corn syrup**, and even **brown sugar** should be avoided as much as possible.

Organic raw cane sugar, **Florida Crystals**, and **turbinado sugar** have gained in popularity and are commonly found in health food stores and restaurants. Although I am not a big fan and don't use them myself, I believe they are a slightly better option than the completely refined stuff, since these kinds of sugars do retain some nutrients and are better for the environment. But they're not healthy.

Coconut palm sugar and **coconut nectar** are my sweeteners of choice and preferable to all of the above due to their low glycemic index and high nutrient content. Because of coconut palm sugar's granular consistency, it can be a good alternative to refined white or brown sugar in cooking. Coconut nectar is a cleaner alternative to high-fructose corn syrup and even agave nectar. Unlike most agave nectars, coconut nectar is raw and therefore contains active enzymes, amino acids, and a nice vitamin and mineral profile. While these are great options from a nutritional perspective, please take note that there are some environmental concerns; it still remains unknown whether the coconut tree can continue producing coconuts after the sap has been removed from its palm.

Maple syrup and **brown rice syrup** are two very common natural sweeteners. While not ideal because they can negatively impact existing digestive issues and have a fairly high glycemic index, they are okay in moderation if they are pure and of a high quality. I lean toward maple syrup over brown rice syrup, as some studies have shown brown rice syrup to contain arsenic.

Raw honey is a far better choice than many of the other sweeteners, especially the unheated varieties, which are rich in antioxidants, enzymes, and various healing cofactors. However, strict vegans see honey as an animal product, and therefore don't include it in their diet.

Raw agave nectar has fast become the sweetener of choice among those looking to avoid refined sugar. I believe it's a better option than refined sugar, yet it still has its issues, including a very high fructose content and dubious production standards. I suggest using it in moderation.

Molasses is also a decent option, favored for its high iron, calcium, and potassium content, as well as its high chromium level, which helps stabilize blood sugars.

Stevia (technically a supplement), is an extract from the sweet leaves of the stevia plant. It is becoming increasingly popular for its highly sugary taste and safeness for diabetics, although some people are not crazy about its aftertaste and inability to mix well in liquids, such as coffee. Don't choose the newer white variety, which is highly refined. Although the stevia plant has been used safely by humans for a long time, the long-term safety of the refined products derived from the plant is still unknown.

Artificial sweeteners, such as Splenda, Equal, or NutraSweet (aspartame) should be avoided. There are more adverse reactions to NutraSweet reported to the FDA than to all other foods and additives combined. Plus, there is even convincing evidence that these artificial sweeteners lead to weight gain. Because they are up to six hundred times sweeter than sugar, they tend to raise our expectations of how sweet foods should be.

Beverages

A sparkling stream of water runs through a picturesque valley. This could be an ad for anything from beer to an energy drink. The point? Advertisers know that we know that water is good for us. So they use it to sell beverages that aren't so good. Read on for details about the drinks you might encounter on a daily basis.

Water should be your beverage of choice, in my opinion; usually it is the most natural and the purest liquid you can get. Drinking plenty of water keeps your body's natural detoxification systems flowing, helps fight cellular inflammation, and balances an acidic environment in the body. It can also have the added benefit of reducing your appetite. Often, we confuse our thirst with hunger, and think we are craving food when in fact what our body needs is water. Next time you find yourself longing for a snack, try drinking a glass of water and see if the craving fades. That being said, however, don't overdo your water consumption. If you are running to the bathroom every ten minutes and your urine is completely clear, you may be in danger of overtaxing your kidneys.

Filtered tap water is the best choice in most situations. It's free, safe, and better for the environment than bottled water (plus, you avoid ingesting chemicals that may leach into the water from the plastic bottle). Opt for filtered water whenever available, and invest in a filtration system for your home. Bottled water tends to be overpriced, and the environmental cost is even higher. Americans use 2 million plastic bottles *every five minutes*. Imagine them all stacked up in a pile. The amount of oil needed to make those bottles equals about 15 million barrels a year. Even recycling them means using more fossil fuels. The only time I advocate choosing bottled water is where the only other option is unfiltered tap water, which is often polluted by chlorine and fluoride, among other contaminants.

Fruit juices are okay to drink but have high fructose levels, which is why I recommend diluting them with water. Freshly squeezed juice is always the best option, but if you buy it bottled, read the label to check that it is not sweetened and ideally not from concentrate. Look for brands that incorporate vegetables into their fruit juices, and if you are making your own fruit juices, try adding a few veggies, such as celery or carrots.

Vegetable juices are a much better choice than fruit juices. They count toward your nutrient intake, especially with dark greens thrown in. Again, opt for fresh over bottled.

COLD-PRESSED JUICES

When making or purchasing juice, cold-pressed is the ideal way to go. Unlike the typical centrifugal juicer that uses heat and static electricity for extraction, cold-pressing mashes the fruit, thereby retaining vital nutrients and preventing oxidation. Cold-pressed juices have a longer shelf life than do other freshly squeezed juices, but still need to be consumed within three days. While cold-pressed juicers are quite pricey, more and more health food stores are stocking prebatched cold-pressed juice.

Sodas and **soft drinks** are composed of unfiltered, artificially carbonated water with added sugar (or worse, corn syrup or artificial sweeteners), flavorings, colorings, preservatives, and sometimes caffeine. In addition, their high phosphoric-acid content is associated with osteoporosis. Not a recipe for health. I recommend avoiding them altogether, especially the diet ones, which are loaded with artificial sweeteners that, research has suggested, may actually cause weight gain. As long as they're sweetened with fruit juice instead of cane sugar, natural sodas are fine to drink in moderation, as they're made from cleaner water and are caffeine-free.

ELECTROLYTES FOR ATHLETES

Looking to replenish those electrolytes after a tough workout? Replace your Gatorade with coconut water now widely available in most grocery stores. It's loaded with electrolytes and a naturally sweet taste to boot. Opt for the plain with no sugars added.

Coffee can provide a much-needed lift. Still, my recommendation is to reduce caffeine consumption with the goal of eventually giving it up altogether. Sure, some people metabolize caffeine better than do others. Coffee beans contain antioxidants, and some recent studies suggest many benefits associated with coffee. However, caffeine in general, and coffee in particular, is also linked to raised blood pressure, insomnia, nervous conditions, osteoporosis, and certain cancers. It is also very acidic and dehydrating. Imbibing caffeine with your meal reduces the availability of minerals in the food—it leaches them out. If you can't resist a cup of coffee now and then, opt for decaf or half-caf and be sure to choose an organic, Fair Trade, or shade-grown version and drink after eating, as a digestive aid of sorts.

COFFEE REPLACEMENT

Raw cacao nibs make a tasty interim crutch for people trying to break their coffee habit. Cacao will give you a lift partially from caffeine, and partially from other natural happiness-inducing chemicals. Plus, it's extraordinarily rich in magnesium and antioxidants (sorry, chocolate bars with their cooked cocoa and sugar don't count as a whole-food alternative to coffee). Restaurants that serve raw or live desserts—meaning enzymes and healthy bacteria are active in the food—often offer a raw cacao–based option, naturally sweetened to boot.

Grain coffee substitutes, such as Teeccino, are caffeine-free yet have coffee's robust taste.

Green tea may be the most healthful, or at least the most benign, of all caffeinated beverages. It contains polyphenols, a type of antioxidant that can reduce blood pressure (note coffee's opposite effect), lower blood-level fats, and combat free radicals. It contains much less caffeine than coffee. In addition, it has theanine, which mitigates some of caffeine's effects to produce a calmer type of energy and prevent a caffeine "hangover."

Black tea has fewer antioxidants and more caffeine than green. But it doesn't contain as much caffeine as coffee, unless it is steeped for an especially long time. Both green and black tea come from the same plant, often one that's been heavily sprayed with pesticides, so seek out an organic version.

White tea has a rich nutritional profile, with less caffeine than green or black varieties. Its high catechin level is said to cleanse the intestines and prevent against oxidation. Plus, because it is harvested early and dried immediately (unlike green or black tea), less oxidation occurs in the processing. White tea is rich in fluoride, and can potentially help prevent the growth of dental plaque. Some studies show that white tea has the ability to kill bacteria, viruses, and fungi with a higher rate of success than any other type of tea making it more effective in preventing cancer cell growth.[1]

Decaffeinated tea or **coffee** is fine to drink if the caffeine has been removed using the Swiss-water process. Otherwise, residue from chemicals used to remove the caffeine might remain—a nonissue if the product is certified organic. Either way, all decaffeinated beverages still contain some traces of caffeine.

Herbal teas may be the best hot drink overall, as they are naturally caffeine-free and boast mild therapeutic benefits. For instance, peppermint and ginger tea are both helpful to drink after a heavy meal, since they aid digestion; chamomile, as you probably know, has calming properties.

Fermented drinks are digestive aids, rich in enzymes and probiotics. They are increasingly available in health food stores, juice bars, and health-conscious restaurants. *Kombucha* is a fermented cold drink rich in enzymes, probiotics, and B vitamins, and is a wonderful aid to digestion and general well-being. Other common kinds of fermented drinks include *amazake*, made from rice; kefir, which is lacto-fermented milk; and traditional-style ginger ale and apple cider, both healthy when made using old-fashioned methods with no sugar added.

Wine is fermented, true, but I believe that its alcohol content tends to neutralize the much-touted health benefits. Although wine has been in the news as being good for you in various small ways, my experience is that people use that as an excuse to drink too much. Even in relatively small amounts, wine is an antinutrient, particularly good at robbing the body of B vitamins. All alcohol can make you accident prone, dehydrated, unable to concentrate, and even aggressive. It should be avoided if you are susceptible to *Candida* overgrowth. Long-term drinking to excess, whether labeled alcoholism or not, can result in liver damage and stomach ulcers, not to mention a host of social and emotional problems.

Still, like coffee, alcohol can be useful in moderation. After a stressful day at work, a relaxing glass of wine can make all the difference to your enjoyment of a meal and your ability to converse with fellow diners. Plus, it can stimulate the digestive process. Red wine in particular provides some antioxidant benefits and is said to be good for the heart in moderate amounts. As with coffee, though, there is no need to rely on wine for your antioxidants; think vegetables and fruits instead.

If you do choose to consume alcohol, organic red wine is the best choice; like other organic goods, these drinks should be free of pesticides. Biodynamic wine is arguably better than regular organic, because biodynamic producers go to extraordinary lengths to create special, pure growing conditions. These wines are increasingly available in specialty wine stores or in health food stores with a wine section.

Specialty wine stores may also offer wines labeled sulfite-free or NSA, meaning "no sulfites added." Sulfites occur naturally on grapes, but many vineyards add more to prevent bacterial growth, oxidation, and a vinegary taste. Many people experience allergic side effects, including headaches, when they consume sulfites, and some connoisseurs prefer the taste of a low-sulfite wine. White wine generally has fewer sulfites than red.

Beer, **ale**, and **lager** are lower in alcohol than wine, but it's still important to watch the amount that you drink.

Hard liquor or **spirits**, such as vodka, tequila, or rum, are much higher in alcohol than both wine and beer, which is why they're often diluted with tonic water or fruit juice. Be especially careful of these because of the high alcohol content.

---

1. For more on the benefits of white tea, see:
http://www.pacificcollege.edu/acupuncture-massage-news/articles/532-health-benefits-of-white-tea.html, http://www.cancer.gov/cancertopics/factsheet/prevention/tea, and http://www.sciencedirect.com/science/article/pii/S13835 71801002005.

CHAPTER 7

Mind-Set Matters: Ingredients of a Healthy Attitude

AS I'VE SAID, I BELIEVE THAT HAVING PRACTICAL
tools and advice is one of the most important factors in creating actual change. But another factor is critical, too: having the
right mind-set. Previously, I discussed some of the motivations that
might inspire you to eat healthier. In this chapter, I'll focus on how to
build healthy habits and a sound mind-set so that the change can easily be
put into action and sustained. If you are already on the path to eating
healthier, you may want to look at this as a friendly reinforcement of your
current way of thinking. Although the issues we will be focusing on in
this chapter are less tangible—thoughts, emotions, cultural beliefs, and
cravings—the advice I give will be very practical and down to earth.

Our relationship to food is one of the most intimate and complex relationships in our life. It forms in early childhood, shaped by our upbringing, our family's economic circumstances, our parents' attitudes, and the
pressures of our peer groups. An unhealthy relationship to food is sometimes exacerbated by the fact that many of us have lost touch with our natural physiological responses to what we eat. For example, some people

are so used to overeating that they don't know what it is like to feel satiated but not overfull. Others tend to be more in touch with their cravings than with their body's actual needs. And all of this is because our culture fosters a lack of awareness of the eating process—we eat in front of our computer or television, as we're walking down the street, or while talking on our cell phone. We are not culturally encouraged to eat mindfully. Traditional cultures created rituals, such as the Japanese tea ceremony or the elaborate multicourse formal dinner, that encouraged slow, mindful eating and appreciation of food, but these have been largely lost in fast-paced contemporary society. Fast food is unconscious food. And without consciousness, the faculty of choice becomes guided by more primitive instincts and habit patterns.

Developing a Healthy Relationship with Food

For some of us, our relationship to food is akin to an unhealthy relationship with another person—it's been the way it is for as long as we can remember, and it's hard to know where to begin untangling the web of emotions and unconscious habits. But don't be intimidated by the task. Some very simple, practical steps that you can take will make a big difference right away. Here are a few that I have found to be most effective.

SET YOUR INTENTION

The first step to having a healthy relationship and sustaining change is to be really clear on your intention. It is important to understand your motivations and deeply commit to eating healthier in a way that is right for you. You should recognize that it might be challenging along the way, but you should also be very confident that you will be able to do it over the long haul.

ACCEPT AND DEPERSONALIZE

For many of us, an unhealthy relationship to food goes together with an equally unhealthy attitude toward our own body and mind. While the desire to improve our physical health, strength, and beauty is a positive thing, the standards we tend to set for ourselves are often unrealistic. We are not all perfect specimens, and there is no ideal to which we should be conforming. Often our ideals are so far away from the reality of our life that we subconsciously feel like a failure before we have even begun. In order to change, it is important that you come to a deep acceptance of your body and mind, with their particular needs and proclivities. This acceptance doesn't mean you don't strive to change, but it will allow you to be patient with yourself. And remember, everyone has challenges. We are all human. Your struggles aren't just *your* struggles, and that craving isn't just *yours*. We tend to victimize ourselves and believe it's harder for us to stay on track than it is for everyone else. This kind of thinking only weakens our will to persevere. Be a warrior, not a victim. Knowing that the process you are experiencing is impersonal makes it much easier.

SEEK SUPPORT

As we have discussed, our relationship to food does not develop in a vacuum. You may come up against resentment and pressure from loved ones, which may act as a deterrent. Don't be discouraged. Remember, change can often make others feel uncomfortable or threatened, especially if they feel pressured to make similar changes. To help you persevere, seek support from others who share your intentions and understand the new values you are striving to embrace. Find a friend or even a professional nutritional consultant or coach who can support you through your transition. Studies have shown that people who have a "buddy" on this journey are much more successful than those who go at it alone.

Try not to impose your choices on others—remember the precept of bio-individuality; what works for your body may not work for theirs. Instead, try to make them understand it isn't personal—your choice to skip your mother's famous apple pie doesn't come from a place of arrogance. By choosing foods that maximize our mental and physical potential, we are choosing a fuller and more dynamic life. Be grateful to yourself for making good choices and be grateful to those who support you in making them.

THE GIFT OF CHOICE

One of the greatest gifts of being human is the ability to make independent, conscious choices. Be grateful for your power of choice, and strive to bring it into alignment with your highest intentions.

CROWD OUT

The word *diet* is laden with negative connotations because it typically describes a restriction of food or calories. I believe this is part of the reason why fad diets are so difficult to maintain. Nearly 65 percent of dieters return to their predieting weight within three years, according to Gary Foster, PhD, clinical director of the Weight and Eating Disorders Program at the University of Pennsylvania. Food is one of life's greatest pleasures, and it is a tragedy how many people miss out on enjoying it because they are so entangled in negative emotions. Eating food (healthy or not) should never be a "crime" or "wrong"; it should be a pleasure and a privilege. By demonizing foods as "bad," we foster negative emotions, such as fear and guilt. And guilt tends to cause counterproductive activities, such as restricting calories, skipping meals, and obsessing over the past. To break the association of diet with deprivation, focus on adding foods that are aligned with your intentions and goals rather than subtracting foods that you think you "shouldn't" eat. Frame your changes as positives rather than negatives. If something is "bad" we consider it "off-limits," and when something is off-limits, human nature seems to make us want it more. Instead of dwelling on what you need to eliminate, simply eat more of the good stuff so that it "crowds out" both the desire and the space for unhealthy foods. Unless you have a serious illness or allergy, there is room for every food in your diet, so long as you practice moderation.

THE 80/20 RULE

No one eats perfectly all the time; it isn't practical (or fun!) to strive for that unrealistic goal. I like to use the "80/20 rule"—eat well 80 percent of the time, and relax a little for the remaining 20 percent. At first, you may need to be satisfied with eating healthier about half of the time, but once you do get to that 50/50 mark, you will have the momentum to go further, slowly, from 60/40 to 70/30 and onward, until you may even hit 90/10. Don't be too extreme right away. Start with a 50 percent goal and see what happens. There are different ways to do this—some people have adopted the idea of "Meatless Mondays," for example. Others like to be more rigorous with their food choices during the week but loosen up on the weekends. Some people find that including little indulgences every day helps them stay on track and avoid bingeing.

Studies show that people who give in to their cravings every once in a while actually maintain a healthier body image and weight than people who don't. For example, if you are with family for the holidays and there is a dish you typically wouldn't eat but is part of your family's tradition, the healthiest choice may be to join your family in sharing that dish. Or if you really crave chocolate, but because it's "bad," decide to eat other foods in its place, only to end up caving in and eating the chocolate anyway, it may have made more sense to just allow yourself the chocolate in the first place, when you probably would have eaten much less. If you always deny yourself the foods you love, the cravings become much stronger and you may grow resentful. When indulging, try choosing high-quality versions of your favorite treats—such as a naturally sweetened dessert or organic potato chips with sea salt—and most important, enjoy it! Don't feel guilty for days afterward. Eat it, enjoy it, and let it go.

Cultivate Awareness
and Foster Patience

Becoming more aware is a foundational part of the Clean Plates approach because it makes you conscious of your choices. Think about your particular habits. Do you eat mindlessly in front of the television? Do you tend to not eat all day and then binge at night? Do you turn to food for comfort when you are feeling stressed, tired, or depressed? Once you've identified these patterns, reflect on where they may stem from. Were they passed on to you from your parents? Are they associated with certain memories of positive or negative situations? Another way to cultivate more awareness is to keep a detailed food journal with your emotions, thoughts, and sensations before and after eating, so that you are more in tune with how certain foods affect you.

Once you've become aware of your habits, you can try different responses to the situations that trigger you to eat unconsciously. For example, if you are stressed, plan to take a walk around the block before you eat anything. Give yourself time to feel the emotions before you pacify them. If you tend to see food as a reward for success, find another way to celebrate your achievements. Pamper yourself with a massage instead of a tub of Häagen-Dazs. And make an effort to eat consciously. Try putting away all of your distractions—stay seated away from your computer or TV while eating and enjoy your food in solitude or with family and friends.

In the midst of your busy, stressful life, you may find the effort needed to remain aware of your choices to be overwhelming and that there are certain areas in which you are really resisting change. Identify these, and don't worry about them for now. Start with areas where there is less resistance. Your successes will give you the motivation to move on to the tougher habits. Also, in bringing consciousness to different areas of your life, you may be surprised at the emotional reactions that are stirred. As we've discussed, food is often related to some deeply rooted emotional and psychological issues. Make space for yourself to experience these coming to the surface—it's a healthy process.

If things aren't happening as quickly as you would have liked, remember that change takes time—especially when habits are deep. Studies have shown that it takes at least thirty days of consistent action to break an old habit and create a new one. The good news is that little changes do make a big difference. The human body is very resilient. Patience and perseverance will pay off.

Healthy Choices

All of the advice I've shared in this chapter should help when you come to the critical moments: the moments of choice. In the end, a healthy relationship to food is one that supports you in making conscious, informed choices on a day-to-day basis, based on your deeper long-term intentions rather than your superficial short-term desires. The ability to make conscious choices is like a muscle that we need to build, through practice and commitment and consistency.

As you do this, you will find that it gets easier. Once you make a commitment to change, and start to follow through on it, you will feel better about yourself. Eating well takes away a lot of the subconscious guilt that can sap your energy, and frees up your attention for the things you care about. A positive momentum starts to build which will inspire you to keep taking steps forward. Life is a precious gift. If you are poorly nourished, you will miss out on its extraordinary potentials. I like to think that every time we put food in our mouth, it is our way of saying "Yes!" to life. Food is our life source. So by choosing foods that maximize our mental and physical potential as human beings, we choose a fuller and more dynamic life. I am grateful for having this human body and mind, which gives me the opportunity to do good in the world. I recognize that my life is intricately interconnected with those around me and the planet we share. Having respect for my own body and taking good care of it is the foundation for having a positive impact on the broader web of life. And food sustains all of it. When you create a healthy relationship to food, you give yourself the energy and the alertness to appreciate and contribute to the unfolding of this human adventure—for yourself, and for future generations.

CHAPTER 8

Your Clean Plates Lifestyle: Putting It All Together

CLEAN EATING IS A JOURNEY—A LIFELONG JOURNEY that will continue to take you into new terrain as your body changes, your tastes evolve, and both you and society at large learn more about nutrition and health. You may be well along on that road—if so, I hope that this book will be a helpful companion as you continue on your way. If you are just setting out, don't panic if you're feeling overwhelmed by all the information you've learned in these chapters—you don't have to embrace it all at once, and no one is expecting you to be eating perfectly (remember the 80/20 rule). If you're inspired by the potential for bringing greater consciousness and intelligence to your food choices, just start taking simple steps.

As you move forward in this journey, think of the Five Precepts as general orienting principles to help you make choices. Let's remind ourselves of what they are:

1. There's more than one right way to eat.

2. The overwhelming majority of your diet should consist of real, high-quality, and whole foods.

3. Everyone would be better off if a larger proportion of his or her diet consisted of plants—mostly vegetables (in particular, leafy greens), and some nuts, seeds, and fruits.

4. If you choose to eat animal products, consume only (a) high-quality and sustainably raised animals (ideally pasture-raised and grass-fed, but at least hormone- and antibiotic-free); and do so (b) in moderation (meaning smaller portions with less frequency) and (c) using the right cooking methods.

5. To feel better immediately, simply reduce your intake of artificial, chemical-laden processed foods, especially poor-quality oils and refined sugars.

I want to make it easy for you to transition—and stick—to healthier eating, in your own home and also in the many other circumstances you will encounter throughout your day. In this chapter, I'll be sharing numerous psychological and social tips for following the precepts outlined here. We'll start with the places your home-cooked meals are born—in your own kitchen, and in the grocery store or farmers' market where you buy your ingredients. Then I'll address some of the more difficult social situations you might find yourself in, and offer tips for staying on track. Lastly, I'll give you some advice on how to eat your food, wherever you may be eating it, for you to get maximum benefits.

Setting Up Your Kitchen

It's a lot easier to cook nutritious and healthy meals when you have the right ingredients and the right tools (especially a good chef's knife) in place. When you make a commitment to change your eating habits, solidify that commitment by having a kitchen cleanup. Get rid of clutter and things you don't use. Invest in a few simple tools to help you cook the kinds of meals you plan to eat. Clean out your cupboards and your refrigerator and freezer, throwing out or donating to a local food bank the foods you don't want to eat any more, whether it's cans of processed soup or frozen dinners, bags of white flour or sugary breakfast cereals. Make plenty of space in your refrigerator for all those fresh veggies you will be eating!

Grocery Shopping

If there is a good health-food oriented market in your area, try to shop there as often as possible—it is worth driving a little farther and paying a little more for the difference in the quality of food. If there is a local farmers' market, even better—you will find that to be a great source for many of the fresh ingredients recommended in this book, and you'll know that they are local as well. (See page 285 for information on how to find farmers' markets.) However, if your choices are limited to the standard supermarket chains, don't worry. An increasing range of healthy choices are available there as well.

When shopping, it always helps to be prepared. Make a list, thinking through what you plan to cook and what ingredients you will need. It can be helpful to keep a list of staples that you can check through each time you shop. Another great tip is to eat before you shop—just as going to a party with an empty stomach increases your likelihood of snacking, going to the grocery store hungry makes it much more likely that you will give in to impulses to buy foods you otherwise might choose to leave on the shelf. Make sure that you give yourself enough time when you are shopping—again, this allows you to make conscious choices, to read the ingredients and pick the best options rather than grabbing the nearest or most familiar brand. Aim to spend the most time in the outer aisles of the grocery store—this is where the minimally processed food usually lives. And if your local store doesn't carry the items you want or the quality you are looking for, ask the store manager. Very often, the manager may be willing to order new items if he or she knows that customers are requesting them. Shop regularly enough that you keep your fridge well stocked with fresh, wholesome, nutritious food. "Shop more, buy less" is a good approach, ensuring that your fresh produce won't go bad.

Tips for Tricky Situations

It's one thing to create a haven for clean eating in the privacy of your own home. It's quite another thing to stay on track in the multitude of different social situations that most of us find ourselves in on a daily basis. Again, remember the 80/20 rule—you don't have to be perfect all the time. That being said, here's some advice for a few of the common scenarios that can present challenges to healthful eating.

BREAKFAST

When you're running late for work or trying to get the kids to school, it can be all too easy to skip breakfast, or just grab something easy, such as a piece of toast or a cereal bar. Studies have shown, however, that people who take the time to eat a good, nutritious breakfast consume less throughout the day and suffer from fewer cravings. Wherever possible, make the time to eat a good, balanced breakfast. Try the Breakfast Experiment, described on page 28, to figure out what's the best kind of breakfast for you. Try eating your leftover grains from the previous night for breakfast with an egg on top, or lentils and greens. Cook extra quinoa during the day that you can heat up with almond milk, nuts, and fruit.

SNACKING

We all, at least occasionally, get the urge to snack, and the candy bars in the vending machine or the cookies at the coffee shop can be very tempting. If you eat good, nutrient-dense meals throughout the day, you will find that you feel much less need to snack. If you do need to snack, make sure you have healthy options on hand, such as baby carrots with homemade hummus (recipe on page 140), nuts and seeds, kale chips (recipe on page 143), or sliced fruit and almond butter. I recommend keeping a bag of nuts and sugar-free, unsulfured[1] dried fruits with you at all times in case of an emergency. Remember also to stay hydrated, so that you don't mistake thirst for hunger.

TRAVELING

Any time you are on the road, it's much harder to control your food choices. Don't be too hard on yourself if it's just an occasional trip, but especially if you are a regular traveler, it's good to be prepared. Take a few minutes before a trip to research food markets and healthy restaurants near the area where you are staying, to reduce the chances that you'll make bad choices in the moment. Think of foods you can easily carry with you, such as bags of nuts and dried fruit, or packets of oatmeal that you can easily eat for breakfast. If you have a long flight ahead of you, take the time to pack a healthy meal to eat on the plane. If you're going to be in one place for a while, consider booking a hotel room or suite with a kitchenette—you can often do this for very little extra cost, and you'll save by preparing some of your own food instead of eating out three times a day.

PARTIES AND BARS

Social situations like these can be tough, but again, don't be too hard on yourself. Allow a little indulgence without letting yourself go completely. A great strategy I often recommend to clients is to eat a good meal before going to a party or meeting friends for drinks—that way, you'll be full and less tempted to munch. And sip your drinks slowly.

EATING OUT

Eating out with others in a good restaurant is one of the great pleasures of life. Wherever possible, check the menus online before you make a reservation, so that you choose somewhere with plenty of healthful options. Visit www.cleanplates.com for my recommendations in several major cities, and download the Clean Plates app for your smartphone so that good advice is always in your purse or pocket. Even with the best intentions, however, you will occasionally end up at a restaurant that does not serve healthy food and/or with a group of diners who do not share your dietary goals. In those instances, you can stay on track by asking for a special order or combination of side dishes, such as vegetables and a whole grain. Or try asking for an entrée-size version of a healthy-looking appetizer salad. Most restaurants are quite accommodating. Other good ideas include asking for the salad dressing or sauce on the side, so you can control how much you use, and asking to substitute brown rice for white, or green veggies for French fries. Lastly, remember, just because the bread is complimentary does not mean that you have to eat it. Likewise, try to ignore those fortune cookies or mints that arrive with the bill.

HOW TO EAT

Whatever you choose to eat, and wherever you choose to eat it, *how* you eat also plays an important role. Here are a few helpful tips:

Chew: Sounds obvious, but you'd be surprised how many people don't, at least not properly. Thorough mastication helps your body digest nutrients better—and makes your food taste better. To see just how little chewing we all do, try chewing ten to twenty times per mouthful, or until the food becomes liquid. You'll be surprised how difficult it is!

Eat slowly: Pause between bites to savor the flavors and check in with your stomach to ask, "Are you full yet?" This will make your meal last longer and help prevent the discomfort and weight gain associated with overeating.

Don't overeat: Eating slowly and chewing properly helps prevent this, but note how much you cook in the first place. Practice portion control. Whether you're cooking a meal at home or eating in a restaurant, it's unnecessary to have an appetizer and dessert as well as an entrée.

Avoid distractions: If you're not good at blocking out extraneous noise and distractions, you might want to eat in silence or alone occasionally. But given that most meals are a fun, shared experience, try to dine with people who don't give you indigestion. Keep heated debates to a minimum so that you can chew and assimilate the food properly. Reading and television are also distracting.

Don't eat under stress: Anxiety and anger mess with the digestive function, as part of the fight-or-flight response. Eating under such circumstances can cause indigestion. At such times you will be tempted to go for comfort foods or to overeat to numb your feelings.

Practice gratitude: Be thankful for your food and for all the people and forces that brought it to your plate: the sun that shone down on it, the farmer who grew it, the person who cooked it (which may be yourself!). Taking a moment to give thanks will calm you and remind you of your connection to the whole. It will also enable you to feel grateful for real, healthy food and simple pleasures.

Enjoy: Whatever you choose to eat—even if you know it is not perfectly healthy—allow yourself to enjoy it. Guilt is a stressor that makes you, and your digestive system, unhappy.

And remember, whatever you do, eat your veggies!

---

1. Sulfur compounds can be used as a preservative for dried fruit, but have been linked to adverse reactions).

CHAPTER 9

The Recipes

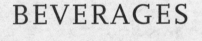

BEVERAGES

SEASONAL FRUIT SPARKLING SODA

COCONUT HOT COCOA

ORANGE, HERB, AND HONEY ICED TEA

MAPLE GINGER LEMONADE

APPLE-CUCUMBER-LIME AGUA FRESCA

BANANA ALMOND KEFIR SHAKE

BASIC BERRY SMOOTHIE

CHOCOLATY SUPERFOODS SMOOTHIE

Seasonal Fruit Sparkling Soda

HERE'S A SIMPLE AND EASY WAY TO TURN A BASIC FRUIT JUICE INTO A special, festive refreshment, with a recipe that can be used any time of year to take advantage of different fruits and juices in season. I particularly recommend serving it at parties—a tall glass of the bubbly, fruity tonic is a great way to greet your guests.

If you like, make a double or even triple batch of the honey syrup, which makes successive batches of the soda even easier to whip up.

MAKES ABOUT 2 QUARTS/1.9 L

1 cup/240 mL raw honey (see note)

3 cups/710 mL sparkling water

2 cups/475 mL organic no-sugar-added seasonal fruit juice (see Seasonal Fruit Ideas, next page), ideally freshly juiced

Ice

Seasonal fresh fruit, for garnish (see Seasonal Fruit Ideas, next page)

In a medium saucepan over high heat, combine 2 cups/475 mL of filtered tap water and the honey, stirring to dissolve the honey. Bring to a boil, remove from the heat, and set aside to cool to room temperature.

In a 2-quart/2 L pitcher, combine the sparkling water, fruit juice, and honey syrup to taste. Serve over ice, garnished with fresh fruit.

> **Some raw honeys are solid at room temperature and others are pourable.** Because it's easier to measure, I recommend using pourable raw honey for the recipes in this book.

SEASONAL FRUIT IDEAS

Spring
- Use tangerine juice; garnish with tangerine segments.
- Use equal parts orange and strawberry juice; garnish with whole strawberries.
- Use equal parts apple and kiwi juice; garnish with kiwi slices.

Summer
- Use equal parts raspberry and blueberry juice; garnish with whole raspberries and blueberries.
- Use nectarine juice; garnish with whole cherries.
- Use equal parts apricot and plum juice; garnish with apricot and plum slices.
- Use honeydew juice; garnish with cantaloupe balls.
- Use watermelon juice; garnish with lime slices.

Fall
- Use pear juice, garnish with diced pear.
- Use apple juice; garnish with apple slices and orange segments.
- Use equal parts apple and grape juice; garnish with red and green grapes.

Winter
- Use blood orange juice; garnish with blood orange segments.
- Use Meyer lemon juice; garnish with Meyer lemon and lime slices.
- Use equal parts apple and pomegranate juice; garnish with apple slices and pomegranate arils.

OTHER WAYS TO VARY YOUR SODA

- Use still water instead of sparkling.
- Infuse the honey syrup with other flavors—for example, heat a few cinnamon sticks, herb sprigs, ginger slices, some citrus zest, or some dried lavender in the saucepan with the water and honey (strain the solids out after the syrup has cooled).

Coconut Hot Cocoa

MAKING REAL HOT CHOCOLATE IS PRETTY SIMPLE REALLY. DO IT ONCE and you'll never be tempted to buy a mix again. This version, using coconut milk instead of cow's milk and grain-sweetened chocolate instead of sugar-sweetened, is a deliciously unusual treat that won't act as heavily on your blood sugar levels—and it tastes like a candy bar in a cup.

SERVES 4

4 cups/950 mL coconut milk (see notes)

8 ounces/225 g grain-sweetened semisweet chocolate or chocolate chips, chopped (for example, SunSpire brand)

$\frac{1}{2}$ teaspoon pure vanilla extract

$\frac{1}{8}$ teaspoon ground cinnamon

In a medium saucepan over medium-high heat, heat the coconut milk until small bubbles appear around the edges of the pan (do not boil). Remove from the heat and add the chocolate, whisking until the mixture is smooth (return to low heat if necessary). Stir in the vanilla and cinnamon. Serve hot.

> **You can find coconut milk in the natural foods section, or wherever your** market stocks the nut milks and soy milks. It's packaged in a box or carton.
>   To make this recipe vegan and dairy-free, use vegan chocolate chips.

Orange, Herb, and Honey Iced Tea

YOU PROBABLY KNOW THAT WHEN YOU COMBINE HOT WATER AND TEA leaves, the leaves infuse the water with their medicinal properties and flavors. But why stop at tea? This recipe adds medicinal herbs and flavors, including citrus zest, basil, and mint, creating a super-flavorful citrus- and herb-infused treat.

MAKES 2 QUARTS/1.9 L

4 large oranges

2 cups/40 g packed fresh basil leaves, chopped roughly, plus sprigs for garnish

2 cups/40 g packed fresh mint leaves, chopped roughly, plus sprigs for garnish

8 green tea bags

1 cup/240 mL raw honey (see note on page 106) or raw agave nectar, or more to taste

Ice

Zest the oranges. Juice the oranges to yield 1 cup/240 mL of juice. Set the zest and juice aside separately.

In a medium saucepan over high heat, combine 3 cups/710 mL of water with the orange zest, basil, mint, and tea bags. Bring to a boil, cover, remove from the heat, and let steep for 10 minutes.

Strain the tea mixture through a fine-mesh strainer into a 2-quart/2 L pitcher, pressing on the solids. Add the honey, stirring to dissolve. Stir in the orange juice and 3 cups/710 mL of cold water. Add more honey to taste, then refrigerate until thoroughly chilled.

Serve over ice, garnished with mint and basil sprigs.

Maple Ginger Lemonade

GO LEMONADE ONE STEP BETTER, BY USING NATURALLY SWEET MAPLE syrup and adding good-for-what-ails-you ginger. The result is a kind of crazy cross between lemonade and ginger ale—that's crazy good.

MAKES 2 QUARTS/1.9 L

1 (2-inch/5 cm) piece fresh ginger, cut into 6 or 8 slices

1 cup/240 mL pure maple syrup

1 cup/240 mL freshly squeezed lemon juice (from 6 to 8 lemons),
   plus 1 lemon for garnish, sliced

Ice

In the bowl of a food processor, combine the ginger with $1/2$ cup/120 mL of water and process to finely chop the ginger, scraping down the bowl as necessary. Strain the ginger water through a fine-mesh strainer into a 2-quart/2 L pitcher, pressing on the solids. Stir in the maple syrup, lemon juice, and 5 cups/1.2 L of cold water.

Serve over ice, garnished with lemon slices.

Apple-Cucumber-Lime Agua Fresca

INSPIRED BY LATIN *AGUA FRESCAS*, THIS DRINK IS A LITTLE BIT SWEET, A little bit tart, a little bit fruity, and a little bit herbal. Serve it with Huevos Rancheros (page 130), Flank Steak and Chimichurri Salad (page 184), Grilled Veggie Soft Tacos (page 225), or Griled Salmon with Strawberry Avocado Salsa (page 234).

MAKES 2 QUARTS/2 L

2 large sweet-crisp apples, such as Fuji, cored and cut into
  rough 1-inch/2.5 cm pieces

1 large cucumber, peeled and cut into rough 1-inch/2.5 cm pieces

1 cup/240 mL freshly squeezed lime juice (from 8 to 12 limes)

^{1}/$_2$ cup/120 mL raw agave nectar, or more to taste

2 tablespoons packed fresh cilantro leaves, plus sprigs for garnish

In the jar of a blender, combine the apple, cucumber, lime juice, agave, cilantro, and 4 cups/950 mL of water and puree until smooth. Strain through a medium-mesh strainer into a 2-quart/2 L pitcher, pressing on the solids. Add more agave to taste, then refrigerate until thoroughly chilled.

Serve garnished with cilantro sprigs.

Banana Almond Kefir Shake

THICK, FRUITY, AND UTTERLY SATISFYING, HERE'S A MILK SHAKE WITH flavors that both kids and grown-ups will love. Plus it's jam-packed with probiotics. Enjoy it for breakfast, as a snack, or as a simple-yet-special dessert.

SERVES 2

3 medium-size bananas, peeled, broken into large chunks, and frozen

1 cup/240 mL unsweetened almond milk

1 cup/240 mL unsweetened grass-fed organic kefir

¹/₈ teaspoon pure almond extract (optional)

In the jar of a blender, combine the bananas, almond milk, kefir, and extract (if using), and puree until smooth. Serve immediately.

> **To make this recipe vegan, substitute coconut milk, coconut kefir, or more** almond milk for the kefir.
>
> For more about why nut milks are a good alternative to cow's milk, see page 69.

Basic Berry Smoothie

WHEN BERRIES ARE IN SEASON, STOCK UP, KEEPING WHAT YOU DON'T eat right away in the freezer and enabling you to enjoy farmers' market–quality, antioxidant-rich berries all year long.

SERVES 1

1½ cups/170 g frozen strawberries, blueberries, raspberries, or blackberries, or a combination

1 cup/240 mL grass-fed organic plain yogurt or kefir

Coconut nectar (see page 82) or other natural sweetener to taste (optional)

In the jar of a blender, combine the berries and yogurt and puree until smooth. Add coconut nectar to taste, if desired, and serve.

> **If your fruit isn't frozen, just add some ice cubes.**
> To make this recipe vegan, substitute coconut milk or coconut kefir for the yogurt.

WAYS TO VARY YOUR SMOOTHIE

Try different fruits
• In addition to berries, use peaches, apricots, or nectarines in the summer; use apples, pears, or persimmons in the fall; and use bananas or citrus fruits in the winter and spring.

Try different liquids
• Use milk instead of the yogurt—try regular milk, nut milk, or coconut milk.
• Use juice instead of the yogurt—try orange, apple, cranberry, pomegranate, apricot, or even vegetable juices, such as carrot, cucumber, or celery.
• Use a combination of yogurt and juice.

Include other flavors
• Add grated fresh ginger, a pinch of cinnamon, a splash of pure vanilla extract, or mint leaves.

Increase the nutrition
• Add whole leaves of kale or spinach (removing any thick ribs or stems), flaxseeds, or dried seaweed.

Chocolaty Superfoods Smoothie

I THINK OF THIS AS SORT OF A "KITCHEN SINK" SMOOTHIE. IT'S GOT A little bit of a lot of things that are especially good for you—including antioxidant-rich berries and cacao, vitamin-packed greens, and heart-healthy coconut oil and seeds—yet the seemingly varied ingredients come together deliciously.

SERVES 1

1^1/$_2$ cups/170 g frozen strawberries

1 cup/240 mL coconut milk (see note on page 108)

2 large leaves collards, kale, or chard, ribs removed,
   leaves torn into large pieces

2 tablespoons unsweetened raw cacao powder

2 tablespoons coconut nectar (see page 82), or more to taste

2 tablespoons virgin coconut oil (optional)

1 tablespoon chia or hemp seeds

In the jar of a blender, combine the strawberries, coconut milk, greens, cacao powder, coconut nectar, coconut oil, and seeds and puree until smooth. Add more coconut nectar to taste and serve.

> **If your fruit isn't frozen, just add some ice cubes.**
>   For more about why coconut oil is good for you, see page 78.

EGGS, BREAKFAST, AND BREADS

VANILLA PECAN GRANOLA WITH STEEL-CUT OATS

CRANBERRY PEAR PARFAIT

QUINOA CARROT MUFFINS

APPLE AND APPLESAUCE BRAN MUFFINS

ZUCCHINI, WALNUT, AND FLAXSEED TEA BREAD

BUTTERMILK BUCKWHEAT PANCAKES

MORNING MISO SOUP

KAMUT AND BROWN RICE BREAKFAST BOWL

COMFORTING QUINOA CEREAL

HUEVOS RANCHEROS

POTATO, LEEK, AND SPINACH FRITTATA

SHIRRED EGGS WITH ASPARAGUS
AND GOAT CHEESE

Vanilla Pecan Granola with Steel-Cut Oats

USING STEEL-CUT OATS INSTEAD OF ROLLED OATS ADDS TO THE nutritional benefits of this granola, and it also makes for a crispy, crunchy twist on the usual texture. Adding pure vanilla extract and pecans gives it perceived sweetness, so the actual sweetener (the coconut nectar) can be kept to a minimum. All in all, a great granola that you'll find lots of great ways to enjoy.

MAKES ABOUT 4½ CUPS/550 G

2 cups/340 g steel-cut oats, soaked overnight in the refrigerator and drained

1¼ cups/140 g coarsely chopped pecans

¾ cup/60 g unsweetened flaked or shredded coconut

½ teaspoon ground cinnamon

¼ teaspoon fine sea salt

¼ cup/60 mL coconut nectar (see page 82)

2 tablespoons organic neutral-flavored oil, such as grapeseed

½ teaspoon pure vanilla extract

Preheat the oven to 300°F/150°C. Line a large, rimmed baking sheet with parchment paper or a silicone mat.

Spread out the oats in an even layer on the prepared baking sheet and bake, stirring about every 15 minutes, until dry and lightly browned, about 60 minutes.

Meanwhile, in a large bowl, combine the pecans, coconut, cinnamon, and salt. In a small bowl, combine the coconut nectar, oil, and vanilla.

Stir the toasted oats into the pecan mixture (leave the oven on). Add the coconut nectar mixture, stirring to thoroughly combine. Transfer the oat mixture to the lined baking sheet and spread it out evenly. Bake until nicely browned and dry to the touch, 30 to 35 minutes, stirring and respreading halfway through (the granola may not be crisp—it'll crisp as it cools).

Transfer the baking sheet to a wire rack to cool completely.

WAYS TO VARY YOUR GRANOLA

Change the nuts
• Use chopped walnuts, sliced almonds, cashews, pistachios, or peanuts—
   or a combination—instead of the pecans.

Change the flavoring
• Use almond or orange extract instead of the vanilla—or use orange or lime zest.

Add other goodies
• Add spices such as allspice, ginger, cardamom, or nutmeg, and seeds such as sunflower seeds, sesame seeds, pumpkin seeds, or ground flaxseeds, along with the
   nuts; add dried fruits, such as raisins, chopped apricots, or goji berries while the
   granola is cooling.

Variations
• Use almonds, almond extract, and dried cranberries to make cranberry almond
   granola.
• Use walnuts, vanilla extract, and dried apples and raisins to make apple walnut
   granola.
• Use macadamia nuts, ginger, banana chips, and chopped dried mango, pineapple,
   or papaya to make tropical granola.
• Use cashews, sesame seeds, cinnamon, raisins, and dried apricots to make Indian-
   inspired granola.
• Use hazelnuts, vanilla extract, dried cherries, and cacao nibs to make chocolate
   cherry hazelnut granola.

Cranberry Pear Parfait

A PRETTY, AND FESTIVE, WAY TO ENJOY FRUIT AND YOGURT. WHEN pears aren't in season, try it with apples, oranges, peaches, berries, or other favorite fruits.

SERVES 4

1 cup/240 mL cranberry sauce (see page 278 to make your own)
1 cup/140 mL grass-fed organic plain yogurt or kefir
4 medium-size pears, cored and diced
¹/₂ cup/55 g naturally sweetened granola (see page 117 to make your own)

In a medium bowl, combine the cranberry sauce and yogurt. Place about half of the pears in the bottom of four parfait glasses or tall tumblers. Top each glass with ¼ cup/60 mL of the yogurt mixture. Repeat, making another layer each of pears and the yogurt mixture. Top with the granola and serve.

> **To make this recipe gluten-free, use gluten-free granola.**

Quinoa Carrot Muffins

QUINOA NOT ONLY ADDS HIGH-QUALITY PROTEIN TO THESE MUFFINS, it also keeps them deliciously moist.

MAKES 1 DOZEN MUFFINS

4 ounces/115 g unsalted grass-fed organic butter, melted, plus more as needed

2 large organic, pasture-raised, or antibiotic-free eggs

$^3/_4$ cup/180 mL grass-fed organic plain yogurt or kefir

1 teaspoon pure vanilla extract

$1^3/_4$ cups/215 g spelt flour

$^1/_2$ cup/75 g coconut palm sugar (see page 82)

2 teaspoons ground cinnamon

1 teaspoon aluminum-free baking soda

$^1/_2$ teaspoon fine sea salt

$1^1/_2$ cups/270 g cooked quinoa (see page 275 for how to cook grains)

1 cup/85 g shredded carrots

$^2/_3$ cup/90 g unsweetened and unsulfured raisins or dried currants

$^2/_3$ cup/80 g chopped walnuts, toasted (see notes)

Preheat the oven to 450°F/230°C. Coat twelve standard-size muffin cups with butter.

In a large bowl, whisk the eggs, yogurt, butter, and vanilla. Set aside. In a medium bowl, combine the flour, sugar, cinnamon, baking soda, and salt. Add the flour mixture to the egg mixture, stirring until just shy of combined. Gently stir in the quinoa, carrots, raisins, and walnuts, stirring just until combined.

Fill the prepared muffin cups to slightly rounded over the top. Bake until the muffin tops are golden brown and set, 15 to 18 minutes. Transfer to a wire rack and let cool for 10 minutes. Remove the muffins from the pan and return them to the rack to cool thoroughly.

> **If you like, you can substitute cracked wheat for the quinoa.**

To toast nuts

Preheat the oven to 350°F/175°C. Spread the nuts onto a rimmed baking sheet and cook, stirring occasionally, until lightly browned and fragrant, 6 to 10 minutes depending on the type of nuts and the size of the pieces. When they're close to being done, watch them carefully—nuts go from toasted to burnt very quickly.

To toast seeds

In a small skillet over medium heat, stir the seeds until lightly browned, and depending on the seeds, fragrant. It should take 1 to 3 minutes, depending on the type and amount of seeds. Transfer to a plate and set aside to let cool.

Apple and Applesauce Bran Muffins

A SUPER SIMPLE RECIPE THAT YOU CAN CHANGE AND ADAPT, DEPENding on your mood and what's in the cupboard.

MAKES 1 DOZEN MUFFINS

1½ cups/80 g wheat bran

1¼ cups/155 g spelt flour

1½ teaspoons aluminum-free baking soda

¼ teaspoon fine sea salt

Organic neutral-flavored high-heat cooking oil, such as grapeseed, as needed

⅔ cups/160 mL grass-fed organic plain yogurt or kefir

½ cup/120 mL coconut nectar (see page 82)

¼ cup/85 g unsweetened or homemade applesauce
  (see page 279 to make your own)

1 large organic, pasture-raised, or antibiotic-free egg

½ small apple, cored, sliced thinly, then slices cut in half crosswise

Preheat the oven to 450°F/230°C.

In a large bowl, combine the wheat bran and ½ cup/120 mL of boiling water. Set aside for 10 minutes.

Meanwhile, in a medium bowl, combine the flour, baking soda, and salt. Coat twelve standard-size muffin cups with oil. Set the flour mixture and muffin pan aside.

Add the yogurt, coconut nectar, applesauce, and egg to the bran mixture, stirring to thoroughly combine. Add the flour mixture, stirring until just shy of combined. Add the apple, stirring just until combined.

Fill the prepared muffin cups to slightly rounded over the top. Bake until the tops are browned and set, 15 to 18 minutes. Transfer to a wire rack and let cool for 10 minutes. Remove the muffins from the pan and return them to the rack to cool thoroughly.

IDEAS FOR MUFFIN MIX-INS

- Chopped, toasted nuts, such as walnuts, almonds, or pecans
- Dried fruits, such as raisins, cranberries, or cherries
- Toasted seeds, such as pumpkin, sunflower, or sesame
- Spices, such as cinnamon, ginger, or cloves

Zucchini, Walnut, and Flaxseed Tea Bread

A LITTLE BIT OF A TWIST ON THE FLAVORS AND TEXTURES OF CARROT cake, this is a full-flavored, cinnamon-laced bread. Enjoy it as a tea cake or occasional morning treat.

MAKES ONE 8 BY 4 BY 3-INCH/20 BY 10 BY 7.5 CM LOAF

1¼ cups/155 g spelt flour

¼ cup/30 g ground flaxseeds

1½ teaspoons aluminum-free baking soda

1 teaspoon ground cinnamon

1 teaspoon ground ginger

¼ teaspoon fine sea salt

1 cup/150 g coconut palm sugar (see page 82)

2 large organic, pasture-raised, or antibiotic-free eggs

¼ cup/60 mL organic neutral-flavored oil, such as grapeseed,
　　plus more as needed

1 cup/100 g shredded zucchini

1 cup/100 g chopped walnuts, toasted (see note on page 122)

Preheat the oven to 350°F/175°C. Oil an 8 by 4 by 3-inch/20 by 10 by 7.5 cm loaf pan. Cut a piece of parchment paper to fit the bottom of the pan and press it into the pan.

In a medium bowl, combine the flour, flaxseeds, baking soda, cinnamon, ginger, and salt. Set aside. In a large bowl, whisk ¼ cup/60 mL of water with the sugar and eggs. Whisk in the oil. Add the flour mixture to the egg mixture. Stir in the zucchini and walnuts.

Transfer the mixture to the prepared pan and bake until a toothpick inserted into the center comes out clean, 40 to 45 minutes. Let the bread cool in the pan on a wire rack for 10 minutes, then unmold and return the bread to the rack to cool completely.

For more about why flax is good for you, see page 51.

Buttermilk Buckwheat Pancakes

THESE PANCAKES HAVE A SATISFYINGLY EARTHY FLAVOR, PLUS BLOOD sugar-stabilizing properties, thanks to the buckwheat. They're not particularly sweet, but you can make them more so with syrup. They're also good topped with nut butter, honey, and a sprinkling of raisins.

SERVES 4 TO 6

1 cup/120 g spelt flour

1 cup/125 g buckwheat flour

2 tablespoons coconut palm sugar (see page 82)

1 tablespoon aluminum-free baking powder

$^1/_2$ teaspoon fine sea salt

$2^1/_2$ cups/590 mL grass-fed organic buttermilk, plus more as needed

3 large organic, pasture-raised, or antibiotic-free eggs

$^1/_4$ teaspoon pure vanilla extract

6 tablespoons/70 g unsalted grass-fed organic butter, plus more as needed, melted, divided

Pure maple syrup, for serving

Preheat the oven to 250°F/120°C. Place a large, rimmed baking sheet in the oven.

In a large bowl, combine the spelt flour, buckwheat flour, sugar, baking powder, and salt. In a medium bowl, combine the buttermilk, eggs, vanilla, and $^1/_4$ cup/60 mL of the melted butter. Add the buttermilk mixture to the flour mixture, stirring until just combined (a few lumps are okay). Add more buttermilk as needed for desired consistency.

On a griddle or in a large skillet over medium heat, heat the remaining 2 tablespoons of butter. Use $^1/_4$ cup/60 mL of batter for each pancake, making as many pancakes as you can comfortably fit without crowding the griddle. Cook until bubbles start to form on the tops and the bottoms are nicely browned, 2 to 3 minutes. Turn and cook until browned and cooked through, 1 to 2 minutes.

Transfer the cooked pancakes to the baking sheet in the oven and repeat with the remaining batter, adding more of the butter to the griddle or skillet as needed.

Serve the pancakes hot, passing the maple syrup at the table.

IDEAS FOR PANCAKE MIX-INS

- Sliced bananas, apples, peaches, or strawberries
- Whole raspberries, blueberries, or blackberries
- Chopped toasted hazelnuts or walnuts, or sliced toasted almonds
- Toasted sesame, sunflower, or pumpkin seeds
- A pinch of cinnamon or nutmeg

Morning Miso Soup

PART OF A TYPICAL JAPANESE BREAKFAST, MISO SOUP IS A WONDERFULLY nurturing way to start the day. Note that it's best to keep the miso separate from the soup until right before serving, because heat can compromise miso's fermented soybean health benefits.

SERVES 6

$^1/_4$ cup/6 g wakame (see notes)

6 cups/1.4 L dashi (see page 280 to make your own) or organic reduced-sodium chicken or vegetable stock, divided (see notes)

$^1/_2$ cup/145 g organic white miso

1 medium-size carrot, cut into matchsticks

8 ounces/115g non–genetically modified or organic soft tofu, drained and cut into $^1/_2$-inch/1.25 cm cubes

4 medium-size scallions, sliced thinly on the diagonal

Organic naturally brewed soy sauce or organic wheat-free tamari, for serving

In a small bowl, combine the wakame with enough warm water to cover it by 1 inch/2.5 cm. Set aside for 15 minutes, then drain, discarding the liquid.

In a medium saucepan over medium-high heat, bring 5$^1/_2$ cups/1.3 L of the dashi to a boil.

Meanwhile, in a small bowl, combine the miso and the remaining $^1/_2$ cup/120 mL of dashi, stirring until smooth. Set aside.

Add the carrot to the boiling dashi. Lower the heat to a simmer and cook until the carrot is crisp-tender, 1 to 2 minutes. Stir in the wakame, tofu, and scallions and simmer until heated through, about 1 minute.

Divide the miso mixture among serving bowls. Top with the soup mixture and serve, passing the soy sauce at the table.

Wakame is a dried sea vegetable that comes in both sheets and small, shriveled pieces— use the shriveled pieces for the recipes in this book. You can find wakame in the ethnic or Asian section at most natural foods supermarkets.

When using store-bought stocks and broths, read the label to make sure they don't contain any added sugar. You'd be surprised how often sweeteners end up in places where you'd never expect them!

This recipe is designed so that you can make just one serving at a time if you'd like. Just make the soup base, let it cool to room temperature, then chill it in the refrigerator. Also refrigerate the miso mixture. For each serving, heat about 1¼ cups/295 mL of the soup base. Place 2½ tablespoons of the miso mixture in a serving bowl, top with the warm soup, and serve.

Kamut and Brown Rice Breakfast Bowl

A LITTLE LIKE RICE PUDDING, THIS WARM, COZY BREAKFAST—WHICH IS ideal for a cool morning—is chock-full of whole grains, which should keep you well satisfied until lunch. It has an exotic flair, thanks to allspice, cardamom, apricots, and pistachios. That said, you can vary it with whatever combination of spices, dried fruits, and nuts you have on hand. You can also substitute farro for the kamut, or try it with a dollop of plain yogurt or a splash of kefir on top.

SERVES 4 TO 6

2¾ cups/650 mL coconut milk, plus more as needed
  (see note on page 108)

⅔ cup/140 g kamut, soaked overnight in the refrigerator and drained

⅔ cup/140 g short-grain brown rice, soaked overnight in the refrigerator
  and drained

¼ teaspoon ground allspice

¼ teaspoon ground cardamom

¼ cup/35 g chopped unsweetened, unsulfured dried apricots (see note)

¼ cup/35 g unsweetened and unsulfured raisins

2 tablespoons coconut palm sugar (see page 82), pure maple syrup, or
  raw agave nectar, plus more as needed

Fine sea salt to taste

¼ cup/30 g chopped pistachio nuts

In a medium saucepan over high heat, bring the coconut milk to a boil. Add the kamut, rice, allspice, and cardamom and return to a boil. Lower the heat to a simmer, cover, and cook until the kamut and rice are almost tender (there will still be some liquid), about 20 minutes.

Stir in the apricots, raisins, and sugar. Cover and cook until the fruit is plump, the kamut and rice are tender, and almost all of the liquid is absorbed, about 5 minutes. Add salt to taste.

Transfer the mixture to serving bowls and sprinkle with the pistachios. Serve immediately, passing additional coconut milk and sugar at the table.

For more about why unsulfured dried fruit is good for you, see page 104.

Comforting Quinoa Cereal

ALTHOUGH IT'S SERVED WARM, THIS EASY QUINOA DISH IS MEANT to be enjoyed as you'd eat a cold breakfast cereal—pour on the milk (or something like it), top with fresh fruit and perhaps a little sweetener, and dig in. Simple, satisfying, and devoid of all those sugars, additives, and preservatives.

SERVES 4 TO 6

1½ cups/265 g quinoa, soaked overnight in the refrigerator and drained

½ teaspoon ground cinnamon

Fine sea salt to taste

1 cup/115 g berries or chopped fresh fruit

Grass-fed organic milk, unsweetened nut milk,
  or coconut milk, for serving (see note on page 108)

Coconut palm sugar (see page 082), pure maple syrup,
  or raw agave nectar, for serving

In a medium saucepan over medium-high heat, bring 2¼ cups/530 mL of water to a boil. Add the quinoa and cinnamon and return to a boil. Lower the heat to a simmer, cover, and cook until the quinoa is tender and the liquid is absorbed, 8 to 10 minutes. Add salt to taste.

Transfer the quinoa to serving bowls and top with the fruit. Serve immediately, passing the milk and sweetener at the table.

WAYS TO ENHANCE YOUR QUINOA CEREAL

- Add flavors to the saucepan with the quinoa, such as orange zest, sliced fresh ginger, vanilla extract, cacao powder, nut butter, or dried fruits, such as currants, raisins, or chopped dried apples.
- Add toppings such as chopped toasted nuts, toasted seeds, coconut flakes, or cacao nibs.

Huevos Rancheros

WHO DOESN'T LIKE HUEVOS RANCHEROS? AND IF YOU CUT DOWN ON the cheese and load up on the beans and veggies—as this recipe does—it can make for an amazingly healthy brunch. I also like it as breakfast-for-dinner, especially at the end of a long and satisfying weekend.

SERVES 4

1 medium-size tomato, cut into $^1/_4$-inch/0.65 cm dice

$^1/_4$ medium-size red onion, cut into 1/4-inch/0.65 cm dice

$^1/_4$ cup/10 g chopped fresh cilantro

2 cups/175 g cooked, drained black or pinto beans, plus $^1/_2$ cup/120 mL cooking liquid (see page 277 for how to cook beans)

1$^1/_2$ teaspoons ground coriander

1$^1/_2$ teaspoons ground cumin

Fine sea salt to taste

Freshly ground black pepper to taste

8 (5-inch/13 cm) organic corn, sprouted-grain, or brown rice tortillas

2 tablespoons organic neutral-flavored oil, such as grapeseed, divided, plus more as needed

8 large organic, pasture-raised, or antibiotic-free eggs

$^1/_2$ cup/60 g crumbled *queso fresco*, *cojita*, or feta cheese

$^1/_2$ medium-size avocado, pitted and sliced thinly

Hot sauce, for serving

Preheat the oven to 250°F/120°C. Place a large, rimmed baking sheet on a rack in the oven.

Meanwhile, in a small bowl, combine the tomato, onion, and cilantro. Set aside. In a medium saucepan, combine the beans, cooking liquid, coriander, and cumin and use a potato masher or fork to mash to a chunky consistency. Bring to a boil over medium-high heat, lower the heat to a simmer, cover, and cook until thickened and heated through, about 3 minutes. Remove from the heat and add salt and pepper to taste. Set aside (keep covered).

Heat a large skillet over medium heat. Working in batches, place one or two tortillas at a time in the pan and cook until warm and softened, 30 to 60 seconds per side. Transfer the warm tortillas to the oven. Repeat with the remaining tortillas.

Return the skillet to medium heat and heat 1 tablespoon of the oil. In another large skillet over medium heat, heat the remaining 1 tablespoon of oil. Crack four eggs into each skillet and cook until just set on the bottom, about 2 minutes. Sprinkle with salt and pepper, cover the skillets, and cook until the eggs are at the desired doneness, about 2 minutes.

Arrange two tortillas on each plate. Top with the bean mixture, two eggs, tomato mixture, cheese, and avocado. Serve immediately, passing the hot sauce at the table.

Potato, Leek, and Spinach Frittata

YOU CAN CHANGE THE VEGETABLES IN THIS RECIPE, DEPENDING ON what's in season. Remember to precook any ingredients that you wouldn't want to eat raw—they won't get much more cooked once they get mixed together with the eggs.

SERVES 6 TO 8

2 tablespoons organic extra-virgin olive oil

6 ounces/170 g yellow-fleshed sweet potatoes, cut into $\frac{1}{2}$-inch/1.25 cm dice

2 medium-size leeks, white and light green parts only, quartered lengthwise and cut into $\frac{1}{2}$-inch/1.25 cm slices

12 large organic, pasture-raised, or antibiotic-free eggs

$\frac{1}{2}$ cup/120 mL grass-fed organic milk or unsweetened nut milk

4 teaspoons chopped fresh thyme

$1\frac{1}{2}$ teaspoons fine sea salt

1 teaspoon freshly ground black pepper

1 cup/125 g grated Parmesan cheese, divided

2 cups/30 g loosely packed spinach leaves

In a medium, ovenproof skillet over medium heat, heat the oil. Add the potatoes and cook, stirring occasionally, for 2 minutes. Add the leeks and cook, stirring occasionally, until all the vegetables are tender, about 6 minutes.

Meanwhile, in a medium bowl, whisk the eggs. Whisk in the milk, thyme, salt, pepper, and $^3/_4$ cup/90 g of the cheese.

Add the egg mixture to the skillet, stirring gently to evenly distribute the vegetables. Lower the heat to medium-low and cook without stirring until the eggs are set around the edges, about 10 minutes.

Meanwhile, preheat a broiler and arrange a rack about 8 inches from the heating element.

Scatter the spinach leaves on top of the frittata, pressing them down to slightly submerge, and sprinkle on remaining $^1/_4$ cup/35 g of cheese. Place the skillet under the broiler and broil until the eggs are set and the top of the frittata is golden brown, about 5 minutes.

Transfer the frittata skillet to a wire rack (careful, the handle and pan will be hot) and let cool for 10 minutes.

Cut the frittata into eight to ten wedges. Serve warm or room temperature.

WAYS TO VARY YOUR FRITTATA

- Use baby artichokes, asparagus, and peas in the spring; zucchini, corn, and tomatoes in the summer; and butternut squash, broccoli, and caramelized onions in the fall and winter.
- Basil, rosemary, oregano, sage, and marjoram are all great with eggs—or try a combination.
- Instead of Parmesan, try shredded Cheddar or Gruyère, crumbled goat cheese or queso fresco, or grated pecorino or Asiago.
- Start by sautéing crumbled breakfast sausage or Italian sausage, or ground chicken, pork or beef: Remove with a slotted spoon before sautéing the vegetables, then add back with the egg mixture.

Shirred Eggs with Asparagus and Goat Cheese

ALTHOUGH I DON'T RECOMMEND EATING A LOT OF IT, ENJOYING A high-quality cream in moderation is okay—and here, just a little helps keep the eggs soft and, well, lusciously creamy.

SERVES 8

Fine sea salt

1½ cups/165 g ½-inch/1.25 cm asparagus pieces

Unsalted grass-fed organic butter, for coating ramekins

½ cup/120 mL grass-fed organic heavy cream

⅔ cup/90 g crumbled goat cheese

8 large organic, pasture-raised, or antibiotic-free eggs

Freshly ground black pepper

1 tablespoon chopped fresh flat-leaf parsley

1½ teaspoons chopped fresh tarragon

1½ teaspoons chopped or crumbled wakame (see note on page 127)

Preheat the oven to 325°F/160°C.

Set a medium saucepan of well-salted water (1½ teaspoons of fine sea salt per quart/950 mL) over high heat and bring to a boil. Cook the asparagus until just tender, 1 to 2 minutes. Drain, rinse with cool water, and drain again. Pat dry with a kitchen towel and set aside.

Coat eight ½-cup/120 mL ramekins with butter. Arrange the ramekins on a rimmed baking sheet and place 1½ teaspoons of cream in the bottom of each. Top with the asparagus and cheese, dividing them evenly. Gently crack an egg into each ramekin and sprinkle with salt and pepper. Drizzle each ramekin with 1½ teaspoons of cream and bake until the eggs are softly set, 20 to 25 minutes.

Sprinkle with the parsley, tarragon, and wakame and serve.

SNACKS AND APPETIZERS

ROASTED PECANS WITH ROSEMARY,
OLIVE OIL, AND SEA SALT

SPICED MIXED NUTS WITH DRIED FRUIT

KITCHEN SINK ALMOND BUTTER SNACK BARS

ROASTED EGGPLANT DIP

WHITE BEAN DIP WITH GARLIC AND PARSLEY

HUMMUS

BLACK AND WHITE SESAME SEED CRACKERS

KALE CHIPS

SMASHED AVOCADO TOASTS

DEVILED FARM-FRESH EGGS WITH SPRING HERBS

GREEN APPLE CARPACCIO WITH
GOAT CHEESE AND ARUGULA

HIRAMASA TARTARE WITH AVOCADO

BROWN RICE SPICY SUSHI ROLL

FARRO CAKES WITH CURRIED YOGURT

GLUTEN-FREE CHICKEN MEATBALLS

Roasted Pecans with Rosemary, Olive Oil, and Sea Salt

DON'T LET THE SIMPLICITY OF THIS RECIPE FOOL YOU. THESE NUTS ARE simultaneously salty, rich, crunchy, and deliciously complex, thanks to the rosemary. Keep them on hand for an easy, yet thoroughly enticing, snack.

MAKES 3 CUPS/300 G

3 cups/300 g raw pecan halves

2 tablespoons organic extra-virgin olive oil

1 tablespoon chopped fresh rosemary

Fine sea salt to taste

Preheat the oven to 375°F/190°C.

Arrange the pecans on a large, rimmed baking sheet and bake until browned and fragrant, about 12 minutes.

While the nuts are still warm, return them to the bowl and add the oil, rosemary, and salt to taste, tossing to evenly coat. Return the mixture to the baking sheet, set the sheet on a wire rack, and let cool to room temperature.

Spiced Mixed Nuts with Dried Fruit

PART OF WHAT MAKES THIS NUT MIX SO ADDICTIVE IS THE CHINESE five-spice blend that seasons it, a warm, sweet-but-not-too-spicy combination that typically includes star anise, cinnamon, cloves, fennel, and pepper. You'll find Chinese five-spice blend in the spice section or the Asian food section of most major supermarkets. (And you can also enjoy it in the Spiced Braised Short Ribs with Red Cabbage, page 255.)

MAKES ABOUT 6 CUPS (WEIGHT DEPENDS ON TYPE OF NUTS AND FRUITS)

1 organic, pasture-raised, or antibiotic-free egg white

4 cups mixed raw nuts (weight depends on type of nuts)

¹/₃ cup/45 g coconut palm sugar (see page 82)

1 teaspoon Chinese five-spice blend (see above)

2 teaspoons coarse sea salt

2 cups mixed unsweetened, unsulfured dried fruit, larger pieces cut into bite size (weight depends on type of fruit)

Preheat the oven to 250°F/120°C.

In a medium bowl, combine the egg white and 1 tablespoon of water, whisking until foamy. Add the nuts, tossing to coat. Transfer the nuts to a strainer, shake them, then let them drain for at least 2 minutes.

Wipe out the bowl and add the sugar, five-spice blend, and salt, mixing to combine. Add the nuts, tossing to thoroughly and evenly coat. Spread the nuts in a single layer on a rimmed baking sheet and bake for 40 minutes.

Use a metal spatula to stir the nuts. Spread them out again, lower the oven temperature to 200°F/95°C, and bake until the nuts are dry, about 30 minutes.

Remove the nuts from the oven and stir them again. Scatter the dried fruit on top and transfer the baking sheet to a wire rack to cool completely.

You can use any combination of nuts you like—walnuts, pecans, hazelnuts, pistachios, almonds, cashews, peanuts, you name it—plus any combination of dried fruits. You can also vary the recipe by using different spices and spice blends:

- Curry powder
- Garam masala
- Cinnamon, ginger, and clove

- Cumin and cayenne
- Chili powder
- Star anise and black pepper

Kitchen Sink Almond Butter Snack Bars

THIS SNACK—WHICH IS GREAT AS A LATE MORNING OR AFTERNOON pick-me-up, or to take along on a hike or picnic—is kind of a cross between a granola bar and a Rice Krispies Treat. Using puffed brown rice cereal instead of oats not only gives the bars the aura of a nostalgic childhood treat, but it keeps them gluten-free.

MAKES ONE 8-INCH/20 CM SQUARE PAN

2 cups/30 g puffed brown rice cereal

$^1/_2$ cup/60 g naturally sweetened unsulfured dried cranberries

$^1/_2$ cup/60 g raw cacao nibs

$^1/_2$ cup/40 g unsweetened shredded coconut

$^1/_4$ cup/35 g sesame seeds, toasted, divided (see note on page 122)

$^2/_3$ cup/160 mL organic almond butter

$^2/_3$ cup/160 mL coconut nectar (see page 82)

Line an 8-inch/20 cm square baking pan with parchment or waxed paper, letting it hang a bit over the sides. Set aside.

In a medium bowl, combine the cereal, cranberries, cacao nibs, coconut, and 3 tablespoons of the sesame seeds. Set aside.

In a medium saucepan over medium heat, combine the almond butter and coconut nectar, stirring until blended. Remove from the heat and stir in the cereal mixture. Transfer the entire mixture to the prepared pan, spreading it out evenly. Sprinkle with the remaining 1 tablespoon of sesame seeds, pressing them to adhere, and refrigerate until firm, about an hour.

Use the parchment to transfer the bars from the baking pan to a cutting board. Cut into squares and serve.

Roasted Eggplant Dip

BESIDES BEING AN EASY-TO-MAKE AND WHOLLY SATISFYING DIP, THIS IS also nice stirred into rice or grains, or dolloped on top of steamed or roasted veggies.

MAKES ABOUT 2¼ CUPS/520 G

1 large eggplant (about 1 pound/455 g)
1 medium-size red bell pepper
10 large leaves fresh basil, plus sprigs for garnish
¼ cup/60 mL organic extra-virgin olive oil
2 teaspoons freshly squeezed lemon juice, or more to taste
2 garlic cloves
Fine sea salt to taste
Freshly ground black pepper to taste

Preheat the oven to 400°F/205°C.

Place the whole eggplant and whole bell pepper on a large, rimmed baking sheet and roast until the eggplant is very tender through to the center, about 40 minutes. Set aside until cool enough to handle.

Trim the top off the eggplant, then chop the eggplant into large chunks.

Transfer to the bowl of a food processor. Trim, seed, and peel the bell pepper, then transfer it to the food processor with the eggplant. Add the basil, oil, lemon juice, and garlic and process to make a smooth puree, scraping down the bowl as necessary. Add more lemon juice, salt, and black pepper to taste.

Serve warm or room temperature, garnished with the basil sprigs.

White Bean Dip with Garlic and Parsley

IF YOU GET INTO COOKING YOUR OWN BEANS INSTEAD OF BUYING canned—which I definitely hope this book will inspire you to do—you'll occasionally have extra on hand. This recipe is a great way to take advantage of that, using them up and making a great appetizer or snack in the process.

MAKES ABOUT 2 CUPS/475 ML

2 cups/350 g cooked, drained cannellini beans, plus ¼ cup/60 mL cooking liquid (see page 277 for how to cook beans)

¼ cup/5 g packed flat-leaf parsley leaves, plus chopped parsley for garnish

1 tablespoon raw apple cider vinegar

1 tablespoon organic extra-virgin olive oil

6 garlic cloves, or more to taste

Fine sea salt to taste

Freshly ground black pepper to taste

In the bowl of a food processor, combine the beans, cooking liquid, parsley, vinegar, oil, and garlic and process to a puree, scraping down the bowl as necessary. Add more garlic, salt, and pepper to taste.

Hummus

SURE, YOU CAN BUY HUMMUS AT ALMOST ANY FOOD STORE THESE days, in a myriad of flavors. But why not skip the processed stuff made with inflammatory oils and God-knows-what else, and treat yourself to homemade? It's exceptionally easy to throw together, and simple to customize to your taste.

MAKES ABOUT $2^2/_3$ CUPS/630 ML

2 cups/370 g cooked, drained garbanzo beans (chickpeas), plus $^1/_2$ cup/120 mL cooking liquid, or more as needed (see page 277 for how to cook beans)

$^1/_2$ cup/120 mL raw tahini (see note)

6 tablespoons/90 mL freshly squeezed lemon juice (from 2 or 3 lemons), or more to taste

$^1/_4$ cup/60 mL organic extra-virgin olive oil

2 garlic cloves

Fine sea salt to taste

In the bowl of a food processor, combine the chickpeas, cooking liquid, tahini, lemon juice, oil, and garlic and process to a puree, scraping down the bowl as necessary. Add more cooking liquid as needed for desired consistency. Add more lemon juice and salt to taste.

Tahini is a paste made of ground sesame seeds. You can find it in the ethnic or health food section of most major supermarkets and natural foods stores.

WAYS TO VARY YOUR HUMMUS

- Use lime juice instead of lemon.
- Add roasted red peppers, artichoke hearts, or red onion.
- Add herbs, such as basil, cilantro, mint, or dill.
- Add a little sesame oil, a pinch of cayenne pepper, or a dash of hot sauce.
- Increase the garlic.
- Garnish with a drizzle of olive oil or roasted garlic oil (see page 281 to make your own), chopped fresh herbs, chopped fresh tomato, or a sprinkle of paprika.

Black and White Sesame Seed Crackers

WHETHER YOU'RE GLUTEN-FREE OR NOT, YOU'LL ENJOY THE SLIGHTLY nutty flavor and pleasantly sandy texture of these crackers. They're a little on the thick side, making them sturdy enough for all your favorite dips, toppings, and spreads—but they're also great on their own.

MAKES ABOUT 2 DOZEN

$^1\!/_2$ cup/50 g almond meal or almond flour (see notes)

$^1\!/_2$ cup/55 g organic amaranth flour, plus more as needed (see notes)

$^1\!/_2$ cup/55 g arrowroot powder

1 tablespoon aluminum-free baking powder

$^1\!/_2$ teaspoon fine sea salt

$1^1\!/_2$ teaspoons black sesame seeds, divided

$1^1\!/_2$ teaspoons white sesame seeds, divided

$^1\!/_4$ cup/60 mL plus $1^1\!/_2$ teaspoons organic extra-virgin olive oil

$^1\!/_2$ teaspoon coarse sea salt

Preheat the oven to 350°F/175°C.

In a large bowl, combine the almond meal, amaranth flour, arrowroot, baking powder, fine sea salt, 1 teaspoon of the black sesame seeds, and 1 teaspoon of the white sesame seeds. Add $^1\!/_4$ cup/60 mL of the oil and $^1\!/_4$ cup/60 mL of water and stir until a shaggy dough forms. Transfer the dough to a work surface lightly dusted with amaranth flour and knead a few times, until the mixture comes together.

Pat the dough into a rectangle, then roll it out to about 12 inches/30 cm long and 8 inches/20 cm wide, sprinkling a little amaranth flour under the dough as needed and pressing together any tears or cracks. Brush the dough with the remaining $1^1\!/_2$ teaspoons of oil and sprinkle with the coarse salt, the remaining $^1\!/_2$ teaspoon of black sesame seeds, and the remaining $^1\!/_2$ teaspoon of white sesame seeds. Cut the dough into twenty-four 2-inch/5 cm squares, then use a spatula to carefully transfer the crackers to a large, rimmed baking sheet. Bake until lightly browned at the edges, 25 to 30 minutes.

Transfer the baking sheet to a wire rack and let the crackers cool completely.

You can find almond meal, sometimes called almond flour, at some supermarkets and at most natural foods supermarkets. You can also make your own by using a food processor to finely grind toasted, skinned almonds.

You can find amaranth flour at most natural foods supermarkets.

WAYS TO VARY YOUR CRACKERS

Instead of the sesame seeds, try:
• Chopped fresh herbs
• Orange or lemon zest
• Other seeds, such as caraway, fennel, or poppy seeds

Kale Chips

THE NOTION OF KALE CHIPS IS ALMOST OXYMORONIC, BUT THEY truly are a healthy snack, rich in vitamins, nutrients, and heart-healthy fat. Note that you can make these chips with all kinds of kale—curly, dino, whatever—but if your leaves are super large or particularly thick, they might take a little longer to cook.

MAKES ABOUT 8 CUPS/80 G

12 large leaves kale, ribs removed, leaves cut or torn into
   1-to 2-inch/2.5 to 5 cm pieces

3 tablespoons organic extra-virgin olive oil

1 teaspoon coarse sea salt, plus more to taste

Preheat the oven to 275°F/135°C. Arrange a rack in the upper half of the oven and another in the lower half.

In a very large bowl, combine the kale, oil, and salt. Arrange the mixture on two large, rimmed baking sheets in an even layer and bake until crisp, 30 to 35 minutes, stirring and rotating the position of the baking sheets halfway through.

Transfer to a wire rack and let cool to room temperature. Add more salt to taste and serve.

Smashed Avocado Toasts

CASUAL ENOUGH FOR AN AFTERNOON SNACK, DRESSY ENOUGH FOR company, this recipe features toasted sprouted bread topped by a delightfully unusual, Asian-inspired twist on guacamole.

SERVES 4

2 medium-size ripe avocados, pitted and peeled

1 tablespoon unseasoned rice vinegar

1½ teaspoons toasted sesame oil

1 teaspoon prepared wasabi paste

Fine sea salt to taste

4 slices sprouted-grain bread, halved or quartered on a diagonal

1 cup/20 g lightly packed watercress leaves

1 scallion, sliced thinly on a diagonal

1 teaspoon chia seeds

In a medium bowl, combine the avocado, rice vinegar, sesame oil, and wasabi paste, using a fork to mash to a chunky consistency. Add salt to taste and set aside.

Toast the bread until it's to your liking.

Arrange the watercress on the toasts and top with the avocado mixture. Sprinkle with the scallions and chia seeds and serve.

> **To make this recipe gluten-free, use gluten-free bread.**

Deviled Farm-Fresh Eggs with Spring Herbs

HERE'S A REFRESHING TWIST ON TYPICAL DEVILED EGGS, ADDING A burst of flavor and nutrients with herbs, including chives, parsley, and cilantro. The recipe also replaces the usual mayonnaise with yogurt or kefir, omitting a processed food and providing a probiotics boost in the process.

MAKES 2 DOZEN

1 dozen large organic, pasture-raised, or antibiotic-free eggs

$^1/_2$ cup/60 mL grass-fed organic plain yogurt or kefir

2 tablespoons chopped fresh chives

2 tablespoons chopped fresh flat-leaf parsley

2 teaspoons chopped fresh cilantro

$^1/_8$ teaspoon cayenne pepper, or more to taste

Fine sea salt to taste

Freshly ground white pepper to taste

Place the eggs in a large pot and cover with cold water by 1 inch/2.5 cm. Bring to a boil over high heat, then cover, remove from the heat, and let stand 10 minutes.

Meanwhile, prepare a bowl of ice water.

Transfer the eggs to the ice water and let stand for 5 minutes.

Peel the eggs and halve them lengthwise. Carefully remove the yolks and transfer them to a bowl, setting the whites aside. Add the yogurt, chives, parsley, cilantro, and cayenne to the bowl with the yolks and mash with a fork. Add more cayenne, salt, and pepper to taste.

Spoon the yolk mixture into the egg whites. Arrange on a platter and serve.

> **These eggs are purposefully not completely hard-cooked, because** slightly undercooking helps avoid oxidation. For more about why that's a good thing, see page 73.

Green Apple Carpaccio with Goat Cheese and Arugula

SORT OF A CROSS BETWEEN TRADITIONAL CARPACCIO AND A FRUIT salad, this dish is a nice twist on the expected. If you want, you can core the apple before cutting it crosswise into thin slices.

You can vary this recipe by changing the apple slices to orange slices.

SERVES 4

¼ cup/60 mL organic extra-virgin olive oil

4 teaspoons raw apple cider vinegar

Fine sea salt to taste

Freshly ground black pepper to taste

2 small tart green apples, such as Granny Smith or Pippin

3 cups/40 g loosely packed arugula leaves

½ cup/60 g crumbled goat cheese (optional)

¼ cup/30 g thinly sliced red onion

2 tablespoons chopped hazelnuts, toasted (see page 122)

In a medium bowl, whisk together the oil and vinegar. Add salt and pepper to taste. Set aside.

Cut the apples crosswise (through the core) into thin slices, discarding the seeds—each slice should be one round cross-section of the apple. Arrange the apple slices on plates or a platter and drizzle with about half of the dressing.

Add the arugula to the bowl with remaining dressing and toss. Arrange the arugula on top of the apples, top with goat cheese (if using), red onion, and hazelnuts, and serve.

> **To make this recipe raw, don't toast the nuts.**

Hiramasa Tartare with Avocado

A NATIVE NEW YORKER AND WINNER OF FOOD NETWORK'S NEXT IRON Chef competition, Marc Forgione is also the youngest American chef to earn a prestigious Michelin star three years in a row. His self-titled Manhattan restaurant, showcasing a contemporary approach to New American cuisine and an often-changing menu, highlights sustainable ingredients at their peak. Impressive and refined, this tartare of Hiramasa has quickly become one of the eatery's signature starters.

SERVES 4

$1/2$ medium-size avocado, pitted, peeled, and cut into $1/2$-inch/1.25 cm dice

1 teaspoon freshly squeezed lime juice

Fine sea salt to taste

12 ounces/340 g sustainably sourced Hiramasa (yellowtail), cut into $1/2$-inch/1.25 cm dice

2 tablespoons finely diced cucumber

1 cup/240 mL plus 3 tablespoons organic extra-virgin olive oil, divided

2 tablespoons raw honey (see note on page 106)

2 tablespoons mustard oil (see note)

2 tablespoonsorganic teriyaki sauce

4 small radishes, cut into small matchsticks

$1/2$ cup/10 g lightly packed fresh micro cilantro or other microgreens

1 tablespoon pine nuts, toasted (see note on page 122)

In a small bowl, combine the avocado, lime juice, and salt to taste. In a medium bowl, combine the Hiramasa, cucumber, 3 tablespoons of the olive oil, and salt to taste. In another medium bowl, whisk together the honey, mustard oil, teriyaki sauce, and the remaining 1 cup/240 mL of olive oil.

Place a 3-inch/7.5 cm ring mold in the bottom of a chilled shallow bowl. Layer with one-quarter of the avocado mixture and one-quarter of the fish mixture, packing the mold tightly. Remove the mold and repeat with three more chilled shallow bowls. (If you don't have a ring mold, use a 3-inch/7.5 cm–diameter ramekin and fill it with one-quarter of the fish mixture, then one-quarter of the avocado mixture. Overturn it into chilled shallow bowl and repeat with three more chilled shallow bowls.) Rewhisk the honey sauce and pour it into the bowls, dividing it evenly. Arrange the radishes and micro cilantro on top of the fish and sprinkle the pine nuts on top of the sauce.

You can find mustard oil at specialty food stores.

Brown Rice Spicy Sushi Roll

NORI, THE SEAWEED PAPER USED TO WRAP SUSHI AND OTHER SEA vegetables, has a unique nutritional profile. Add the other veggies in the recipe, and this dish becomes a power-packed snack, appetizer, or light meal.

MAKES 4 ROLLS

1 cup/190 g short-grain brown rice or brown sushi rice, soaked overnight in the refrigerator and drained

3 tablespoons unseasoned rice vinegar

$^1/_2$ teaspoon coconut palm sugar (see page 82)

$^1/_8$ teaspoon fine sea salt

$^1/_3$ cup/80 mL grass-fed organic plain yogurt or kefir

$^1/_2$ teaspoon cayenne pepper, or more to taste

4 (7$^1/_2$ by 8$^1/_2$-inch/19 by 21.5 cm) sheets nori

1 cup/30 g sunflower sprouts, bean sprouts, alfalfa sprouts, or microgreens

$^1/_2$ small cucumber, peeled, halved lengthwise, seeded, and cut lengthwise into thin slices

$^1/_2$ small carrot, cut into matchsticks

$^1/_2$ avocado, pitted, peeled, and cut lengthwise into eight slices

Organic naturally-brewed soy sauce or organic wheat-free tamari, for serving

Wasabi paste, for serving

Pickled ginger, for serving

In a medium saucepan over high heat, bring 1¾ cups/415 mL of water to a boil. Add the rice, return to a boil, lower the heat to a simmer, and cover. Cook until the rice is tender and the liquid is absorbed, 30 to 35 minutes. Remove from the heat and let stand, covered, for 5 minutes.

Meanwhile, in a small bowl, combine the vinegar, sugar, and salt.

Transfer the rice to a medium bowl and stir in the vinegar mixture. Cover with a damp kitchen towel and set aside to cool.

In a small bowl, combine the yogurt and cayenne, adding more cayenne to taste. Set aside.

Place a bamboo sushi mat on a work surface, with the sticks in the mat parallel to you. Place a sheet of nori on the mat, shiny side down, shorter edge toward you. Have a small bowl of water nearby.

Dampen your hands in the water, shaking off the excess. Use your fingers to press ¾ cup of rice onto the nori, covering three-quarters of the length of the sheet and the entire width, leaving 2 or 3 inches from the farthest edge uncovered. (If the rice sticks to your hands as you work, rewet them in the water.) Drizzle a scant tablespoon of the yogurt mixture on top of the rice in a line parallel to you, about 1 inch from the closest edge. Top with one-quarter of the sprouts, one-quarter of the cucumber, one-quarter of the carrot, and one-quarter of the avocado.

Holding the fillings firmly in place with your fingertips, use your thumbs to lift the edge of the mat closest to you up and over, enclosing the fillings. Squeeze gently to make a compact roll. Raise the end of the mat slightly to avoid rolling it in with the nori, and continue rolling, squeezing occasionally, until the sushi is completely rolled in a tight cylinder. If necessary, dampen the furthest edge of nori with water to help it seal, then set the roll aside for a minute or two. Using a sharp knife, slice the roll into eight pieces. Repeat with the remaining ingredients, making four rolls total.

Serve the sushi with the soy sauce, wasabi, and pickled ginger on the side.

> **Because soy sauce is a processed food, use it sparingly.**
> Look for pickled ginger with no added sweeteners; many brands include high-fructose corn syrup.
> If you'd like, you can add cooked shrimp or crab or raw fish to these rolls.

Farro Cakes with Curried Yogurt

HERE, THE EXOTIC FLAVORS OF AN INDIAN CURRY MEET A CRAB CAKE-like dish, resulting in an earthy and bright appetizer or light entrée. The farro is purposefully a little overcooked to help make it sticky enough to mold into a disc.

SERVES 4

$^2/_3$ cup/125 g farro, soaked overnight in the refrigerator and drained

Pinch of fine sea salt, plus more to taste

$^1/_4$ cup/60 mL organic extra-virgin olive oil, divided

1 cup/120 g diced fennel (about 1 bulb)

$^1/_2$ cup/65 g diced shallots (2 or 3)

2 lemons

$^2/_3$ cup grass-fed organic plain yogurt

1 garlic clove, minced

$^1/_2$ teaspoon curry powder

Freshly ground black pepper to taste

1 cup/65 g whole wheat panko

2 tablespoons chopped fresh flat-leaf parsley

2 large organic, pasture-raised, or antibiotic-free eggs, lightly beaten

2 tablespoons unsalted grass-fed organic butter

8 large butter lettuce leaves

In a medium saucepan, combine the farro with $1^1/_3$ cups/315 mL of water and a pinch of salt. Bring to a boil over medium-high heat and lower the heat to a simmer. Cover and cook until the farro is very tender and the liquid is absorbed, about 30 minutes. Drain the farro, if necessary, transfer to a large bowl, and set aside to cool.

Meanwhile, in medium skillet over medium heat, heat 2 tablespoons of the oil. Add the fennel and shallots and cook, stirring occasionally, until tender, about 3 minutes. Remove from the heat and set aside to cool.

Zest 1 lemon. Juice the zested lemon to yield 1½ teaspoons of juice (save any remaining juice for another use). In a small bowl, combine the zest, juice, yogurt, garlic, curry powder, and salt and pepper to taste. Cut the remaining lemon into eight wedges. Set the yogurt and lemon wedges aside.

Add the fennel and shallots to the farro. Add the panko, parsley, and salt and pepper to taste. Stir in the eggs. Using moist hands, shape the mixture into eight cakes, each about ¾ inch/2 cm thick.

Heat 1 tablespoon of oil and 1 tablespoon of butter in each of two medium skillets over medium heat. Carefully add four cakes to each skillet. Cook until golden brown and cooked through, 3 to 4 minutes per side.

Arrange the butter lettuce leaves and lemon wedges on plates or a platter. Top with the farro cakes. Spoon the curried yogurt on top and serve.

Gluten-Free Chicken Meatballs

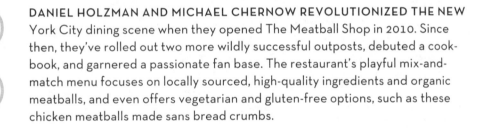

DANIEL HOLZMAN AND MICHAEL CHERNOW REVOLUTIONIZED THE NEW York City dining scene when they opened The Meatball Shop in 2010. Since then, they've rolled out two more wildly successful outposts, debuted a cook-book, and garnered a passionate fan base. The restaurant's playful mix-and-match menu focuses on locally sourced, high-quality ingredients and organic meatballs, and even offers vegetarian and gluten-free options, such as these chicken meatballs made sans bread crumbs.

MAKES 20 MEATBALLS

2 tablespoons extra-virgin olive oil

⅔ cup/80 g cooked brown basmati rice (see page 276 for how to cook rice)

2 pounds/905 g organic ground chicken, ideally dark or thigh meat

½ cup/30 g chopped fresh flat-leaf parsley

⅓ cup/45 g brown rice flour

¼ cup/60 mL dry white wine (see note)

2 organic, pasture-raised, or antibiotic-free eggs, lightly beaten

1 tablespoon fine sea salt

1 teaspoon ground fennel

1 teaspoon freshly ground black pepper

Preheat the oven to 400°F/205°C. Coat a 9 by 13-inch/25 by 35 cm baking pan with the oil.

Place the rice in a food processor and process to finely chop, scraping down the bowl as necessary. Transfer the rice to a large bowl and add the chicken, parsley, flour, wine, eggs, salt, fennel, and pepper, gently mixing until well combined.

With damp hands, roll the mixture into 1$\frac{1}{2}$-inch/4 cm balls, arranging them in the prepared baking pan. Bake until an internal thermometer in a meatball reads 165°F/75°C, about 20 minutes. Let cool for 5 minutes before serving.

> **Although I don't recommend wine for everyday use, for special occasions it's okay.** Other times, substitute stock.

SOUPS, SALADS, AND SIDES

CAULIFLOWER SOUP WITH ROASTED GARLIC OIL

BEANS AND GREENS SOUP

CHILLED SPRING PEA SOUP WITH PEEKYTOE
CRAB, ALMONDS, AND GREEK YOGURT

SUMMER VEGETABLE AND LENTIL SOUP

SIMPLE SOUP WITH CARROTS, PARSNIPS,
AND SCALLIONS

WATERMELON GAZPACHO

CHUNKY CORN CHOWDER

ROASTED TOMATO SOUP

SPRING SLAW

CRISPED CUCUMBERS WITH CILANTRO

HEIRLOOM TOMATOES WITH BASIL VINAIGRETTE

RAW CAULIFLOWER TABBOULEH

SWEET POTATO SALAD
WITH SCALLIONS AND SEAWEED

QUINOA SALAD WITH ARUGULA AND GRAPES

BROCCOLI PASTA SALAD

GREEN LENTIL SALAD WITH KALE,
CARROTS, ASPARAGUS, AND DIJON DRESSING

MUSTARD GREENS SALAD WITH ROASTED
BEETS AND TOASTED PISTACHIOS

KALE SALAD

COLD VEGETABLE SALAD WITH
ALMOND BUTTER SAUCE

WARM SPINACH SALAD WITH POTATO,
ZUCCHINI, AND SALMON

ARUGULA WITH CHICKEN AND BLUEBERRIES

FLANK STEAK AND CHIMICHURRI SALAD

GRILLED CORN WITH FLAVORED GRASS-FED BUTTER

GREEN BEAN SUCCOTASH WITH
COLLARDS AND BLACK-EYED PEAS

HOME-FERMENTED SAUERKRAUT

BRAISED BABY ARTICHOKES

CARAMELIZED ROASTED ENDIVE

BROCCOLI WITH OLIVE OIL AND LEMON

SAUTÉED SHAVED BRUSSELS SPROUTS WITH
SHALLOTS AND ALMONDS

RAINBOW CHARD AND RADICCHIO SAUTÉ

ROASTED CARROTS AND PARSNIPS
WITH GARLIC, CITRUS, AND SAGE

TERIYAKI-GLAZED BABY BOK CHOY

BRAISED GREENS WITH NORI

SMOKY-SWEET GLAZED CARROTS

RATATOUILLE

GARLIC MASHED BUTTERNUT SQUASH

MASHED CELERIAC

SWEET POTATO OVEN FRIES

Cauliflower Soup with Roasted Garlic Oil

HERE'S AN EXCELLENT EXAMPLE OF HOW QUICK AND EASY IT IS TO make a warming homemade soup. It's lusciously creamy even though it's dairy-free—and it's finished with a drizzle of always-welcome roasted garlic oil.

SERVES 4 TO 6

3 tablespoons organic extra-virgin olive oil

5 cups/455 g small cauliflower florets (from 1 small head)

1 large yellow onion, cut into $^1/_4$-inch/0.65 cm dice

8 garlic cloves, minced

2 teaspoons coarsely chopped fresh oregano leaves

2 teaspoons coarsely chopped fresh sage leaves

4 cups/950 mL organic reduced-sodium chicken or
   vegetable stock (see note on page 127)

Fine sea salt to taste

Freshly ground black pepper to taste

3 tablespoons Roasted Garlic Oil (page 281)

In a large saucepan or small stockpot over medium heat, heat the olive oil. Add the cauliflower and cook, stirring occasionally, until lightly browned, 5 to 7 minutes. Stir in the onion, garlic, oregano, and sage and cook, stirring occasionally, until the onion is very tender and the entire mixture is beginning to brown, 8 to 10 minutes.

Add the stock, scraping up any browned bits on the bottom of the pot. Bring to a boil, lower the heat to a simmer, and cook until the cauliflower is very tender, about 5 minutes.

Working in batches if necessary, transfer the soup to a blender or food processor, or use an immersion blender, and puree (be careful—the mixture will be hot), scraping down the bowl or jar as necessary.

Reheat the soup if necessary and add salt and pepper to taste. Serve hot, drizzled with the garlic oil.

HOW TO MAKE HOMEMADE SOUP

Using the same basic method as for the cauliflower soup, you can make homemade soup from almost any vegetable. Here's how:

1. Dice up some vegetables.
   Do one type of vegetable or a combination. Mushrooms—mixed or all one type—for mushroom soup. Carrots and parsnips for carrot-parsnip soup. Potatoes and leeks for potato-leek soup.

2. Heat a stockpot, add a little fat, and sauté the vegetables.
   Use olive oil or a neutral-flavored oil, such as grapeseed, enough to coat the bottom of the stockpot. If you're doing more than one type of vegetable, add them to your stockpot according to how long they'll take to cook—add the longest-cooking vegetables first and the quickest-cooking vegetables last, the goal being that they're all tender at the same time.

3. Add liquid to cover.
   The liquid can be stock, broth, water, wine, or a combination. How much? Err on the side of caution. You can always add more later to thin out your soup. Bring to a boil, lower the heat to a simmer, and cook until the vegetables are tender.

4. If you want, puree all or part of your soup.
   If you don't puree it, your soup will have a thin broth with pieces of vegetables floating in it. A quick puree will yield a creamy soup. Puree half to two-thirds of the soup for the best of both worlds.

5. Season to taste.
   Salt and pepper—but especially salt—can make the difference between your vegetable soup's tasting like dishwater and tasting divine.

- Onion, shallot, or garlic is almost never a bad idea. Add these aromatics to the sauté.
- Herbs can give your soup more dimension of flavor. Add heartier ones, such as thyme and rosemary, to the sauté. Add delicate ones, such as parsley and cilantro, either before pureeing or before seasoning.
- Other enhancements include cream, crème fraîche, buttermilk, yogurt, or kefir for creamy notes; citrus zest for light, citrusy freshness; and a touch of soy sauce or tamari for low, savory oomph. Stir in any or all before pureeing or before seasoning.
- Herbs, crème fraîche, flavored oils, and shaved, grated, or crumbled cheese make nice garnishes.

Beans and Greens Soup

THIS IS ONE OF MY ALL-TIME FAVORITE BEAN SOUPS—HEARTY, SATISFYING, and with a delightfully unusual flavor. The turmeric provides anti-inflamatory nutrients and mushroomy *arame* adds minerals.

SERVES 8 TO 10

1 tablespoon organic extra-virgin olive oil

1 large yellow onion, cut into $^1/_2$-inch/1.25 cm dice

2 garlic cloves, minced

1 teaspoon ground turmeric

$^1/_4$ teaspoon cayenne pepper

6 cups/1.4 L organic reduced-sodium chicken or vegetable stock (see note on page 127)

$3^1/_2$ cups/620 g cooked, drained small white beans, plus $1^1/_2$ cups/355 mL cooking liquid (see page 277 for how to cook beans)

4 ounces/115 g collard, kale, chard, chicory, dandelion, or mustard greens, or a combination

1 medium-size carrot, cut into ¹⁄₄-inch/0.65 cm dice

¹⁄₄ cup/6 g packed *arame* (dried seaweed)

2 teaspoons raw apple cider vinegar, or more to taste

Fine sea salt to taste

In a large saucepan or small stockpot over medium heat, heat the oil. Add the onion and cook, stirring occasionally, until lightly browned, 6 to 8 minutes. Add the garlic, turmeric, and cayenne and cook, stirring occasionally, until the garlic is tender but not browned, about 2 minutes. Stir in the stock and bean cooking liquid, scraping up any browned bits in the pot, increase the heat to high, and bring to a boil. Add the beans and return to a boil. Lower the heat to a simmer and cook for 15 minutes.

Meanwhile, cut any tough ribs from the greens, then cut the ribs crosswise into ¹⁄₂-inch/1.25 cm pieces. Slice the remaining leaves crosswise into 1¹⁄₂- to 2-inch/4 to 5 cm by ¹⁄₄-inch/0.65 cm strips (you should have about 4 cups).

Add the greens' ribs and carrots and simmer until almost tender, about 6 minutes. Add the greens' leaves and *arame* and cook until the ribs, carrots, and leaves are tender, about 5 minutes.

Stir in the vinegar. Add more vinegar and salt to taste. Serve hot.

> **For more about why beans are good for you, see page 58.**

Chilled Spring Pea Soup with Peekytoe Crab, Almonds, and Greek Yogurt

AS ONE OF NEW YORK CITY'S PREMIER MICHELIN-STARRED RESTAURANTS, Rouge Tomate is critically acclaimed for its menu of seasonally inspired culinary offerings and locally sourced ingredients. Focusing on sustainable practices and environmentally friendly techniques, executive chef Jeremy Bearman puts his signature twist on modern American cuisine with vibrant, flavorful dishes—such as this creamy chilled soup with fresh peekytoe crab.

SERVES 6

2 tablespoons organic extra-virgin olive oil

1 large spring onion, white and light green parts only, cut into ¹/₂-inch/1.25 cm dice (see notes)

2 garlic cloves, sliced thinly

3 cups/710 mL grass-fed organic milk

¹/₂ medium-size purple potato, peeled and cut into ¹/₂-inch/1.25 cm dice

Fine sea salt to taste, plus more as needed

1 cup/130 g shelled peas, ideally fresh

1 cup/110 g sugar snap peas

8 ounces/225 g pea shoots (see notes)

10 fresh mint leaves

Freshly ground black pepper to taste

1 lemon

8 ounces/225 g sustainably sourced crab, ideally peekytoe

1 tablespoon chopped fresh chives

2 teaspoons almond oil

¹/₂ cup/120 mL Greek-style grass-fed organic plain yogurt

¹/₄ cup/30 g slivered almonds, toasted (see note on page 122)

In a medium saucepan over medium-low heat, heat the olive oil. Add the spring onion and garlic and cook, stirring occasionally, until tender, about 5 minutes. Add the milk, potato, and 1 cup/240 mL of water and bring to a boil over medium heat. Lower the heat to a simmer and cook until the potato is very tender, about 5 minutes. Set aside.

Prepare a bowl of ice water. Set aside.

In a large saucepan or small stockpot of well-salted boiling water (1 1/2 teaspoons of fine sea salt per quart/950 mL), cook the shelled peas until tender but still nicely green, 1 1/2 to 2 minutes. Use a slotted spoon to transfer them to the ice water.

Add the sugar snap peas to the boiling water and cook until tender but still nicely green, 1 1/2 to 2 minutes. Use a slotted spoon to transfer them to the ice water.

Add the pea shoots to the boiling water and cook until tender but still nicely green, about 5 minutes. Drain and add the pea shoots to the ice water.

Drain the peas, snap peas, and pea shoots and transfer them to the jar of a blender. Add the mint leaves and the potato mixture and process to a puree.

Strain the puree through a fine-mesh sieve into a large mixing bowl, pressing the solids with the back of a spoon or ladle. Place this bowl in a larger bowl filled with ice water, to chill the soup quickly and help preserve the color. Add water if necessary to reach the desired consistency. Add salt and pepper to taste. Set aside, stirring occasionally, until the soup is thoroughly chilled.

Meanwhile, zest the lemon. Juice the lemon to yield 1 teaspoon of juice. In a medium bowl, combine the lemon zest, lemon juice, crab, chives, and almond oil. Set aside.

Just before serving, stir the yogurt into the soup, and if necessary, more salt and pepper to taste. Divide the soup among shallow bowls and mound some of the crab mixture in the center of each. Garnish with the almonds and serve.

Spring onions are small young onions—sort of like giant scallions with a more bulbous base. Look for them at farmers' markets and specialty food stores in the springtime.

Pea shoots are tendrils from pea plants. Look for them at Asian markets, farmers' markets, natural foods stores, and specialty food stores.

To make this recipe vegetarian, omit the crab mixture. To make it vegan and dairy-free, use nut milk or coconut milk for the milk and coconut yogurt for the yogurt.

Summer Vegetable and Lentil Soup

THIS SOUP IS BRIMMING WITH BIG CHUNKS OF SUMMERY ABUNDANCE— including bell pepper, tomato, green beans, summer squash, and zucchini. Earthy lentils nicely complement all that brightness, and the tiniest bit of sesame oil brings it all together. Yes.

SERVES 8 TO 12

12 ounces/340 g tomatoes, seeded and cut into large chunks

4 garlic cloves

2 tablespoons organic extra-virgin olive oil

$^1/_2$ medium-size red bell pepper, cored and cut into $^1/_2$-inch/1.25 cm dice

$^1/_2$ medium-size yellow bell pepper, cored and cut into $^1/_2$-inch/1.25 cm dice

$^1/_2$ medium-size yellow onion, cut into $^1/_2$-inch/1.25 cm dice

9 cups/2.1 L organic reduced-sodium chicken or vegetable stock (see note on page 127)

$1^1/_2$ cups/295 g dried lentils

6 sprigs fresh thyme

$^1/_2$ teaspoon toasted sesame oil

4 ounces/115 g green beans, cut into $^3/_4$-inch/2 cm lengths

1 cup/150 g fresh organic corn kernels

1 medium-size yellow squash, quartered lengthwise and cut into $^1/_2$-inch/1.25 cm slices

1 medium-size zucchini, quartered lengthwise and cut into $^1/_2$-inch/1.25 cm slices

Fine sea salt to taste

Freshly ground black pepper to taste

Place the tomatoes and garlic in the bowl of a food processor and process to a puree, scraping down the bowl as necessary. Set aside.

In a large saucepan or small stockpot over medium heat, heat the oil. Add the bell peppers and onion and cook, stirring occasionally, until the vegetables are crisp-tender, 3 to 4 minutes. Add the pureed tomatoes and cook, stirring occasionally, until the liquid is evaporated and the tomato bits start to stick and brown in the pot, about 10 minutes.

Stir in the stock, lentils, thyme, and sesame oil, scraping up any browned bits in the pot. Increase the heat to high, bring to a boil, and lower the heat to a simmer. Cook for 5 minutes. Add the green beans and cook for 5 minutes. Add the corn, squash, and zucchini and cook, adjusting the heat to maintain a simmer, until the lentils and vegetables are tender, 10 to 15 minutes.

Remove the thyme sprigs, add salt and black pepper to taste, and serve hot.

Simple Soup with Carrots, Parsnips, and Scallions

HERE'S A SOUP THAT'S BEAUTIFUL IN ITS SIMPLICITY—A BASIC BROTH brimming with a sweet and springlike combination of tender vegetables. It'd be great as a first course to a rich, hearty meal or alongside a roasted sweet potato. It's also a perfect food for when you're feeling under the weather and just want something light and comforting.

SERVES 6 TO 8

2 tablespoons organic extra-virgin olive oil

1 medium-size celery stalk, cut into $^1/_4$-inch/0.65 cm dice

$^1/_2$ large yellow onion, cut into $^1/_4$-inch/0.65 cm dice

$1^1/_2$ teaspoons fennel seeds, toasted (see page 121 for how to toast seeds)

8 ounces/225 g carrots, cut into $^1/_4$-inch/0.65 cm dice (about $3^1/_4$ cups)

8 ounces/225 g parsnips, cut into $^1/_4$-inch/0.65 cm dice (about $3^1/_4$ cups)

6 cups/1.4 L organic reduced-sodium chicken or vegetable stock (see note on page 127)

Fine sea salt to taste

Freshly ground black pepper to taste

2 medium-size scallions, cut into $^1/_2$-inch/1.25 cm lengths, for garnish

In a large saucepan or small stockpot over medium heat, heat the oil. Add the celery and onion and cook, stirring occasionally, for 4 minutes. Add the fennel seeds, carrots, and parsnips and continue to cook, stirring occasionally, until the onion is tender, about 4 minutes. Add the stock, bring to a boil over high heat, lower the heat to a simmer, and cook until all the vegetables are tender, about 5 minutes.

Add salt and pepper to taste. Serve hot, garnished with the scallions.

WAYS TO ENHANCE YOUR SOUP

- Add shredded cooked chicken.
- Add cooked quinoa, millet, or couscous.
- Add chopped fresh herbs, such as parsley, tarragon, dill, or cilantro.
- Add wakame or other sea vegetables.

Watermelon Gazpacho

THIS BRIGHT, BEAUTIFULLY RUBY-PINK SOUP IS A NICE ADDITION TO ANY summer party or backyard barbecue, and it takes just minutes to make. Instead of serving it in bowls, you can also serve it in small shot glasses—this recipe will make about twenty-four ¼-cup shooters.

SERVES 4 TO 6

3 limes, divided

1 pound/455 g tomatoes, cut into rough 1-inch/2.5 cm dice

½ jalapeño pepper, seeded

Pinch of cayenne pepper, or more to taste

4½ pounds/2 kg seedless watermelon, rind removed, cut into rough 1-inch/2.5 cm dice

Fine sea salt to taste

Zest two of the limes. Juice the zested limes to yield 2 tablespoons of juice. In the bowl of a food processor or the jar of a blender, combine the lime juice, lime zest, tomatoes, jalapeño, and cayenne and process to a puree, scraping down the bowl or jar as necessary. Add the watermelon and process to make a chunky puree, scraping down the bowl or jar as necessary (you may have to do this in batches). Cover and refrigerate until well chilled, at least an hour.

Add salt and more cayenne to taste. Slice the remaining lime. Serve the soup garnished with the lime.

Chunky Corn Chowder

A WONDERFUL WAY TO ENJOY SUMMER CORN, THIS IS A RELATIVELY traditional chowder recipe with one key difference—it uses vitamin-packed sweet potatoes instead of starchy white potatoes. The change is so barely noticeable that I'm hoping it inspires you to make healthful switches in other dishes.

SERVES 6 TO 8

6 large ears organic white or yellow corn, or a combination

4 tablespoons/55 g unsalted grass-fed organic butter or olive oil

4 medium-size shallots, cut into ¼-inch/0.65 cm dice (about 1 cup)

4½ cups/1 L organic reduced-sodium chicken or vegetable stock (see note on page 127)

1 pound/455 g yellow-fleshed sweet potatoes, cut into ½-inch/1.25 cm dice (about 1 cup)

½ cup/80 mL grass-fed organic milk or nondairy milk

Fine sea salt to taste

Freshly ground white pepper to taste

2 tablespoons chopped fresh basil

2 tablespoons chopped fresh chives

Cut the kernels from the corn cobs, then cut or break the corn cobs in half. Set the kernels and corn cobs aside.

In a large saucepan or small stockpot over medium heat, melt the butter. Add the shallots and cook, stirring occasionally, until tender, 3 or 4 minutes. Add the corn kernels, corn cobs, stock, and potatoes and bring to a boil over high heat. Lower the heat to a simmer and cook until the potatoes and corn are very tender, about 10 minutes.

Remove the corn cobs from the pot. Transfer about half of the soup to a food processor or blender and process to a puree. Return the mixture to the pot, along with the milk.

Add salt and pepper to taste and serve hot, garnished with the basil and chives.

Roasted Tomato Soup

DEDICATED TO RAISING THE STANDARD OF VEGETARIAN COOKING IN the United States, Ann Gentry founded Santa Monica's Real Food Daily—the only area restaurant serving a completely vegan menu using foods grown exclusively with organic farming methods. She's since opened two more Southern California locations, cementing her reputation as L.A.'s most celebrated gourmet vegan chef. Curl up with Ann's comforting Roasted Tomato Soup from her book *Vegan Family Meals, Real Food for Everyone* (Andrews McMeel Publishing, 2011). The soup is best eaten the day it is made, but it can be covered and refrigerated for up to one day. To rewarm, bring the soup to a simmer over medium heat, stirring occasionally and adding water to thin the soup to the desired consistency.

SERVES 6 TO 8

4 pounds/1.8 kg ripe tomatoes, quartered

$^1/_4$ cup/60 mL balsamic vinegar

12 large garlic cloves, chopped

6 tablespoons/90 mL organic extra-virgin olive oil, divided

Fine sea salt to taste

Freshly ground black pepper to taste

2 medium-size red onions, cut into $^1/_2$-inch/1.25 cm dice

$^1/_4$ cup/10 g chopped fresh basil

2 tablespoons finely chopped fresh flat-leaf parsley

$4^1/_2$ teaspoons finely chopped fresh sage

Preheat the oven to 500°F/260°C.

In a large bowl, combine the tomatoes, vinegar, garlic, $^1/_4$ cup/60 mL of the olive oil, and a generous sprinkle of salt and pepper. Transfer the mixture, along with any accumulated juices, to a large, rimmed baking sheet. Arrange the tomatoes in a single layer, skin side down, and roast until charred on the edges, about 40 minutes. Set aside to cool slightly, then slip the skins off the tomatoes.

In a large saucepan or small stockpot over medium heat, heat the remaining

2 tablespoons olive oil. Add the onions and cook, stirring often, until very soft, about 10 minutes. Add the basil, parsley, and sage and cook, stirring occasionally, for about 1 minute. Stir in the roasted tomatoes, along with any accumulated juices, and 5 cups/1.2 L of water. Bring to a boil, lower the heat to a simmer, and cook gently to allow the flavors to blend, about 8 minutes. Add more salt and pepper to taste. Serve hot.

Spring Slaw

WHEN I GET BORED WITH LEAFY GREEN SALADS, I TURN TO SLAW TO satisfy my cravings for crisp, cool, vegetable sides. This one is abundant with springtime vegetables and herbs, but you can easily change and adapt it to the season.

SERVES 8 TO 10

Fine sea salt to taste, plus more as needed

6 thin asparagus spears, trimmed and cut into 1-to 1¹⁄₂-inch/2.5 to 4 cm lengths

¹⁄₂ cup/65 g fresh or frozen peas

8 cups or 1 (10-ounce/285 g bag) finely shredded green cabbage

1 medium-size carrot, shredded

¹⁄₂ medium-size fennel bulb, halved, cored, and sliced thinly

4 medium-size scallions, sliced thinly

2 tablespoons thinly sliced fresh mint leaves

2 tablespoons chopped fresh flat-leaf parsley

1 tablespoon chopped fresh dill

¹⁄₄ cup/60 mL organic extra-virgin olive oil

¹⁄₄ cup/60 mL raw apple cider vinegar

Zest of 1 medium-size orange

Freshly ground black pepper to taste

In a medium saucepan of well-salted boiling water ($1^{1}/_{2}$ teaspoons of fine sea salt per quart/950 mL), cook the asparagus and the peas until just tender, 1 to 2 minutes. Drain, rinse with cool water, and drain again. Pat dry with a kitchen towel and set aside.

In a large bowl, combine the asparagus, peas, cabbage, carrot, fennel, scallions, mint, parsley, and dill. In a small bowl, combine the oil, vinegar, and orange zest. Add the dressing to the slaw mix, tossing to combine. Add salt and pepper to taste. Cover and refrigerate until well chilled before serving.

> **To make this recipe raw, leave the asparagus and peas uncooked.**

SEASONAL SLAW IDEAS

Summer
- Instead of the asparagus, peas, carrot, and fennel, use shredded zucchini, thinly sliced bell peppers, and chopped tomato.
- Instead of the mint, parsley, and tarragon, use basil or cilantro.

Fall
- Use small florets of broccoli and cauliflower (and blanch them à la the asparagus) and thinly sliced Brussels sprouts.
- Use tarragon or sage.

Winter
- Use orange segments or apples cut into matchsticks.
- Instead of herbs, add orange, lemon, or lime zest.

- Add crumbled cheese, such as blue cheese or goat cheese.
- Add unsweetened, unsulfured dried fruits, such as raisins or currants.
- Add chopped nuts, such as hazelnuts or pine nuts.
- Add baby spinach or arugula leaves or shredded greens, such as kale or chard.
- Replace some or all of the green cabbage with red cabbage.
- Use different vinegars, or use orange, lemon, or lime juice instead of vinegar.
- If you like your slaw creamy, use grass-fed, organic sour cream, plain yogurt, or kefir instead of some of the vinegar.

Crisped Cucumbers with Cilantro

A REFRESHING SUMMER SIDE DISH, THESE CUCUMBERS GO PARTICULARLY well with seafood. They're also nice alongside grain dishes or piled on top of salad greens. Salting makes them deliciously crisp and beautifully translucent.

Note that the recipe needs to be started at least a couple of hours before you plan to serve it.

SERVES 4

$1\frac{1}{2}$ pounds/680 g cucumbers, peeled, halved lengthwise, seeded, and sliced thinly on a diagonal (about 4 cups)

$1\frac{1}{2}$ teaspoons coarse sea salt

$\frac{1}{3}$ cup/60 mL raw apple cider vinegar

2 teaspoons raw agave nectar

$\frac{1}{4}$ teaspoon toasted sesame oil

1 garlic clove, minced

$\frac{1}{4}$ small red onion, sliced thinly

Fine sea salt to taste

Freshly ground white pepper to taste

2 tablespoons chopped fresh cilantro

In a large bowl, toss the cucumbers and coarse sea salt. Transfer to a colander and set the colander in a bowl. Set aside at room temperature for 1 to 2 hours, tossing and pressing down on the cucumbers occasionally to help drain their liquid.

In a large, nonreactive bowl, combine the vinegar, agave, oil, and garlic. Stir in the cucumbers, onion, and salt and pepper to taste. Cover and refrigerate until well chilled.

Drain off all but a little of the accumulated liquid, add the cilantro, and serve.

Heirloom Tomatoes with Basil Vinaigrette

ARE THERE ANY TWO INGREDIENTS THAT ARE AS GOOD TOGETHER AS tomatoes and basil? I think not—especially when the tomatoes are full-flavored heirlooms and it's the peak of the season.

The dressing is basically a simple vinaigrette pureed with basil leaves, and it would be good on almost any summery veggies. Try it with sliced cucumbers, blanched green beans, grilled eggplant and zucchini, or a green salad.

SERVES 6

$^1/_2$ cup/15 g packed fresh basil leaves

$^1/_4$ cup/60 mL raw apple cider vinegar

$1^1/_2$ teaspoons coconut nectar (see page 82)

$^1/_2$ cup/120 mL organic extra-virgin olive oil

$2^1/_4$ pounds/1 kg heirloom tomatoes (6 medium-size), cored and cut into $^1/_2$-inch/1.25 cm slices

1 medium-size shallot, chopped finely

Fine sea salt to taste

Freshly ground black pepper to taste

In the bowl of a food processor, combine the basil, vinegar, and coconut nectar and process to chop the basil, scraping down the bowl as necessary. With the motor running, slowly drizzle in the oil. Set aside.

Arrange the tomatoes on plates or a platter and sprinkle with the shallot and salt and pepper to taste. Drizzle the basil vinaigrette on top and serve.

Raw Cauliflower Tabbouleh

SINCE OPENING IN 2005, M CAFÉ HAS SUCCESSFULLY INTRODUCED contemporary macrobiotic cuisine to mainstream Los Angeles dining. Featuring a balanced, nutritious, and creative menu, M Café focuses on whole natural foods—without using any refined sugars, eggs, dairy, red meat, or poultry. To reap all the healthy benefits of macro cooking at home, try the café's simple twist on tabbouleh.

SERVES 6 TO 8

2 to 3 lemons, as needed

2 pounds/905 g cauliflower, cored and cut into large bite-size pieces

1 large cucumber, halved lengthwise, seeded, and cut into $^1/_4$-inch/0.65 cm dice

1 large tomato, cut into $^1/_4$-inch/0.65 cm dice

$^3/_4$ cup/40 g chopped fresh flat-leaf parsley

$^1/_2$ cup/20 g chopped fresh dill

1 tablespoon chopped fresh mint leaves

2 tablespoons organic extra-virgin olive oil

Fine sea salt to taste

Zest one of the lemons. Juice the zested lemon along with enough remaining lemons to yield $^1/_3$ cup/80 mL of lemon juice. Set the zest and juice aside.

Place the cauliflower in the bowl of a food processor and process to finely chop into small, grainlike pieces, scraping down the bowl as necessary. Cover a work surface with a clean, dry tea or kitchen towel and turn out the cauliflower onto the towel. Twist the cauliflower in the towel to extract any moisture. Transfer the squeezed cauliflower to a large mixing bowl and add the lemon zest, lemon juice, cucumber, tomato, parsley, dill, mint, and olive oil. Add salt to taste.

Serve immediately at room temperature or chilled.

Sweet Potato Salad with Scallions and Seaweed

A NICE ALTERNATIVE TO THE USUAL POTATO SALAD, THIS VERSION IS colorful, nutritious, and tasty. Mineral-rich wakame adds a little crunch when it's first mixed in, and over time it softens to become pleasantly chewy.

SERVES 6 TO 8

1 1/2 pounds/680 g yellow- or orange-fleshed sweet potatoes, or a combination, cut into 1-inch/2.5 cm dice

Zest and juice of 2 lemons (for about 1/4 cup/60 mL of juice)

3 tablespoons organic extra-virgin olive oil

4 medium-size scallions, sliced thinly

1/4 cup/8 g wakame (see note on page 127)

Fine sea salt to taste, plus more as needed

Freshly ground black pepper to taste

Place the potatoes in a large saucepan or small stockpot of cold, well-salted water (1 1/2 teaspoons of fine sea salt per quart/950 mL) and bring to a boil over high heat. Lower the heat to a simmer and cook until the potatoes are tender, 6 to 8 minutes.

In a large bowl, combine the lemon zest, juice, and oil.

Drain the potatoes and add them to the bowl, stirring to thoroughly combine. Set aside to cool to room temperature.

Add the scallions, wakame, and salt and pepper to taste. Serve chilled or room temperature.

Quinoa Salad
with Arugula and Grapes

I LOVE WHOLE-GRAIN SALADS BECAUSE THEY COMBINE THE COMFORTING quality of grains with the refreshing quality of a salad. This one has both sweet and savory notes, and can be served as a side dish or light entrée.

SERVES 8 TO 10

$^1/_2$ cup/120 mL unseasoned rice vinegar

$^1/_3$ cup/80 mL organic neutral-flavored oil, such as grapeseed

1 tablespoon raw agave nectar

4$^1/_2$ cups/550 g cooked, cooled quinoa (see page 275 for how to cook grains)

2 cups/30 g baby arugula leaves

2 cups/300 g halved red or green grapes, or a combination

$^1/_4$ small red onion, sliced thinly

$^1/_2$ cup/70 g pine nuts, toasted (see note on page 122)

2 medium-size scallions, sliced thinly

Fine sea salt to taste

Freshly ground black pepper to taste

In a large bowl, combine the vinegar, oil, and agave. Add the quinoa, stirring to thoroughly combine. Add the arugula, grapes, onion, pine nuts, and scallions.

Add salt and pepper to taste and serve chilled or room temperature.

Broccoli Pasta Salad

AFTER ESTABLISHING HIMSELF IN SOME OF NEW YORK CITY'S MOST high-profile kitchens and debuting his cookbook *Inspired by Ingredients*, chef Bill Telepan opened new American restaurant Telepan in 2005. Since then, the elegant Upper West Side eatery has been widely celebrated by diners and critics for its seasonal menu and use of fresh, local ingredients. In his simple and skillful preparations, Bill allows the natural flavors of food to emerge—as in his bright and tangy Broccoli Pasta Salad.

SERVES 6 TO 8

1 tablespoon balsamic vinegar

1 tablespoon red wine vinegar

$^1/_2$ small garlic clove, mashed into a paste

6 tablespoons/90 mL organic extra-virgin olive oil

Fine sea salt to taste, plus more as needed

8 ounces/225 g penne, fusilli, or farfalle pasta (brown rice, whole wheat, or your favorite variety)

8 ounces/225 g broccoli, cut into large florets

1 cup/160 g cooked, drained white beans (see page 277 for how to cook beans)

$^1/_2$ cup/75 g sliced kalamata olives

$^1/_2$ medium-size red bell pepper, cored and cut into $^1/_2$-inch/1.25 cm dice (optional)

$^1/_4$ cup/5 g torn fresh basil leaves

$1^1/_2$ teaspoons chopped fresh oregano (optional)

In a small bowl, whisk together the balsamic vinegar, red wine vinegar, and garlic. Whisk in the oil. Add salt to taste and set aside.

In a medium saucepan of lightly salted boiling water ($^3/_4$ teaspoon of fine sea salt per quart/950 mL), cook the pasta according to the package directions. When the pasta is about 2 minutes from being done, add the broccoli and cook until the pasta is al dente and the broccoli is tender. Drain the pasta mixture and rinse with cold water until cool, 3 to 4 minutes. Drain again.

Transfer the pasta mixture to a large bowl and add the beans, olives, red pepper (if using), basil, oregano (if using), and dressing to taste. And salt to taste.

Set aside for at least 30 minutes to let the flavors develop before serving.

Green Lentil Salad with Kale, Carrots, Asparagus, and Dijon Dressing

A GREAT SOURCE OF PROTEIN, THIS REFRESHING—YET HEARTY—DISH can be made with brown or pink lentils. But green du Puy lentils are less likely to get mushy, so they make for a more toothsome, satisfying salad.

SERVES 10 TO 12

2 cups/475 mL organic reduced-sodium chicken or vegetable stock (see note on page 127)

1 cup/210 g green du Puy lentils

6 ounces/170 g carrots, cut into $1/4$-inch/0.65 cm dice

6 ounces/170 g asparagus, cut into $1/2$-inch/1.25 cm lengths

6 tablespoons/90 mL organic extra-virgin olive oil

3 tablespoons raw cider vinegar

1 teaspoon whole-grain Dijon mustard

4 large leaves kale, ribs removed, leaves chopped into $1/2$-inch/1.25 cm pieces

$1/4$ medium-size red onion, cut into $1/4$-inch/0.65 cm dice

4 teaspoons chopped fresh tarragon

Fine sea salt to taste

Freshly ground black pepper to taste

In a medium saucepan over medium-high heat, combine the stock and lentils and bring to a boil. Lower the heat to a simmer, cover, and cook until the lentils are about 6 minutes from being tender, about 15 minutes. Add the carrots, cover, and cook for 3 minutes. Add the asparagus, cover, and cook until the lentils are tender but not mushy, the vegetables are tender, and the liquid is absorbed, about 3 minutes.

Meanwhile, in a large bowl, whisk together the oil, vinegar, and mustard.

Drain the lentil mixture, if necessary, then add it to the bowl, stirring to thoroughly combine. Set aside to cool to room temperature.

Add the kale, onion, and tarragon. Add salt and pepper to taste and serve chilled or room temperature.

> **A larger portion of this salad would make a nice light meal. If you want to beef it up** even more, serve it over spinach or arugula leaves and top it with a softly poached egg or two. It's also nice as a bed for pan-sautéed, grilled, or roasted meats and seafood.

Mustard Greens Salad with Roasted Beets and Toasted Pistachios

THIS EASY-TO-DIGEST SALAD HAS A DEFINITE KICK FROM THE MUSTARD greens, but it's softened by the sweet beets and nutty pistachios.

SERVES 4

1 pound/455 g beets, ideally a combination of colors and about the same size, greens trimmed (save the greens for another use)

¼ cup/60 mL pistachio oil (see notes)

2 tablespoons organic extra-virgin olive oil

¼ cup/60 mL white or golden balsamic vinegar (see notes)

1 medium-size shallot, minced

Fine sea salt to taste

Freshly ground black pepper to taste

6 cups/85 g baby mustard greens (see notes)

¼ cup/30 g chopped pistachios, ideally unsalted, toasted (see note on page 122)

Preheat the oven to 400°F/205°C.

Wrap the beets in foil, then place them on a rimmed baking sheet. Roast until the beets are tender all the way through (check with the tip of a knife), 45 to 90 minutes depending on the size of the beets. Remove from the oven, open the foil, and set aside until cool enough to handle.

Meanwhile, in a small bowl, combine the oils, vinegar, and shallot.

Rub the skin off the beets and trim the stems. Cut the beets into wedges, transfer to a medium bowl, and drizzle with about one-third of the dressing. Add salt and pepper to taste and set aside.

In a large bowl, combine the mustard greens with the remaining dressing and salt and pepper to taste. Arrange the salad on plates or a platter, top with the beets and pistachios, and serve.

You can find white or golden balsamic vinegar in most supermarkets and wherever regular balsamic is sold.

You can find pistachio oil at many specialty food stores—ideally, look for a toasted oil, which will have a more nutty flavor—or you can substitute another nut oil or olive oil.

Look for baby mustard greens with the loose lettuces and packaged salad greens at your supermarket. If you can't find them, substitute full-grown mustard greens, which are usually near the chard, kale, and other leafy greens. Remove the ribs and cut or tear the remaining leaves into bite-size pieces.

OTHER WAYS TO ENJOY ROASTED BEETS

- Serve them as a warm side dish, drizzled with olive oil and sprinkled with chopped fresh herbs.
- Serve them as a cold side dish, drizzled with vinegar and sprinkled with crumbled goat cheese.
- Add them to other green, bean, or grain salads.
- Mash them into mashed cauliflower or sweet potatoes.
- Add them to a smoothie.

Kale Salad

A SMALL NEIGHBORHOOD SPOT IN NEW YORK CITY'S EAST VILLAGE, Northern Spy Food Co. is known for serving locally sourced meals at reasonable prices. Built around seasonality and quality, chef Hadley Schmitt's menu incorporates the finest ingredients from area purveyors and growers. Whenever possible, he lets the natural flavor of the food shine—such as in this robust raw kale salad studded with roasted butternut squash, toasted almonds, and crumbled cheese.

SERVES 2

¾ cup/90 g ½-inch/1.25 cm diced kabocha or butternut squash

2 tablespoons plus 1½ teaspoons extra-virgin olive oil, divided, or more to taste

2½ cups/45 g chopped or shredded kale, ideally Tuscan or black kale

¼ cup/35 g whole almonds, toasted (see note on page 122)

¼ cup/30 g crumbled aged Cheddar cheese, such as Cabot Clothbound Cheddar

1 tablespoon freshly squeezed lemon juice, or more to taste

Fine sea salt to taste

Freshly ground black pepper to taste

Pecorino or other hard cheese, for shaving (optional)

Preheat the oven to 375°F/190°C.

In a medium bowl, combine the squash and 1½ teaspoons of the oil. Arrange in a single layer on a small, rimmed baking sheet and bake until tender, 10 to 12 minutes. Set aside to cool to room temperature.

In a large bowl, combine the squash, kale, almonds, and Cheddar cheese. Add the lemon juice and remaining 2 tablespoons of oil and toss to combine. Add more lemon juice, more oil, and salt and pepper to taste.

Arrange the salad on plates or a platter, garnish with shaved pecorino cheese (if using), and serve.

Cold Vegetable Salad with Almond Butter Sauce

KNOWN AS *GADO GADO* **IN INDONESIA, WHERE IT'S SERVED AS A MAIN** dish, this salad is a nice change from leafy greens–type salads. And while most of the ingredients here are relatively traditional, you can definitely change and adapt the recipe to your tastes. Try adding other vegetables, either fresh or blanched and cooled, but also pieces of tempeh or rice.

SERVES 4

Fine sea salt to taste, plus more as needed

12 ounces/340 g yellow-fleshed sweet potatoes, cut into
    ¹/₂-inch/1.25 cm slices

6 ounces/170 g green beans, ideally Chinese long beans, cut into
    2-inch/5 cm lengths

2 large carrots, cut diagonally into ¹/₄-inch/0.65 cm slices

¹/₄ medium-size green or red cabbage, cored and cut into
    ¹/₂-inch/1.25 cm shreds

¹/₂ cup/120 mL organic reduced-sodium chicken or vegetable stock
    (see note on page 127)

¹/₄ cup/60 mL mirin (Japanese rice cooking wine) (see notes)

¹/₂ cup/200 g organic almond butter (see notes)

1 tablespoon unseasoned rice vinegar

1 tablespoon toasted sesame oil

1 tablespoon organic naturally brewed soy sauce or organic
    wheat-free tamari

1 teaspoon finely grated fresh ginger

1 garlic clove, minced

¹/₈ teaspoon crushed red pepper flakes

2 medium-size tomatoes, cut into wedges

¹/₂ medium-size cucumber, cut into ¹/₄-inch/0.65 cm slices

3 soft-cooked organic, pasture-raised, or antibiotic-free eggs,
    peeled and cut into quarters (optional) (see notes)

In a large pot of boiling, well-salted boiling water (1½ teaspoons of fine sea salt per quart/950 mL), cook the potatoes until tender, about 5 minutes. Use a slotted spoon to transfer the potatoes to a large paper towel–lined plate or platter. Set aside.

Add the green beans to the boiling water and cook until tender, about 3 minutes. Use a slotted spoon to transfer to the plate with the potatoes.

Add the carrots to the boiling water and cook until tender, about 3 minutes. Use a slotted spoon to transfer to the plate with the potatoes.

Add the cabbage to the boiling water and cook until just slightly limp, 1 to 2 minutes. Drain the cabbage and add it to the plate with the potatoes. Set aside to cool to room temperature, then if you'd like to serve the vegetables cold, refrigerate until chilled.

Meanwhile, in a medium saucepan over medium heat, combine the stock, mirin, almond butter, vinegar, sesame oil, soy sauce, ginger, garlic, and pepper flakes. Bring to a gentle boil, stirring until the mixture thickens, just a few seconds. Remove from the heat, add salt to taste, and set aside to cool to room temperature.

Arrange the potatoes, green beans, carrots, cabbage, tomatoes, cucumber, and soft-cooked egg (if using) on plates or a platter, keeping the different items in separate piles. Drizzle with the sauce and serve. Alternatively, serve the sauce on the side.

> **The sauce for this dish is typically made with peanut or cashew butter, but we're using** almond butter. For more about why almond butter is good for you, see page 51.
>
> You can find mirin in the Asian or ethnic food section of most major supermarkets. If you'd rather avoid wine, substitute stock.
>
> Ideally, slightly undercook your hard-cooked eggs, to help avoid oxidation. For more about why that's a good thing, see page 73.

Warm Spinach Salad with Potato, Zucchini, and Salmon

BESIDES SALMON AND WARM VEGETABLES, THIS ENTRÉE-SIZE SALAD features fresh herbs, scallions, and a lemony vinaigrette. If you don't have already-cooked salmon, just grill or pan-sauté salmon fillets for 3 or 4 minutes per side, until they're barely opaque throughout. (Remember, the less your fish is cooked, the greater its health benefits.)

SERVES 4

2 lemons

$^1/_4$ cup/60 mL organic extra-virgin olive oil

3 small zucchini

Fine sea salt to taste, plus more as needed

8 ounces/225 g red potatoes, cut into $^1/_2$-inch/2.5 cm wedges

8 medium-size scallions, sliced thinly

3 tablespoons coarsely chopped fresh flat-leaf parsley, plus sprigs for garnish

3 tablespoons coarsely chopped fresh basil, plus sprigs for garnish

1 pound/455 g cooked sustainably-sourced salmon, broken into large chunks

Freshly ground black pepper to taste

12 cups/170 g spinach leaves

Use a vegetable peeler to cut the colored part of the peel from half of one of the lemons. Cut the peel crosswise into thin slices and place it in a large bowl. Juice the lemons to yield $^1/_4$ cup/60 mL of juice. Add the juice to the bowl. Add the oil and set aside.

Cut the zucchini into $1^1/_2$-inch/4 cm lengths. Cut each length into $^1/_4$-inch/0.65 cm sticks. Set aside.

In a large pot of well-salted boiling water ($1^1/_2$ teaspoons of fine sea salt per quart/950 mL), cook the potatoes until tender, about 5 minutes. Use a slotted spoon to remove the potatoes, shake off any excess water, and transfer them to the bowl.

Add the zucchini to the boiling water and cook until tender, about 1 minute. Drain well and transfer the zucchini to the bowl. Add the scallions, parsley, and basil. Gently fold in the salmon. Add salt and pepper to taste.

Arrange the spinach on plates or a platter and top with the salmon mixture. Garnish with the herb sprigs and serve warm.

HOW TO MAKE A BASIC VINAIGRETTE

1. Combine one part acid with two or three parts oil.
2. Adjust to taste with more acid or more oil.
3. Add salt and pepper to taste now, or add it to the finished, tossed salad.

WHAT'S AN ACID?
- The acid in a vinaigrette can be vinegar—including balsamic, wine, rice, or cider vinegars—or lemon, lime, or orange juice. Or a combination.

WHAT KIND OF OIL?
- The oil in a vinaigrette can be olive oil, a nut oil, or a seed oil—all of which will add flavors to your vinaigrette—or a neutral-flavored oil, such as grapeseed. Or a combination.

OTHER ADDITIONS
- Chopped shallots, citrus zest, herbs, and a dab of Dijon mustard are all nice additions to a vinaigrette.
- Adding buttermilk, sour cream, plain yogurt, or an egg yolk or two will make a creamy vinaigrette.
- Sweeteners, such as maple syrup or raw agave, will help balance acidity.
- Other juices generally act like mild acids, requiring less oil to balance your vinaigrette.

OTHER THOUGHTS
- If you season your vinaigrette with salt and pepper, be aggressive—it should be enough to season the whole salad.
- Using a blender to combine your acid and oil will help keep it from separating.
- Toss salads with vinaigrette just before serving.

Arugula with Chicken and Blueberries

THIS ENTRÉE SALAD IS FIRING ON ALL CYLINDERS. IT'S FULL OF NUTRIENT-rich foods—arugula, blueberries, nuts—and also jam-packed with fruity, savory, earthy, and refreshing flavors and textures. It's also nice enough to serve for company, but simple enough for a weeknight meal. Enjoy.

SERVES 4

$^1\!/_3$ cup/80 mL plus 2 tablespoons organic extra-virgin olive oil, divided

4 boneless, skinless organic chicken breast halves (about $1^3\!/_4$ pound/795 g)

Fine sea salt to taste

Freshly ground black pepper to taste

$^1\!/_4$ cup/60 mL raw apple cider vinegar

1 medium-size shallot, minced

2 teaspoons raw honey (see note on page 106)

12 cups/140 g loosely packed arugula leaves

$1^1\!/_2$ cups/205 g blueberries

$^3\!/_4$ cup/85 g crumbled blue cheese (optional)

$^1\!/_2$ cup/50 g sliced raw almonds, toasted (see note on page 122)

In a very large skillet over medium heat, heat 2 tablespoons of the oil. Sprinkle the chicken with salt and pepper and cook until cooked through, 5 to 6 minutes per side. Transfer the chicken to a cutting board and let it rest, covered loosely with foil, for 5 minutes.

Meanwhile, in a small bowl, combine the vinegar, shallot, honey, and the remaining $^1\!/_3$ cup/80 mL of oil. In a large bowl, combine the arugula, blueberries, and cheese (if using), with the dressing and salt and pepper to taste. Arrange the salad on plates or a platter.

Slice the chicken and arrange it on the salad. Sprinkle with the almonds and serve.

Flank Steak and Chimichurri Salad

CHIMICHURRI IS LIKE A PARSLEY-AND-OREGANO PESTO, WITH A TOUCH of vinegar and a mild chile pepper kick. In South America, it's traditionally served with grilled meats, but here it's thinned out a bit to make an herb-packed—and highly medicinal—dressing for a meaty entrée-size salad.

SERVES 4

1/2 cup/120 mL organic extra-virgin olive oil

1/4 cup/60 mL raw apple cider vinegar

6 garlic cloves

20 sprigs fresh flat-leaf parsley

Leaves from 5 sprigs fresh oregano

1/2 teaspoon crushed red pepper flakes

Fine sea salt to taste

1 pound/455 g grass-fed flank steak

Freshly ground black pepper to taste

12 cups/170 g lightly packed spring mixed greens

1 cup/145 g halved cherry tomatoes

1 medium-size zucchini, halved lengthwise and sliced thinly

1/2 medium-size red onion, halved and sliced thinly

In the bowl of a food processor, combine the oil, vinegar, garlic, parsley, oregano, and red pepper flakes and process to a puree, scraping down the bowl as necessary. Add salt to taste and set aside.

Prepare a grill to high heat and lightly oil the grate. Sprinkle the steak with salt and black pepper and grill to desired doneness, about 5 minutes per side for medium-rare. Remove the steak from the grill and let it rest, covered loosely with foil, for 5 minutes.

Meanwhile, in a large bowl, combine the greens, cherry tomatoes, zucchini, and onion with the dressing and salt and black pepper to taste. Arrange the salad on plates or a platter.

Thinly slice the steak crosswise and arrange on the salad. Drizzle with additional dressing and serve.

Grilled Corn with Flavored Grass-Fed Butter

I KNOW THAT THE TYPICAL WAY TO ENJOY FRESH CORN IS TO BOIL IT, but grilling adds a whole new dimension to corn's sweet flavors. Try this as a side dish to other grilled entrées, such as Grilled Veggie Soft Tacos with Cilantro Slaw and Spiced Crema (page 225), Rosemary-Stuffed Grilled Trout with Fennel Relish (page 233), or Big Beef Burgers with Grilled Onions and (Sometimes) Blue Cheese Sauce (page 251).

SERVES 6

6 medium-size ears fresh organic corn
Flavored butter (page 282)

Prepare the grill to medium-hot. Carefully peel back the husks from the corn and remove the silks. Pull the husks back over the kernels.

Place the corn on the grill and cook, turning occasionally, until the husks are charred in spots and the kernels are hot, 10 to 12 minutes.

Pull back or remove the husks. Serve the corn with the butter on the side.

Green Bean Succotash with Collards and Black-Eyed Peas

HERE'S A TASTY TWIST ON A TRADITIONAL SOUTHERN SIDE DISH, ONE that's beautifully colorful. It'd nicely complement grilled or pan-seared chicken or fish, but in a larger portion, it'd also make a good vegetarian main dish. To vary it, use different kinds of beans and greens.

SERVES 6 TO 8

Fine sea salt to taste, plus more as needed

2 large leaves collard greens, ribs removed, leaves cut into 1½-inch/4 cm by ¼-inch/0.65 cm strips

6 ounces/170 g green beans, cut into ½-inch/1.25 cm lengths

2 tablespoons organic extra-virgin olive oil

½ medium-size red onion, cut into ¼-inch/0.65 cm dice

1½ cups/225 g organic corn kernels

1 cup/170 g cooked, drained black-eyed peas (see page 277 for how to cook beans)

½ cup/120 mL organic reduced-sodium chicken or vegetable stock (see note on page 127)

4 medium-size scallions, sliced thinly

Freshly ground black pepper to taste

In a medium saucepan of well-salted boiling water (1½ teaspoons of fine sea salt per quart/950 mL), cook the collards and green beans until the vegetables are crisp-tender, 2 to 3 minutes. Drain and set aside.

In a large skillet over medium-high heat, heat the oil. Add the onion and cook, stirring occasionally, until starting to become translucent, about 2 minutes. Add the corn and cook, stirring occasionally, until the onion and corn are crisp-tender, about 2 minutes. Add the collards, green beans, black-eyed peas, and stock and cook, stirring, until the vegetables are tender and the stock is almost entirely evaporated, 3 to 5 minutes. Remove from the heat and add the scallions and salt and pepper to taste. Serve hot.

Home-Fermented Sauerkraut

IT'S ALMOST MAGIC TO TURN RUN-OF-THE-MILL CABBAGE INTO amazingly-good-for-you sauerkraut, yet the process is nothing more than an age-old food preservation method—fermentation. All it takes is a few ingredients plus time and patience, and your reward is a taste and texture that store-bought sauerkraut can only dream of.

Because what we're dealing with is, basically, controlled spoilage, be sure that all your equipment—utensils, containers, dish towels, hands—is scrupulously clean at every point in the process, including your tasting of the sauerkraut during the fermentation process.

MAKES 4 TO 5 CUPS/500 TO 625 G

10 teaspoons fine sea salt, divided (see notes)
2 pounds/905 g green cabbage, cored and shredded finely
1 to 2 tablespoons flavoring ingredients (see sidebar)

In a bowl or measuring cup, combine 5 teaspoons of the salt with 4 cups/475 mL of lukewarm water, stirring to dissolve the salt. Set aside to cool to room temperature.

Meanwhile, in large mixing bowl, combine the cabbage, remaining 5 teaspoons of salt, and flavoring ingredients, if you like, stirring to thoroughly combine. Transfer to a large, nonreactive container, packing it down. Let stand for 15 minutes, so the cabbage can release some of its juices.

Check to see if the juices are enough to cover the cabbage. If not, add enough of the salt water mixture to cover. Cover the top of the cabbage with a double layer of cheesecloth, tucking it in at the edges. Set a plastic, glass, or ceramic plate on top of the cabbage, ideally one that fits just inside the container, to keep the cabbage submerged. Place something heavy on top of the plate, such as a bowl or a lidded jar filled with water. Cover the entire setup loosely with a clean kitchen towel and set it aside in a cool place (no warmer than 75°F) for 3 to 6 weeks, checking the sauerkraut a few times a week to skim any foam from the surface and rinse the plate. When the bubbling stops, the fermentation is complete and the sauerkraut is done, although you can taste it any time during the process, and if it's done to your liking, it's done.

Transfer the sauerkraut to an airtight container and store it in the refrigerator.

While my preference is for you to always use fine sea salt, in this recipe it's especially important—"regular" or iodized table salts have additives that can affect the fermentation process.

For more about why fermented foods are good for you, see page 47.

WAYS TO FLAVOR YOUR SAUERKRAUT

Although it's not necessary to add any flavoring ingredients, if you like, you can add 1 to 2 tablespoons of whole spices, just one or a combination. Here are a few ideas:

- Peppercorns
- Juniper berries
- Caraway, fennel, cumin, coriander, dill, celery, or anise seeds

- Bay leaves
- Cinnamon sticks
- Whole cloves or allspice

Braised Baby Artichokes

DON'T BE INTIMIDATED BY THE IDEA OF TACKLING BABY ARTICHOKES. They take a little time to prepare for cooking, but there's nothing difficult about it. Once prepped, cooking is quicker because the 'chokes are smaller—and eating is easier because all the tough parts have been removed.

You can serve these babies as a side dish, or spooned on top of fish or chicken. But they're also amazing in a green salad, scattered over spelt pizza, or tossed with brown rice pasta.

SERVES 4

2 tablespoons freshly squeezed lemon juice (from 1 or 2 lemons), divided

2 pounds/905 g baby artichokes (18 to 20)

2 tablespoons organic extra-virgin olive oil

4 garlic cloves, minced

²/₃ cup/160 mL organic reduced-sodium chicken or vegetable stock (see note on page 127)

1 tablespoon chopped fresh thyme

2 tablespoons unsalted grass-fed organic butter (optional)

Fine sea salt to taste

Freshly ground black pepper to taste

Fill a large bowl with 6 cups/1.4 L cold water and add 1 tablespoon of the lemon juice. Working with one artichoke at a time, snap off the outer leaves until you reach leaves that are three-quarters yellow and one-quarter green (you'll take off about three outer layers of leaves). Trim the top, removing the green part and spines. Trim any browned part off the stem, then trim around sides of the stem with a paring knife or vegetable peeler, removing the tough green parts and creating a stubby cone shape at the base of the artichoke. Halve the artichoke lengthwise (or quarter if large), then place it in the lemon water to help keep it from browning.

When ready to cook, drain the artichokes. In a medium skillet over medium-high heat, heat the oil. Add the artichokes and garlic and cook, stirring occasionally, until the artichokes begin to brown, 3 to 5 minutes. Add the stock, thyme, and the remaining 1 tablespoon of lemon juice. Bring to a boil, lower the heat to a simmer, cover, and cook until the artichokes are tender, about 5 minutes.

Use a slotted spoon to transfer the artichokes to a medium bowl. Set aside. Increase the heat under the skillet to high and cook the liquid until it's reduced by half, 2 to 3 minutes. Remove from the heat and add the butter (if using), stirring until it melts. Return the artichokes to the pan and toss with the sauce. Add salt and pepper to taste.

Serve hot or room temperature.

Caramelized Roasted Endive

YOU MIGHT BE USED TO ENJOYING FIBER-RICH ENDIVE RAW, AS IN SALADS. But it's also great cooked—the leaves becoming soft and succulent with a mildly buttery flavor.

SERVES 4 TO 6

2 tablespoons unsalted grass-fed organic butter

2 tablespoons organic extra-virgin olive oil

6 medium-size heads endive (about 1¼ pounds/565 g) red, white, or a combination, trimmed and halved lengthwise

Fine sea salt to taste

Freshly ground black pepper to taste

1 teaspoon chopped fresh flat-leaf parsley

Preheat the oven to 450°F/230°C.

In a very large, oven-proof skillet over medium heat, heat the butter and oil. Add the endive, cut side down, and cook until browned, 3 to 5 minutes. Turn the endive and sprinkle with salt and pepper. Place the skillet in the oven and roast until the endive is tender, 8 to 10 minutes.

Remove the skillet from the oven (careful, the handle will be very hot). Sprinkle with parsley and more salt and pepper to taste and serve.

> **To make this recipe vegan, substitute olive oil for the butter.**
> You can change up this very basic recipe simply and easily—just change the parsley to chopped fresh basil, cilantro, tarragon, sage, oregano, marjoram, or really any herb you like.

Broccoli with Olive Oil and Lemon

THIS IS ONE OF THOSE VERY BASIC RECIPES WHERE REALLY GOOD, high-quality ingredients will make a difference. So buy the broccoli—a great source of diindolylmethane (DIM), a phytonutrient that plays a role in healthy hormone balance—at the farmers' market, where you can look the person who grew it in the eye and thank him or her for taking the time to grow delicious food for you. Use your best olive oil. And then, as you sit down to eat, savor the satisfaction of simple foods well prepared.

SERVES 4 TO 6

Fine sea salt to taste, plus more as needed

1 pound/455 g broccoli, cut into large florets

3 tablespoons organic extra-virgin olive oil

Zest of 1 lemon

Freshly ground black pepper to taste

In a large saucepan of well-salted boiling water ($1\frac{1}{2}$ teaspoons of fine sea salt per quart/950 mL), cook the broccoli until crisp-tender, 2 to 3 minutes. Drain and transfer to a large bowl. Add the oil, lemon zest, and salt and pepper to taste.

Serve hot.

Sautéed Shaved Brussels Sprouts with Shallots and Almonds

BRUSSELS SPROUTS CAN BE A BIT BITTER—I THINK THAT'S WHY SOME people don't like them. But here, any bitterness is countered with lemon juice, fresh dill, and toasted almonds. The result is a really good, completely health-conscious vegetable dish.

Even if you haven't liked Brussels sprouts before, you're in for a pleasant surprise.

SERVES 4

1 pound/455 g Brussels sprouts, trimmed, outer leaves removed

2 tablespoons organic extra-virgin olive oil

6 medium-size shallots, sliced thinly (about 1 cup/100 g)

3 garlic cloves, sliced thinly

2 tablespoons freshly squeezed lemon juice (from 1 or 2 lemons)

1 1/2 teaspoons chopped fresh dill

1/4 cup/25 g sliced raw almonds, toasted (see note on page 122), divided

Fine sea salt to taste

Freshly ground black pepper to taste

Use a food processor fitted with a slicing disk to thinly slice the Brussels sprouts. (Alternatively, slice thinly by hand or with a mandoline.) Set aside.

In a large skillet over medium heat, heat the oil. Add the shallots and cook, stirring occasionally, until almost translucent, about 3 minutes. Add the garlic and cook, stirring occasionally, for 1 minute. Add the Brussels sprouts and cook, stirring occasionally, until tender, about 8 minutes. Remove from the heat and add the lemon juice, dill, and 3 tablespoons of the almonds, scraping up any browned bits in the skillet. Add salt and pepper to taste.

Transfer to a serving bowl or plates, sprinkle with the remaining 1 tablespoon of almonds, and serve.

> **Vary this recipe by using different combinations of citrus juice, herbs, and nuts.**

Rainbow Chard and Radicchio Sauté

ONE WAY TO ENSURE EATING A GOOD VARIETY OF VITAMINS AND minerals is to eat a lot of colorful foods, and this recipe is definitely colorful, as well as tasty. The chard is earthy, the radicchio is pleasantly bitter, and the dish is finished with just the right amount of sweet and sour notes.

Enjoy it with a pile of roasted vegetables, halved roasted acorn squash, or a simply prepared piece of fish, chicken, or meat.

SERVES 4

1 pound/455 g rainbow chard

2 tablespoons organic extra-virgin olive oil

1 medium-size yellow onion, halved and cut into $^1/_4$-inch/0.65 cm slices

4 garlic cloves, minced

1 large head radicchio, cored, cut into 1-inch/2.5 cm wedges, leaves separated

1 tablespoon balsamic vinegar, or more to taste

2 tablespoons unsweetened and unsulfured raisins or dried currants

2 tablespoons chopped pecans, toasted (see note on page 122)

Fine sea salt to taste

Freshly ground black pepper to taste

Cut the ribs from the chard and chop them crosswise into 1-inch/2.5 cm lengths. Cut the leaves crosswise into 1-inch/2.5 cm–thick strips. Set the ribs and leaves aside.

In a large saucepan or small stockpot over medium heat, heat the oil. Add the onion and garlic and cook, stirring occasionally, until the onion is tender, about 4 minutes. Add the chard ribs, cover, and cook, stirring occasionally, until tender, about 6 minutes. Working in batches, add the chard leaves and radicchio, stirring until wilted before adding the next batch. Re-cover and cook, stirring often, until the vegetables are tender, 8 to 10 minutes. Remove from the heat and add the vinegar and currants. Add more vinegar and salt and pepper to taste.

Transfer the mixture to a serving bowl. Sprinkle with the pecans and serve.

Roasted Carrots and Parsnips with Garlic, Citrus, and Sage

ROASTED ROOT VEGETABLES ARE AN IDEAL WINTER SIDE DISH, AND when they become brown and caramelized, they have a sweetness that can satisfy your sugar cravings.

Usually, it's plenty to toss them with just olive oil, salt, and pepper, but when you want a bit more, this is your dish. The citrus adds brightness, the sage adds softness, and when are whole roasted garlic cloves not a good thing?

SERVES 6

1 pound/455 g carrots, cut diagonally into ¹/₄-inch/0.65 cm slices

1 pound/455 g parsnips, cut diagonally into ¹/₈-inch/0.3 cm slices

20 garlic cloves

¹/₂ lemon, cut crosswise into ¹/₈-inch/0.3 cm slices (peel and all)

¹/₂ medium-size orange, halved lengthwise and cut crosswise into ¹/₈-inch/0.3 cm slices (peel and all)

¹/₄ cup/60 mL organic extra-virgin olive oil

1 tablespoon chopped fresh sage

Fine sea salt to taste

Freshly ground black pepper to taste

Preheat the oven to 375°F/190°C. Arrange a rack in the upper half of the oven and another in the lower half.

In a large bowl, combine the carrots, parsnips, garlic, lemon, orange, and oil. Divide the mixture between two large, rimmed baking sheets, spreading it out in an even layer. Roast for 20 minutes.

Toss the vegetables and switch the position of the baking sheets. Roast until the vegetables are tender and browned at edges, about 20 minutes.

Sprinkle with the sage and salt and pepper to taste. Serve warm or room temperature.

Teriyaki-Glazed Baby Bok Choy

THIS VERSATILE SIDE DISH IS DELICATE ENOUGH TO COMPLEMENT grain dishes and poached or steamed chicken or fish, but also flavorful enough to work with grilled meats. You can make it more substantial by serving it on a bed of rice or rice noodles. Or add some protein to the stir-fry—I like tempeh, shrimp, or pork.

SERVES 4 TO 6

2 tablespoons raw honey (see note on page 106)

2 tablespoons mirin (Japanese rice cooking wine) (see note on page 180)

1 tablespoon organic naturally brewed soy sauce or organic wheat-free tamari

1 teaspoon toasted sesame oil

$^1/_2$ teaspoon crushed red pepper flakes

1 teaspoon arrowroot powder

2 tablespoons organic high-heat cooking oil, such as grapeseed

3 medium-size shallots, cut into $^1/_4$-inch/0.65 cm slices

$1^1/_2$ pounds/680 g baby bok choy, cut lengthwise (through the core) into $^1/_2$-inch/1.25 cm slices

In a medium bowl, whisk together the honey, mirin, soy sauce, sesame oil, and red pepper flakes. Whisk in the arrowroot. Set aside.

In a large wok or skillet over medium-high heat, heat the oil. Add the shallots and stir-fry for 2 minutes. Add the bok choy and stir-fry until crisp-tender, 6 to 8 minutes. Rewhisk the honey mixture and add it to the wok. Cook, stirring to evenly coat, until the sauce is thickened and the bok choy is tender, about 1 minute.

Serve hot.

> **To make this recipe vegan, use coconut nectar instead of the honey.**

BASIC ROASTED VEGETABLES

There's almost nothing better than beautifully caramelized roasted vegetables. Here's how to make them.

1. **Preheat the oven to 375°F/190°C.**
   Use a slightly lower temperature, about 350°F, if the vegetables are dense, such as winter squash, or if they're are in large pieces. Use a slightly higher temperature, about 400°F, if the vegetables are porous, such as eggplant, or they're cut in small pieces.

2. **Cut each type of vegetable so that its pieces are about the same size.**
   This helps them cook evenly.

3. **Toss the vegetables with olive oil.**
   Add salt and pepper now or add it to the finished, roasted vegetables.

4. **Spread out the vegetables in an even layer on a large, rimmed baking sheet.**
   Make sure the baking sheet isn't too crowded. Room around the vegetables helps them brown, and browning adds flavor. If necessary, use a second baking sheet.

5. **Bake until tender and browned, tossing halfway through.**
   Note that if you're doing more than one type of vegetable, you should add the different types to the oven according to how long they'll take to become tender—add the longest-cooking vegetables first and the quickest-cooking vegetables last, the goal being that they're all done at the same time.

Braised Greens with Nori

HERE'S A SATISFYINGLY BASIC WAY TO ENJOY GREEN LEAFY VEGETABLES. It's inspired by traditional Southern recipes, but gets a nutritional boost with the addition of nori, the same sea vegetable that's used in sushi.

When you're preparing the greens, they might seem like waaay too much for only four to six people, but they'll cook waaay down.

SERVES 4 TO 6

3 slices thick-cut, nitrite-free bacon, or 6 slices tempeh bacon, cut crosswise into $^1/_4$-inch/0.65 cm strips (optional)

1 or 2 tablespoons organic extra-virgin olive oil (if not using bacon)

1 small carrot, chopped finely

4 garlic cloves, minced

2 pounds/905 g collard, kale, chard, chicory, dandelion, or mustard greens, or a combination, ribs removed, leaves cut or torn into rough 3- or 4-inch/ 8 to 10 cm pieces

2 sheets nori, cut or torn into rough 1-inch/2.5 cm pieces

1 cup/240 mL organic reduced-sodium chicken or vegetable stock (see note on page 127)

Fine sea salt to taste

Freshly ground black pepper to taste

Raw apple cider vinegar to taste

In a large, wide saucepan or small, wide stockpot over medium-low heat, cook the bacon, stirring occasionally, until crisp, 3 to 5 minutes. (If using tempeh, over medium-low heat, heat 2 tablespoons of oil, then cook the tempeh, stirring occasionally, until well browned, 3 or 4 minutes. If using neither, over medium-low heat, heat 1 tablespoon of olive oil.)

Add the carrot and garlic and cook, stirring occasionally, until the carrot is tender, 1 to 2 minutes. Working in batches, add the greens, stirring until wilted before adding the next batch. Once all the greens have been added, add the nori and stock and bring to a boil. Lower the heat to a simmer, cover, and cook until the greens are tender, 10 to 20 minutes depending on the greens.

Add salt, pepper, and vinegar to taste. Serve hot.

For more about why greens are good for you, see page 45.

WAYS TO VARY YOUR GREENS

- Add other vegetables to the initial sauté, such as onions, shallots, chopped celery, diced bell peppers, or mushrooms.
- Add other vegetables with the greens, such as green beans, peas, asparagus, broccoli, cauliflower, or cabbage.
- Add crushed red pepper flakes.
- Garnish with toasted seeds or nuts.
- Drizzle the finished greens with olive oil.

Smoky-Sweet Glazed Carrots

IT'S AMAZING HOW QUICKLY AND EASILY YOU CAN TURN SOMETHING basic into something special. Here, simply sautéed, beta-carotene–rich carrots are coated with a little maple syrup and a sprinkle of smoked paprika, and end up uniquely amazing.

SERVES 4 TO 6

1¼ pounds/565 g carrots

1 tablespoon unsalted grass-fed organic butter

1 tablespoon organic extra-virgin olive oil

2 tablespoons organic reduced-sodium chicken or vegetable stock (see note on page 127)

2 tablespoons pure maple syrup

2 teaspoons smoked paprika

Fine sea salt to taste

Cut the carrots into 2- to 2½-inch/5 to 6 cm lengths. Cut each length into ¼-inch/0.65 cm sticks.

In a large skillet over medium heat, melt the butter and oil. Add the carrots and cook, stirring occasionally, for 2 minutes (adjust the heat as needed to keep the butter from burning). Add the stock, maple syrup, and smoked paprika and cook, stirring occasionally, until the carrots are tender and lightly browned and the liquid has evaporated, 5 to 7 minutes. Add salt to taste and serve hot.

> **To make this recipe vegan and dairy-free, substitute more olive oil for the butter.**

Ratatouille

RATATOUILLE—EGGPLANT, TOMATOES, ZUCCHINI, BELL PEPPER, AND herbs simmered together in olive oil until the whole thing is wonderfully gloppy and unctuous—is summer in a skillet. Although not traditional, this recipe includes mushrooms, adding healthful nutrients along with a nice earthiness.

SERVES 8 TO 12

½ cup/120 mL organic extra-virgin olive oil, divided

1 medium-size yellow onion, cut into ½-inch/1.25 cm dice

1 medium-size red bell pepper, cored and cut into ½-inch/1.25 cm dice

1 medium-size eggplant (about 12 ounces/340 g), cut into ½-inch/1.25 cm dice

8 ounces/225 g brown or cremini mushrooms, halved if large and cut into ¼-inch/0.65 cm slices

1 medium-size zucchini, quartered lengthwise and cut into ¼-inch/0.65 cm slices

2 garlic cloves, minced

1 pound/455 g tomatoes, peeled (optional) and cut into $^1/_2$-inch/1.25 dice

1$^1/_2$ teaspoons chopped fresh thyme

1 teaspoon chopped fresh marjoram (see note)

$^1/_2$ cup/20 g chopped fresh basil

Fine sea salt to taste

In a large skillet over medium heat, heat 2 tablespoons of the oil. Add the onion and bell pepper and cook, stirring occasionally, until the vegetables are crisp-tender, about 4 minutes. Add $^1/_4$ cup/60 mL of the remaining oil. Once it's hot, add the eggplant and mushrooms and cook, stirring occasionally, until the eggplant is softened, about 4 minutes. Stir in the zucchini and garlic and cook, stirring occasionally, until the zucchini is crisp-tender, about 4 minutes. Stir in the tomatoes, thyme, and marjoram and cook, stirring occasionally, until all the vegetables are very tender and the mixture is like a very thick stew, 8 to 10 minutes. Stir in the basil, the remaining 2 tablespoons of oil, and salt to taste.

Serve warm or room temperature.

> **If you can't find fresh marjoram, substitute equal parts oregano and sage.**

WAYS TO ENJOY RATATOUILLE

- As a side dish
- As a snack or appetizer, with crackers or cheese
- As a topping for grains, rice, or beans
- As a topping for a grilled steak, lamb chop, chicken breast, fish fillet, or roasted portobello mushroom

Garlic Mashed Butternut Squash

WITH MORE FLAVOR, COLOR, AND NUTRITION, A LOWER GLYCEMIC index, and plenty of garlic, this mashed potato–like recipe is a great alternative to "regular" mashers.

SERVES 4 TO 6

2 pounds/905 g butternut squash, peeled, seeded, and cut into rough, 1-inch/2.5 cm pieces

8 garlic cloves

1½ teaspoons chopped fresh thyme

2 tablespoons unsalted grass-fed organic butter (optional)

Fine sea salt to taste

Freshly ground black pepper to taste

Place the squash in a large saucepan of cold, well-salted water (1½ teaspoons of fine sea salt per quart/950 mL) and bring to a boil over high heat. Add the garlic, lower the heat to a simmer, and cook until the squash and garlic are very tender, about 15 minutes.

Drain the squash and garlic and return them to the saucepan. Add the thyme and butter (if using) and mash with a potato masher to the desired consistency.

Add salt and pepper to taste and serve hot.

> **If you'd like the squash to be smoother, use a handheld mixer to puree it,** instead of a potato masher.

Mashed Celeriac

WITH FRESH, VERNAL FLAVORS FROM THE CELERIAC—ALSO KNOWN AS celery root—and the creamy texture of mashed potatoes, this would also be a great side dish to Poached Sablefish with Julienned Vegetables and Horseradish Yogurt (page 235), Chicken and Pepper Paprikash (page 237), and Spiced Braised Short Ribs with Red Cabbage (page 255).

SERVES 6

Fine sea salt to taste, plus more as needed

2 pounds/905 g celery root (celeriac), peeled, and cut into $^1/_2$-inch/1.25 cm dice

1 pound/455 g yellow-fleshed sweet potatoes, cut into 1-inch/2.5 cm pieces

4 tablespoons/55 g unsalted grass-fed, organic butter, at room temperature

About $^1/_2$ cup/120 mL grass-fed, organic milk, at room temperature

3 scallions, sliced thinly

Freshly ground black pepper to taste

In a large saucepan of well-salted boiling water (1$^1/_2$ teaspoons of fine sea salt per quart/950 mL), cook the celery root for 10 minutes. Add the potatoes and cook until the vegetables are very tender, about 15 minutes. Drain and return the vegetables to the pot. Add the butter and use a potato masher to mash until the butter is mixed in. Add the $^1/_2$ cup/120 mL of milk and continue mashing to the desired consistency, adding more milk if needed. Add the scallions and salt and pepper to taste.

Serve hot.

Sweet Potato Oven Fries

EVEN THOUGH YOU MIGHT BE ABLE TO SQUEEZE ALL THE POTATOES onto one baking sheet, use two. More room around the fries helps them crisp up better.

SERVES 3 OR 4

1 medium-size yellow-fleshed sweet potato, cut into
  $^1/_4$ by $^1/_4$-inch/0.65 by 0.65 cm sticks
1 medium-size orange-fleshed sweet potato, cut into
  $^1/_4$ by $^1/_4$-inch/0.65 by 0.65 cm sticks
3 tablespoons organic neutral-flavored oil, such as grapeseed
Fine sea salt to taste

Preheat the oven to 450°F/230°C. Arrange a rack in the upper half of the oven and another in the lower half.

In a large bowl, combine the potatoes and oil, tossing to coat thoroughly and evenly. Arrange the potatoes on two large, rimmed baking sheets in an even layer and bake for 15 minutes.

One pan at a time, remove the potatoes from the oven and toss them with a spatula, switching the position of the baking sheets. Rearrange the potatoes in an even layer and bake until crisp outside and cooked through, 10 to 12 minutes.

Add salt to taste and serve hot.

WAYS TO VARY YOUR FRIES

- Add spices, such as chili powder or smoked paprika, along with the oil.
- Add chopped fresh herbs—heartier ones, such as rosemary or thyme, during the last few minutes of cooking; more delicate ones, such as parsley or cilantro, after cooking.
- Toss the finished fries with garlic olive oil.
- Sprinkle the finished fries with *furikake* (a Japanese seasoning blend).

ENTRÉES

CAULIFLOWER CURRY WITH CHARD
AND COCONUT MILK

BARLEY RISOTTO PRIMAVERA

CLASSIC PASTA WITH RED SAUCE

SWISS CHARD AND ROSEMARY PESTO PASTA

RAW PAD THAI

SKILLET CASSEROLE WITH ROOT
VEGETABLES, LEEKS, AND MUSHROOMS

MILLET-STUFFED ACORN SQUASH

SIMPLE, SATISFYING RICE WITH TEMPEH,
BROCCOLI, AND KALE

ROASTED EGGPLANT AND PEPPERS
WITH PARMESAN POLENTA

AVOCADO AND ARUGULA WRAP

GRILLED VEGGIE SOFT TACOS WITH
CILANTRO SLAW AND SPICED CREMA

BLACK BEAN "BURGERS"

THAI-STYLE MUSSELS WITH LEMONGRASS

MISO-GLAZED HALIBUT WITH DAIKON AND CARROTS

ROSEMARY-STUFFED GRILLED TROUT
WITH FENNEL RELISH

GRILLED SALMON WITH
STRAWBERRY AVOCADO SALSA

POACHED SABLEFISH (BLACK COD) WITH
VEGETABLES AND HORSERADISH YOGURT

BAKED WHITE FISH

CHICKEN AND PEPPER PAPRIKASH

MOROCCAN-MARINATED CHICKEN BREASTS
WITH WILTED ONIONS

LAVENDER ROASTED CHICKEN
WITH ROASTED YAMS

TURKEY CHILI VERDE

GLAZED SPARE RIBS

MUSTARD-MAPLE PORK TENDERLOIN
WITH CARROTS, ONION, AND APPLES

SPICE-RUBBED PORK CHOPS WITH
SMOKY CABBAGE AND COLLARDS

GREEK LAMBURGERS WITH
EGGPLANT AND LEMON "AIOLI"

LAMB TIKKA MASALA

BIG BEEF BURGERS WITH GRILLED ONIONS
AND (SOMETIMES) BLUE CHEESE SAUCE

MORE-VEGGIES-THAN-BEEF STEW

MOM'S MEAT LOAF WITH QUINOA

SPICED BRAISED SHORT RIBS WITH RED CABBAGE

GRASS-FED RIB EYES WITH GARLIC-CHIVE BUTTER

Cauliflower Curry
with Chard and Coconut Milk

I ESPECIALLY LIKE THIS CURRY ON A FALL OR WINTER DAY—THE healthful ingredients and mildly spicy flavors are soul warming. Try it served over brown basmati or brown jasmine rice.

SERVES 4 TO 6

8 ounces/225 g chard

2 tablespoons organic high-heat cooking oil, such as grapeseed

2 medium-size yellow onions, cut into ³/₄-inch/2 cm dice

2 pounds/910 g cauliflower, cored and cut into large bite-size florets

4 garlic cloves, minced

2 cups/475 mL coconut milk (see note on page 108)

1¹/₂ cups/355 mL organic reduced-sodium chicken or vegetable stock (see note on page 127)

2 tablespoons curry powder

¹/₄ teaspoon ground cinnamon

¹/₈ teaspoon cayenne pepper

¹/₂ cup/65 g unsweetened and unsulfured raisins

Fine sea salt to taste

¹/₄ cup/20 g unsweetened shredded or flaked coconut

Cut the ribs from the chard and chop them crosswise into 1-inch/2.5 cm lengths. Cut the leaves crosswise into 1-inch/2.5 cm–thick strips. Set the chard ribs and leaves aside separately.

In a large saucepan or small stockpot over medium-high heat, heat the oil. Add the onions and cook, stirring occasionally, for 1 minute. Add the cauliflower and cook, stirring occasionally, until it's beginning to brown, about 4 minutes. Add the garlic and cook, stirring occasionally, until fragrant, about 1 minute. Add the coconut milk, stock, curry powder, cinnamon, and cayenne and bring to a boil. Add the chard ribs and raisins and return to a boil. Lower the heat to a simmer, cover, and cook for 5 minutes. Working in batches, add the chard leaves, stirring until wilted before adding the next batch. Cover and cook until the cauliflower and chard are tender, about 5 minutes. Remove from the heat and add salt to taste.

Serve hot, sprinkled with the coconut.

Barley Risotto Primavera

 JUST LIKE A RICE RISOTTO, THIS RECIPE USES A SHORT, STUBBY GRAIN to achieve risotto's signature creaminess. But hulled barley is a whole grain, whereas white risotto rice has the bran removed—so this version is more nutritious than traditional risotto.

As you stir, the friction of the grains rubbing together releases their starch, which combines with the stock to make a rich-tasting sauce without a lot of rich ingredients.

SERVES 6

2 tablespoons organic extra-virgin olive oil

1 medium-size yellow onion, cut into $^1/_4$-inch/0.65 cm dice

$1^1/_2$ cups/300 g hulled barley, soaked overnight in the refrigerator and drained

$5^1/_2$ cups/1.3 L organic reduced-sodium chicken or vegetable stock, divided (see note on page 127)

1 cup/50 g small bite-size broccoli florets

1 medium-size carrot, cut into $^1/_4$-inch/0.65 cm dice

$^2/_3$ cup/70 g snap peas, sliced on a diagonal

4 scallions, cut on the diagonal into $^1/_4$-inch/0.65 cm pieces

$^1/_2$ cup/60 g grated Parmesan cheese, plus more as needed

$^1/_4$ cup/10 g coarsely chopped fresh flat-leaf parsley

Fine sea salt to taste

Freshly ground black pepper to taste

In a large saucepan or small stockpot over medium heat, heat the oil. Add the onion and cook, stirring occasionally, until very soft, 6 to 8 minutes (adjust the heat to avoid browning). Add the barley and 2$\frac{1}{2}$ cups/590 mL of the stock and bring to a boil over high heat. Lower the heat to a simmer, cover, and cook for 30 minutes.

After about 25 minutes, in a large saucepan over high heat, bring the remaining 3 cups/710 mL of stock to a boil. Lower the heat to very low.

Uncover the barley, and if there is any unabsorbed liquid, stir almost constantly until almost all the liquid has absorbed, adjusting the heat to a steady simmer. Continue adding the hot stock about $\frac{1}{2}$ cup/120 mL at a time, stirring almost constantly until almost all of the liquid is absorbed between additions, for 15 minutes.

Taste the barley for doneness—it's done when tender and very slightly chewy. When the barley is just about done, add the broccoli and carrot and cook for 1 minute. Add the peas and continue cooking and adding stock (you may not need it all), until the barley is done, the vegetables are tender, and just a little liquid remains in the pot.

Remove the risotto from the heat and stir in the scallions, cheese, and parsley. Add salt and pepper to taste and serve, passing additional cheese at the table.

Classic Pasta with Red Sauce

PERHAPS OBVIOUSLY, THIS RECIPE IS BEST MADE IN THE LATE SUMMER, when tomatoes will be at their most flavorful. But if you like, make a double or triple batch of the sauce and stash the leftovers in the freezer—that way, you can enjoy peak-of-season tomatoes all year long.

SERVES 6

1 tablespoon organic extra-virgin olive oil

$^1/_2$ medium-size yellow onion, cut into $^1/_4$-inch/0.65 cm dice

6 garlic cloves, minced

1$^1/_2$ teaspoons fennel seeds

4 pounds/1.8 kg tomatoes, ideally Roma, peeled (optional), halved, seeded, and chopped coarsely

1 tablespoon chopped fresh basil

1 tablespoon chopped fresh oregano

Fine sea salt to taste, plus more as needed

Freshly ground black pepper to taste

1 pound/455 g pasta (brown rice, whole wheat, or your favorite variety)

Grated, shredded, or shaved Parmesan cheese, for serving (optional)

In a large saucepan or small stockpot over medium heat, heat the oil. Add the onion and cook, stirring occasionally, until tender, 4 to 6 minutes (adjust the heat, if necessary, to avoid browning). Add the garlic and fennel seeds and cook, stirring, until fragrant, 30 to 60 seconds. Add the tomatoes and cook, stirring frequently, until the tomatoes release some of their juices, 2 to 3 minutes. Increase the heat to high and bring to a boil. Lower the heat to a simmer and cook, stirring occasionally, until the mixture is saucelike, about 15 minutes. Add the basil, oregano, and salt and pepper to taste. Cover to keep warm and set aside.

In a large pot of boiling, well-salted boiling water (1$^1/_2$ teaspoons of fine sea salt per quart/950 mL), cook the pasta until just shy of al dente.

Drain the pasta and add it to the sauce. Cook over medium heat, tossing the pasta occasionally, until al dente, 3 or 4 minutes. Serve hot, passing the cheese (if using) at the table.

> **To make this a meat sauce, add 8 ounces/225 g of cooked organic ground beef, ground** pork, Italian sausage, or a combination along with the tomatoes.
>
> If your tomatoes aren't particularly flavorful, try adding a touch of apple cider vinegar or your natural sweetener of choice to the sauce.

Swiss Chard and Rosemary Pesto Pasta

ALSO KNOWN AS PLAIN OL' CHARD, SWISS CHARD IS A MEMBER OF THAT all-important leafy greens family of vegetables, so any way to get more of it into your diet is a good thing. This recipe is a little sneaky in that regard—it uses chard leaves as you would basil in a traditional pesto, such that you'd hardly even know you're eating healthy.

Should you have leftovers, use the pesto draped over veggies, grains, meats, chicken, or fish—it's particularly great with salmon or on a portobello mushroom burger.

SERVES 8

4 ounces/115 g chard, ribs removed (see note)

³/₄ cup/105 g pine nuts, toasted (see note on page 122)

¹/₃ cup/40 g grated Parmesan cheese, plus more as needed

¹/₄ cup/7 g packed fresh flat-leaf parsley leaves

2 tablespoons packed fresh rosemary leaves

4 garlic cloves

²/₃ cup/160 mL extra-virgin olive oil

Fine sea salt to taste, plus more as needed

Freshly ground black pepper to taste

1¹/₄ pounds/565 g pasta (brown rice, whole wheat, or your favorite variety)

In the bowl of a food processor, combine the chard, pine nuts, cheese, parsley, rosemary, and garlic and process until finely chopped, scraping down the bowl as necessary. With the motor running, slowly add the oil and process until smooth, scraping down the bowl as necessary. Add salt and pepper to taste.

In a large pot of boiling, well-salted water ($1\frac{1}{2}$ teaspoons of fine sea salt per quart/950 mL), cook the pasta until al dente. Drain, saving $\frac{1}{2}$ cup/120 mL of the cooking water, and return the pasta to the pot. Add the pesto and $\frac{1}{4}$ cup/60 mL of the cooking water, tossing to combine. Add more cooking water, salt, and pepper to taste and serve, passing additional cheese at the table.

> **Choose green types of chard for this recipe. Ruby or red chards will result in a pesto** that's unappealingly brown.

Raw Pad Thai

SINCE OPENING IN MANHATTAN IN 2004, PURE FOOD AND WINE HAS become one of the country's most acclaimed restaurants and continues to revolutionize the world of raw food. Of its entirely plant-based vegan menu, nothing is heated above 118°F, to preserve valuable vitamins, minerals, and enzymes. Co-owner and executive chef Sarma Melngailis shares her kelp noodle pad thai recipe, which proves that raw cuisine can be delicious, inspiring, and much more than just salads.

SERVES 4 TO 6

2 limes

1 (1¹/₂ inch/4 cm) square tamarind pulp (see notes)

¹/₂ medium-size tomato, chopped coarsely

¹/₂ small shallot, quartered

2 tablespoons toasted sesame oil

1¹/₂ teaspoons raw agave nectar

¹/₄ Thai chile, seeded, or more to taste (see notes)

¹/₂ garlic clove

6 tablespoons/90 mL organic naturally brewed soy sauce or organic wheat-free tamari, divided

1 medium-size orange bell pepper, cored and cut into matchsticks

1 medium-size baby bok choy, cut crosswise into ¹/₄-inch/0.65 cm shreds

1 medium-size carrot, cut into matchsticks

1 large king oyster mushroom, cut into ¹/₄-inch/0.65 cm slices

1 cup/90 g snow peas, cut into ¹/₂-inch/1.25 cm pieces

1 medium-size zucchini, cut into matchsticks

3 scallions, sliced thinly

1 tablespoon organic extra-virgin olive oil

2 (12-ounce/340 g) packages kelp noodles, chopped into 4-inch/10 cm pieces (see notes)

Bean sprouts, for garnish

Microgreens, for garnish
Chopped raw cashews, for garnish

Cut one of the limes into wedges. Juice the remaining lime to yield 4 $\frac{1}{2}$ teaspoons of juice. Set the wedges and juice aside separately.

In a small bowl, combine the tamarind pulp with $\frac{1}{2}$ cup/120 mL of very hot water. Use a fork to work the mixture into a paste, removing any seeds. Set aside and let soak for 15 minutes.

In the jar of a blender, combine the tomato, shallot, sesame oil, agave, chile, garlic, 2 tablespoons of the soy sauce, and 1 $\frac{1}{2}$ teaspoons of the lime juice and process to a puree. Add the tamarind mixture and process until very smooth. Add more chile to taste and set aside.

In a large bowl, combine the bell pepper, bok choy, carrot, mushroom, snow peas, zucchini, and scallions. Add the olive oil, remaining $\frac{1}{4}$ cup/60 mL of soy sauce, remaining 1 tablespoon of lime juice, and 2 tablespoons of the pureed sauce, stirring to evenly coat. Chill in the refrigerator for at least an hour.

Add the noodles to the vegetable mixture. Add more sauce to taste, tossing with tongs to evenly distribute.

Serve garnished with bean sprouts, microgreens, cashews, and lime wedges.

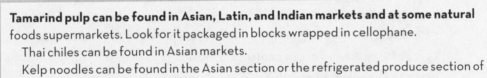

Tamarind pulp can be found in Asian, Latin, and Indian markets and at some natural foods supermarkets. Look for it packaged in blocks wrapped in cellophane.

Thai chiles can be found in Asian markets.

Kelp noodles can be found in the Asian section or the refrigerated produce section of most natural foods supermarkets.

Skillet Casserole with Root Vegetables, Leeks, and Mushrooms

THERE'S SORT OF A RETRO, SEVENTIES HIPPIE VIBE TO THIS BROWN RICE casserole, and I mean that in a good way. It's earthy, rustic, creamy, and hearty, with a nicely unusual combination of vegetables.

Serve it with a green salad or steamed broccoli on the side, or on a bed of braised greens.

SERVES 6 TO 8

2 tablespoons organic extra-virgin olive oil

1 pound/455 g rutabagas, turnips, or a combination, peeled and cut into
  ¹/₂-inch/1.25 cm dice (see note)

6 ounces/170 g white or brown mushrooms, quartered

2 medium-size leeks, white and light green parts only, cut into
  ¹/₂-inch/1.25 cm slices

2 garlic cloves, minced

¹/₄ cup/60 mL organic reduced-sodium chicken or vegetable stock
  (see note on page 127)

3 cups/480 g cooked long-grain brown rice (see page 276 for how to cook rice)

1 cup/225 g grass-fed organic cottage cheese

1 cup/225 g cooked amaranth (see page 275 for how to cook grains)

2 tablespoons chopped fresh thyme

Fine sea salt to taste

Freshly ground black pepper to taste

2 large organic, pasture-raised, or antibiotic-free eggs, lightly beaten

Preheat the oven to 350°F/175°C.

Meanwhile, in a large, ovenproof skillet over medium-high heat, heat the oil. Add the rutabagas and turnips and cook, stirring occasionally, for 3 minutes. Add the mushrooms and cook, stirring occasionally, until the vegetables start to brown, about 2 minutes. Add the leeks and cook, stirring occasionally, until the vegetables are well browned, about 3 minutes. Add the garlic and cook, stirring, until fragrant, 30 to 60 seconds. Add the stock, scraping up any browned bits on the bottom of the skillet, and cook until the liquid is evaporated, about 1 minute. Transfer the mixture to a large bowl.

Add the rice, cottage cheese, amaranth, and thyme, and season with salt and pepper to taste. Stir in the eggs. Transfer the mixture back to the skillet, spreading it out evenly. Place the skillet in the oven and bake until the casserole is browned on top and crusty around the edges, about an hour.

> **When shopping for root vegetables, look for smaller ones—they'll be more tender and** flavorful.

Millet-Stuffed Acorn Squash

BETWEEN THE SQUASH, THE GRAINS, THE SPINACH, AND THE FRESH sage, this dish is both colorful and fall-like. In fact, it'd be a nice addition to the Thanksgiving table, making a nourishing entrée for vegetarians and vegans, and a hearty side dish for omnivores.

SERVES 6

2 tablespoons organic extra-virgin olive oil, plus more as needed

3 small acorn squash, halved lengthwise and seeded

Fine sea salt to taste

Freshly ground black pepper to taste

4 medium-size shallots, cut into ½-inch/1.25 cm dice

8 ounces/225 g fresh shiitake mushrooms, stemmed and sliced thinly

1 tablespoon chopped fresh sage

6 cups/85 g spinach leaves

4 cups/450 g cooked millet (see page 275 for how to cook grains)

⅓ cup/45 g unsweetened and unsulfured raisins or dried currants

2 large organic, pasture-raised, or antibiotic-free eggs, lightly beaten

Preheat the oven to 400°F/205°C. Arrange a rack in the upper half of the oven and another in the lower half. Oil two large, rimmed baking sheets.

Sprinkle the the squash with salt and pepper. Arrange the squash, cut side down, on the prepared baking sheets and roast until tender, about 30 minutes.

Meanwhile, in a large skillet over medium-high heat, heat the oil. Add the shallots and cook, stirring occasionally, for 2 minutes. Add the mushrooms and sage and cook, stirring occasionally, until the vegetables are tender, 4 to 5 minutes. Working in batches, add the spinach, stirring until wilted before adding the next batch. Transfer the mixture to a large bowl.

Add the millet, raisins, and salt and pepper to taste. Stir in the eggs. Use this mixture to stuff the squash halves. Return the squash to the baking sheets and bake until the stuffing is heated through and browned on top, 20 to 30 minutes. Serve hot.

Simple, Satisfying Rice with Tempeh, Broccoli, and Kale

RICE AND STEAMED VEGETABLES IS COMFORT FOOD TO ME—I FIND those basic foods simply prepared just, well, nourishing. This recipe takes that idea one step further, adding a tahini sauce which complements both the rice and veggies so well, you might want to make extra and keep it on hand. (Tahini is a great source of calcium.)

SERVES 4

1 1/2 cups/280 g long-grain brown rice or brown and wild rice blend, soaked overnight in the refrigerator and drained

1/4 cup/60 mL raw tahini (see note on page 140)

1 tablespoon toasted sesame oil

3 tablespoons freshly squeezed lemon juice, divided (from about 2 lemons)

Fine sea salt to taste

Freshly ground black pepper to taste

4 cups/200 g broccoli florets

8 ounces/225 g kale, ribs removed, leaves cut into 1/2-inch/1.25 cm shreds

8 ounces/225 g sliced tempeh, cut into 3/4-inch/2 cm dice

1/4 medium-size red cabbage, cored and cut into 1/4-inch/0.65 cm shreds

1/4 cup/35 g pine nuts, toasted (see note on page 122)

In a medium saucepan over medium-high heat, combine the rice and 2 2/3 cups/630 mL of water and bring to a boil. Lower the heat to a simmer, cover, and cook until the rice is tender and the liquid is absorbed, about 30 minutes.

Meanwhile, in a small bowl, combine the tahini, oil, 2 tablespoons of the lemon juice, 2 tablespoons of water, and salt to taste. Set aside.

When the rice is about 15 minutes from being done, in a large saucepan fitted with a steamer insert, bring the remaining 1 tablespoon of lemon juice and 1 inch/2.5 cm of water and to a boil over high heat. Arrange the broccoli, kale, tempeh, and cabbage in the insert, cover, and steam until the vegetables are tender and the tempeh is heated through, about 5 minutes.

Arrange the rice on plates or a platter and top with the vegetable mixture, tahini sauce, and pine nuts. Pass any remaining tahini sauce at the table.

HOW TO STEAM VEGETABLES

Steaming vegetables results in wonderfully simple, pure, and wholesome flavors. It also helps release some of the nutrients locked in some foods. Here's how to do it.

1. Fit a saucepan with a steamer insert.
If you don't have a steamer insert, try placing a strainer in a saucepan (but make sure the saucepan's lid will still fit relatively well and that the vegetables will be suspended above the boiling water).

2. Add about 1 inch of liquid to the saucepan.
Usually, the liquid is water. But you can flavor your vegetables by using other liquids—such as organic naturally-brewed soy sauce or organic wheat-free tamari, stock, wine, or juice—or by adding other liquids to the water. You can also add seasonings to the liquid, such as peppercorns, cinnamon sticks, and garlic cloves.

3. Cut the vegetables so that they're about the same size.
This helps them cook evenly.

4. Add the vegetables to the steamer insert in an even layer.
This also helps them cook evenly.

5. Cover and steam until tender.
Note that if you're doing more than one type of vegetable, you should add the different types to the steamer insert according to how long they'll take to become tender—add the longest-cooking vegetables first and the quickest-cooking vegetables last, the goal being that they're all done at the same time.

Roasted Eggplant and Peppers with Parmesan Polenta

POLENTA IS A NICE CHANGE OF PACE FROM OTHER STARCHES, SUCH as grains, pasta, or rice, and here it's topped with a colorful and tasty mix of roasted vegetables plus whole cloves of roasted garlic.

Serve with a simple spinach salad or cooked Italian sausages.

SERVES 4 TO 6

1 medium-size red onion

3 medium-size red, yellow, or green bell peppers, or a combination, cored and cut into ¹/₂-inch/1.25 cm strips

24 garlic cloves

3 tablespoons organic extra-virgin olive oil, divided

3 medium-size Asian-style eggplants (about 12 ounces/340 g), cut crosswise into ¹/₂-inch/1.25 cm slices

About 4 cups/950 mL organic reduced-sodium chicken or vegetable stock, plus more as needed (see note on page 127)

1¹/₃ cups/215 g organic polenta (see notes)

1 cup/65 g shredded Parmesan cheese, divided

Freshly ground black pepper to taste

Fine sea salt to taste

2 medium-size tomatoes, cut into ¹/₂-inch/1.25 cm dice

1 tablespoon chopped fresh basil, oregano, or a combination

Preheat the oven to 375°F/190°C. Arrange a rack in the upper half of the oven and another in the lower half.

Keeping the root end intact, cut the onion into twelve wedges (so that each wedge has a bit of root holding it together). In a large bowl, combine the onion, bell peppers, garlic, and 2 tablespoons of the oil. Divide the mixture between two large, rimmed baking sheets, spreading it out in an even layer. Roast for 15 minutes.

In the same large bowl, toss the eggplant with the remaining 1 tablespoon of oil. Divide the eggplant between the baking sheets, toss the vegetables, and switch the position of the sheets. Roast until the vegetables are tender and browned at edges, about 20 minutes.

Meanwhile, in a large saucepan or small stockpot over high heat, bring 4 cups/950 mL of stock to a boil. Gradually add the polenta, whisking constantly. Return to a boil, lower the heat to a simmer, cover, and cook, stirring frequently. Add more stock a few tablespoons at a time if the polenta is too thick and cook until the polenta is tender, about 10 minutes. Remove from the heat and stir in $^3/_4$ cup/50 g of the cheese and salt and black pepper to taste.

Remove the baking sheets from the oven and divide the tomatoes between them, tossing to combine. Add salt and black pepper to taste.

Arrange the polenta in bowls and top with the roasted vegetables. Sprinkle with the remaining $^1/_4$ cup/15 g of cheese and the herbs and serve hot.

You can find polenta at most major supermarkets, often in the same section as the cornmeal. For this recipe, avoid the precooked polenta that comes in a large tube, usually found in the prepared foods section.

To make this recipe vegan and dairy-free, omit the cheese.

Avocado and Arugula Wrap

FOR NEARLY TEN YEARS, CANDLE 79 HAS BEEN NEW YORK CITY'S premier vegan restaurant and one of the country's most celebrated. With a menu of organic, sustainable, and seasonal cuisine, the elegant Upper East Side oasis offers diners a creative and delicious farm-to-table experience. Acclaimed executive chef Angel Ramos takes vegan cooking to new creative heights and his mastery of fusing flavors and textures, such as in this light and refreshing avocado and arugula wrap, perfect for lunch or dinner on a hot day. The almond cheese will likely be one of your favorite recipes: it's a great addition to any salad.

SERVES 4

ALMOND CHEESE
2 cups/195 g sliced almonds

2 teaspoons freshly squeezed lemon juice

1 minced garlic clove

$^1/_2$ teaspoon fine sea salt

Pinch of freshly ground black pepper

PICKLED ONIONS
$^1/_4$ cup/60 mL red wine vinegar

2 tablespoons freshly squeezed lemon juice

$^1/_2$ teaspoon fine sea salt

$^1/_4$ teaspoon ground cumin

1 medium-size red onion, halved and cut into $^1/_4$-inch/0.65 cm slices

WRAPS
4 (10-inch/25 cm) organic corn, sprouted-grain, or brown rice tortillas

8 ounces/225 g baby arugula

2 ripe avocados, peeled, pitted, and sliced

2 ripe heirloom tomatoes, sliced

For the almond cheese: In a large bowl, cover the almonds with warm water and set aside to soak at room temperature for about 4 hours.

Drain the almonds and transfer to a food processor. Add 2 tablespoons of cold water and the lemon juice, garlic, salt, and pepper and process for 8 to 10 minutes until the mixture becomes the texture of a spreadable goat cheese, scraping down the bowl often (if necessary, add water 1 tablespoon at a time). Transfer to a medium bowl and chill in the refrigerator for about 1 hour. This will make 1³/₄ cups/375 g of almond cheese—set aside 1 cup/215 g to use in the wraps and reserve the rest for another use.

For the pickled onions: In a medium bowl, combine 1¹/₂ cups/355 mL of cold water with the vinegar, lemon juice, salt, and cumin. Add the onion and chill in the refrigerator for 3 to 4 hours.

To assemble the wraps: Heat a large skillet over medium heat. Place a tortilla in the skillet and cook until warm and softened, about 30 seconds per side. Transfer to a work surface and arrange one-quarter of the arugula in a line across the tortilla, stopping about 2 inches/5 cm short of one edge. Arrange one-quarter of the avocado, one-quarter of the tomato, one-quarter of the almond cheese (crumble it on), and one-quarter of the pickled onion on the arugula. Fold one side of the tortilla up and over the fillings, tucking in the fillings tightly, then fold in the 2-inch/5 cm edge. Continue rolling the tortilla toward the other side, securing it with a toothpick if necessary.

Repeat with the remaining ingredients.

Grilled Veggie Soft Tacos with Cilantro Slaw and Spiced Crema

THESE TERRIFIC TACOS ARE JAM-PACKED WITH BIG, BOLD FLAVORS AND textures, including zucchini and peppers coated with a chili powder spice rub and grilled. Serve them for family on a weeknight or for company at a backyard barbecue—Apple-Cucumber-Lime Agua Fresca (page 111) would be great alongside.

SERVES 6

3 or 4 limes

1 cup/240 mL grass-fed organic plain yogurt or kefir

2 garlic cloves, minced

$^1/_2$ teaspoon ground turmeric

$^1/_2$ teaspoon crushed red pepper flakes

Fine sea salt to taste

2 tablespoons organic neutral-flavored oil, such as grapeseed,
   plus more as needed

8 cups/285 g or 1 (10-ounce/285 g) bag finely shredded green cabbage

$^1/_2$ small red onion, halved and sliced thinly

1 cup/30 g coarsely chopped fresh cilantro

4 teaspoons smoked paprika

1 tablespoon chili powder

2 teaspoons ground coriander

2 teaspoons ground cumin

2 small green zucchini, cut lengthwise into $^1/_3$-inch/0.75 cm slices

2 small yellow or crookneck squash, cut lengthwise into $^1/_3$-inch/0.75 cm slices

1 medium-size red bell pepper, cored and cut into 1-inch/2.5 cm strips

1 medium-size yellow bell pepper, cored and cut into 1-inch/2.5 cm strips

12 (5-inch/13.5 cm) organic corn, sprouted-grain, or brown rice tortillas

Zest one of the limes. In a small bowl, combine the lime zest, yogurt, garlic, turmeric, red pepper flakes, and salt to taste. Set aside.

Halve and juice the zested lime, plus one more if necessary, to yield 2 tablespoons of juice. In a large bowl, combine the lime juice and oil. Add the cabbage, onion, cilantro, and salt to taste. Cut the remaining two limes into six wedges each. Set the cilantro slaw and lime wedges aside separately.

In a large, shallow bowl, combine the paprika, chili powder, coriander, and cumin. Dredge the vegetables in the spice mixture, arranging them in a single layer on a platter or baking sheet. Sprinkle with salt.

Preheat the grill to medium heat and lightly oil the grate. Grill the vegetables until tender and lightly charred, 2 to 3 minutes per side. Set aside until cool enough to handle, then cut diagonally into $^1/_2$-inch/1.25 cm pieces.

Meanwhile, wrap the tortillas in foil and place them on a cooler part of the grill. Heat until warm, 5 to 8 minutes, turning halfway through.

Divide the vegetables among the tortillas and top with the cilantro slaw and a dollop of the spiced crema. Serve warm, with the lime wedges on the side.

To make this recipe vegan and dairy-free, omit the yogurt and add the other *crema* ingredients to the slaw.

Black Bean "Burgers"

I'M PUTTING *BURGERS* **IN QUOTES HERE BECAUSE THESE AREN'T SO** much burger substitutes as delicious, slightly Southwest-feeling black bean sandwiches. The patties get nicely crisped on the outside, but remain finger-licking soft on the inside.

SERVES 6

³/₄ cup/90 g spelt flour

¹/₂ small tomato, plus additional sliced tomato for serving

¹/₄ small red onion, plus additional sliced onion for serving

2 garlic cloves

1 tablespoon packed fresh oregano leaves

1 teaspoon ground coriander

1 teaspoon ground cumin

¹/₄ teaspoon cayenne pepper

3 cups/565 g cooked, well-drained black beans
  (see page 277 for how to cook beans), divided

Fine sea salt to taste

2 tablespoons extra-virgin olive oil

6 hamburger buns (sprouted wheat, gluten-free,
  or other preferred type), cut sides lightly toasted

Whole-grain mustard, for serving

Green or red leaf lettuce leaves, for serving

Sliced avocado, for serving

Cover a baking sheet or large platter with parchment or waxed paper. Set aside.

In the bowl of a food processor, combine the flour, tomato, onion, garlic, oregano, coriander, cumin, cayenne, and half of the beans and pulse until coarsely chopped, scraping down the bowl as necessary. Transfer to a medium bowl and stir in the remaining beans and salt to taste. Divide the mixture equally into six balls, arranging them on the prepared baking sheet or platter.

With dampened hands, flatten each ball into a patty about 4 inches/10 cm in diameter and ½inch/1.25 cm thick.

Heat 1 tablespoon of oil in each of two medium skillets over medium heat. Carefully add three patties to each skillet (it helps to use the parchment or waxed paper to flip a patty into your hand, one at a time, then carefully place it in the skillet). Cook until well browned, about 3 minutes per side.

Serve the burgers with mustard, lettuce leaves, sliced onion, sliced tomato, and sliced avocado. Serve hot.

> **For a change of pace, try making these burgers with other types of beans, or replace** some of the beans with cooked brown rice.

IDEAS FOR OTHER TOPPINGS

- Grilled or sautéed mushrooms
- Grilled onions
- Spinach or arugula leaves
- Salsa
- Cilantro sprigs

Thai-Style Mussels with Lemongrass

AFTER HONING HIS CRAFT IN SOME OF THE COUNTRY'S BEST KITCHENS and becoming a finalist on *Top Chef*, Ed Cotton made his mark in NYC as executive chef of Plein Sud in Tribeca and is now at Fishtail by David Burke. With a penchant for globally influenced cuisine, Ed elevates zesty Thai-style mussels with fresh herbs, chiles, and a fragrant lemongrass infusion—resulting in a powerfully flavorful entrée that's as easy to make as it is delicious.

SERVES 2

1 lemon

2 large stalks lemongrass

³/₄ cup/180 mL coconut milk (see notes)

1 tablespoon finely chopped galangal (see notes)

¹/₂ green bird's eye or serrano chile, seeded and sliced thinly (see notes)

¹/₂ Kaffir lime leaf (see notes)

Fine sea salt to taste

Freshly ground black pepper to taste

2 tablespoons organic neutral-flavored oil, such as grapeseed

2 tablespoons minced garlic

2 tablespoons minced fresh ginger

2 tablespoons chopped scallion

2 tablespoons minced shallot

2 teaspoons chopped red Thai chile (see note on page 215)

1¹/₂ pounds/680 g cleaned, sustainably sourced mussels

2 cups/70 g thinly sliced fresh Thai basil leaves, divided

Cilantro sprigs for garnish

Zest half of the lemon. Juice the lemon to yield 1 tablespoon of juice. Set the zest and juice aside.

Remove the outer leaves from the lemongrass until you get to the softer, fleshier, pale yellow part. Trim 2 inches/5 cm from the base of the stalk, then thinly slice the remaining stalk about two-thirds of the way from the base to the tip, or until the stalk becomes woody and is no longer pale. Set the sliced lemongrass aside and discard the rest.

In a small saucepan over medium-high heat, combine the coconut milk, galangal, and bird's eye chile and bring to a simmer. Remove from the heat and add the lemon zest, lemon juice, lemongrass, and Kaffir lime leaf. Set aside for 30 minutes, then strain through a fine-mesh strainer. Add salt and pepper to taste and set aside.

In a large skillet over medium-high heat, heat the oil. Add the garlic, ginger, scallion, and shallot and cook, stirring occasionally, until fragrant, about 1 minute. Stir in the red chile. Add the mussels and coconut milk mixture and sprinkle with half of the basil, salt, and pepper. Cover and cook until the mussels have opened, 2 to 3 minutes.

Stir the mussels and transfer to plates or a platter. Sprinkle with the remaining basil, garnish with cilantro sprigs, and serve.

Although I recommend coconut milk for everyday use, for special occasions, use canned coconut milk, as Chef Cotton does, which will have more coconut flavor. Look for BPA-free brands with no added sugars.

Galangal is a root that looks similar to ginger. You can find it in the produce section of some supermarkets, most major natural foods supermarkets, and Asian and Indian markets. If you can't find it, Chef Cotton suggests substituting fresh ginger.

You can find bird's eye chiles and Kaffir lime leaves at Asian markets.

Miso-Glazed Halibut
with Daikon and Carrots

THERE'S NOTHING LIKE THE CLEAN, FRESH FLAVOR OF A PRISTINE piece of fish—and a beautiful halibut fillet is no exception. In this recipe, it gets subtle flavor from a sweet-savory miso mixture and that same mixture serves as a dressing for the radish-carrot garnish.

SERVES 4

Organic neutral-flavored oil, such as grapeseed, as needed

4 (5-to 6-ounce/140 to 170 g) sustainably sourced halibut fillets, about 1 inch/2.5 cm thick

1 lemon, halved

$^{1}/_{4}$ cup/75 g organic white miso

2 tablespoons pure maple syrup

1 tablespoon organic naturally-brewed soy sauce or organic wheat-free tamari

1 cup/115 g shredded daikon radish

1 cup/95 g shredded carrot

1 cup/25 g sunflower sprouts or microgreens

Fine sea salt to taste

2 scallions, sliced thinly

Preheat a broiler and arrange a rack 6 inches/15 cm from the heating element. Lightly oil a rimmed baking sheet and arrange the fish on top. Set aside.

Juice one lemon half to yield 1 tablespoon of juice. In a small bowl, whisk together the lemon juice, miso, maple syrup, and soy sauce. Set aside $^{1}/_{4}$ cup/60 mL of the miso mixture and brush the fish with what remains. Broil until the fish is just cooked through, 8 to 12 minutes.

Meanwhile, in a large bowl, combine the radish, carrot, sprouts, reserved miso mixture, and salt to taste. Transfer to plates or a platter. Cut the remaining lemon half into wedges and arrange alongside the radish mixture.

Arrange the fish on the radish mixture, sprinkle with the scallions, and serve.

SHOPPING FOR SUSTAINABLE SEAFOOD

Here are three great ways to make sure the seafood you're eating—whether it's store-bought or enjoyed in a restaurant—is sustainable.

1. Consult Seafood Watch or Blue Ocean Institute.
You can visit www.seafoodwatch.org or www.blueocean.org, type into the "Search" box any fish you're thinking about, and the website will give that fish a green, yellow, or red light, and explain why. Both organizations also have downloadable pocket guides, which make it easy for you to carry their recommendations around with you, and Seafood Watch has a mobile app, which means the recommendations will always be up-to-date.

2. Look for the Marine Stewardship Council (MSC) label.
Like Seafood Watch and Blue Ocean Institute, the Marine Stewardship Council studies and evaluates the world's seafood, although with slightly different criteria. Unlike Seafood Watch and Blue Ocean Institute, it has a logo—a blue oval with a fish—that certified sources can use on their products. You'll see MSC-labeled fishes at Whole Foods, for example. But note that just because one item at a store or in a restaurant is MSC-certified, it doesn't mean all of them are.

3. Shop and dine at stores and restaurants that sell only sustainable seafood.
This way, once you're in the door, you can choose anything you want. How do you know a shop or restaurant sells only sustainable seafood? Ask. If it does, it will be proud to tell you all about its program. If it doesn't, you'll have given it a reason to consider one.

Rosemary-Stuffed Grilled Trout with Fennel Relish

DOMESTICALLY FARMED RAINBOW TROUT IS CONSIDERED A SUSTAIN-able seafood because it's farmed in an ecologically responsible way. It's also a good nutritional choice because, like salmon, it's loaded with beneficial omega-3 fatty acids. It's the fat that gives trout its wonderfully rich taste. In this recipe, the fennel relish provides a palate-cleansing counterpoint.

SERVES 4

$^1/_2$ cup/60 g finely chopped fennel bulb, plus 2 tablespoons finely chopped feathery fennel fronds

1 large shallot, diced finely

1 tablespoon raw apple cider vinegar

1 tablespoon organic extra-virgin olive oil, plus more as needed

Fine sea salt to taste

Freshly ground black pepper to taste

4 teaspoons chopped fresh rosemary, plus 4 whole sprigs

4 (10- to 12-ounce/285 to 340 g) sustainably sourced whole rainbow trout, cleaned, heads and tails removed if you'd like

In a medium bowl, combine the fennel bulb, fennel fronds, shallot, vinegar, oil, and salt and pepper to taste. Set aside.

Prepare a grill to medium-high heat. Brush both sides of the trout with oil and sprinkle with the chopped rosemary, salt, and pepper. Stuff each trout with a rosemary sprig. Grill the trout until well browned and just cooked through, 3 to 4 minutes per side.

Serve hot, with the fennel relish on top.

> **You can buy whole rainbow trout with bones removed or not—the cooking** time will be the same.

Grilled Salmon with Strawberry Avocado Salsa

SALMON, STRAWBERRIES, AND AVOCADO—YOU COULD HARDLY think up a healthier trio of ingredients. They come together here to create a meal that's so refreshingly different and flavorful, "health food" is about the last thing you'll think of when you enjoy it.

SERVES 4

2 limes

$1/2$ medium-size avocado, peeled, pitted, and cut into $1/4$-inch/0.65 cm dice

6 ounces/170 g strawberries, hulled and cut into $1/4$-inch/0.65 cm dice

$1/4$ small red onion, cut into $1/4$-inch/0.65 cm dice

2 tablespoons chopped fresh cilantro

Fine sea salt to taste

4 (5- to 6-ounce/140 to 170 g) sustainably sourced salmon fillets, about $3/4$-inch/2 cm thick, skin removed if you like

Organic extra-virgin olive oil, for brushing

Freshly ground black pepper

Zest one of the limes. Juice the zested lime to yield 4 teaspoons of juice. In a medium bowl, combine the lime zest, lime juice, avocado, strawberries, onion, cilantro, and salt to taste. Cut the remaining lime into wedges. Set the salsa and lime wedges aside separately.

Prepare a grill to medium-high heat. Brush both sides of the salmon with oil and sprinkle with salt and pepper. Grill the salmon until just cooked through, about 4 minutes per side.

Serve the salmon hot, with the salsa on top and the lime wedges on the side.

Poached Sablefish (Black Cod) with Vegetables and Horseradish Yogurt

FISH IS SO POPULAR THESE DAYS IN ALL KINDS OF PRESENTATIONS and preparations that we've almost forgotten one of the classic ways to enjoy it: poached. In fact, poaching is great for most fish because it'll help keep fish from drying out. It also allows for the naturally clean and delicate flavors of this particular type of fish—which also happens to provide some omega-3 fatty acids—to shine through.

The horseradish yogurt is an easy yet snazzy accompaniment, and a nice juxta-position to the delicate fish. That said, you can use almost any type of large-flake fish fillets—for example, halibut, pollack, or sea bass—for this recipe.

SERVES 4

1 cup/240 mL grass-fed organic plain yogurt

2 tablespoons finely shredded fresh horseradish root, or more to taste

1 teaspoon whole-grain mustard

Fine sea salt to taste

2 cups/475 mL organic reduced-sodium vegetable stock (see note on page 127)

4 (5- to 6-ounce/140 to 170 g) sustainably sourced sablefish fillets (also called black cod), about ³⁄₄ inch/2 cm thick

1 small carrot, cut into matchsticks

1 medium-size celery stalk, sliced thinly on a diagonal

1 tablespoon wakame (see note on page 127)

In a medium bowl, combine the yogurt, horseradish, and mustard, adding more horseradish and salt to taste. Set aside.

In a very large skillet over medium heat, bring the stock to a gentle simmer. Add the fish and adjust the heat to maintain barely a simmer. Cover and cook for 5 min-utes. Add the carrots and celery, nestling them into the liquid. Cover and cook until the vegetables are tender and the fish is barely opaque throughout, about 3 minutes.

Use a slotted spatula to arrange the fish on plates or a platter. Arrange the vegetables on top. Drizzle with some of the horseradish yogurt, sprinkle with the wakame, and serve, passing the remaining horseradish yogurt at the table.

Baked White Fish

CELEBRITY CHEF, SOCIAL ACTIVIST, AND ENTREPRENEUR JAMIE OLIVER has worked tirelessly to raise awareness about the growing obesity epidemic that threatens our children and future generations. As producer and star of the Emmy Award–winning *Food Revolution* series to support better food in schools, Jamie's passion for cooking from scratch continues to inspire people globally. Tap into Jamie's revolution with this wholesome and family-friendly baked fish entrée—he says it's "lovely served with new potatoes and a green salad."

SERVES 4

1 small bunch fresh basil

1 jalapeño or serrano chile

1 tablespoon organic extra-virgin olive oil

3 garlic cloves, sliced thinly

1 (28-ounce/795 g) can diced tomato

Fine sea salt

Freshly ground black pepper

1 tablespoon red wine vinegar

4 (5- to 6-ounce/140 to 170 g) sustainably sourced white fish fillets, such as flounder, tilapia, cod, or sea bass, skin and bones removed

¼ cup/40 g black olives, pitted

Separate the basil leaves from the stalks and finely slice the stalks. Pierce the chile with a knife. In a large skillet over medium heat, heat the olive oil. Add the basil stalks, chile, and garlic and cook, stirring occasionally, until the garlic is tender but not brown, about 1 minute. Add the tomatoes and sprinkle with salt and pepper. Bring to a boil, lower the heat to a simmer, and cook for 30 minutes.

Meanwhile, preheat the oven to 425°F/220°C.

Remove the chile from the tomato mixture. Mash the tomatoes with a wooden spoon to break them up. Stir in the red wine vinegar.

Transfer the tomato mixture to an 8 by 11-inch/20 by 28 cm baking dish. Place the fish fillets on top, then sprinkle with the olives and basil leaves. Bake until the fish is cooked through, about 15 minutes.

Chicken and Pepper Paprikash

A RIFF ON THE HUNGARIAN CLASSIC, THESE MEATY CHICKEN THIGHS are braised with sautéed peppers, onions, and garlic and finished with yogurt and fresh dill. Serve it over brown rice or buttered whole wheat noodles, or with Mashed Celeriac (page 203), so you can sop up every drop.

SERVES 4

Fine sea salt to taste

1 tablespoon organic extra-virgin olive oil

4 (6- to 8-ounce/170 to 225 g) bone-in organic chicken thighs, skin removed

1 medium-size yellow onion, halved and sliced thinly

1 medium-size red bell pepper, cored and sliced thinly

2 garlic cloves, minced

4 teaspoons sweet paprika

$^1/_4$ teaspoon cayenne pepper (optional)

$^3/_4$ cup/180 mL organic reduced-sodium chicken or vegetable stock (see note on page 127)

$^1/_2$ cup/120 mL grass-fed organic plain yogurt

$1^1/_2$ teaspoons chopped fresh dill

In a large skillet over medium-high heat, heat the oil. Sprinkle the chicken with salt and add it to the skillet. Sear the chicken without moving until browned, 3 to 4 minutes. Turn and brown the other side, 3 to 4 minutes. Transfer the chicken to a plate and set aside.

Add the onion and bell pepper to the skillet and cook, stirring occasionally, until the vegetables are starting to soften, about 3 minutes. Add the garlic, paprika, and cayenne (if using), and cook, stirring, until the garlic is fragrant, about 1 minute. Add the stock, scraping up any browned bits on the bottom of the skillet. Nestle the chicken, along with any accumulated juices, back into the skillet and bring to a boil. Lower the heat to a simmer, cover, and cook until the chicken is cooked through and the vegetables are very tender, about 20 minutes.

Remove the chicken from the skillet, arranging it on plates or a platter. Stir the yogurt into the skillet sauce, along with salt to taste.

Use a slotted spoon to arrange the vegetables on top of the chicken. Spoon some of the sauce on top and sprinkle with the dill. Serve hot, passing the remaining sauce at the table.

Moroccan-Marinated Chicken Breasts with Wilted Onions

THIS CHICKEN FEATURES AN EARTHY SPICE BLEND THAT'S A TINY bit hot, thanks to black pepper, but also fragrant and heady thanks to cinnamon, ginger, and nutmeg, to name a few. As wonderfully exotic as it tastes, however, it's easy to make using ingredients you probably already have on hand. Don't you love it when things work out that way?

SERVES 4

1 tablespoon ground cinnamon

1 tablespoon ground coriander

1 tablespoon ground ginger

1½ teaspoons freshly ground black pepper

¾ teaspoon ground nutmeg

¼ teaspoon ground allspice

¼ cup/60 mL organic extra-virgin olive oil, divided

Fine sea salt

4 medium-size boneless, skinless organic chicken breasts

1 medium-size yellow onion, halved and cut into ¹⁄₄-inch/0.65 cm slices

In a small bowl, combine the cinnamon, coriander, ginger, pepper, nutmeg, allspice, and 2 tablespoons of the oil. Arrange the chicken on a plate or platter and spread both sides with the spice paste. Sprinkle both sides with salt. Cover and chill in the refrigerator for at least 4 hours, or overnight.

Preheat the oven to 450°F/230°F and let the chicken come to room temperature.

In a large, ovenproof skillet over medium-high heat, heat the remaining 2 tablespoons of oil. Sear the chicken without moving on one side until browned, 4 to 5 minutes. Turn the chicken, transfer the skillet to the oven, and roast until the chicken is cooked through, 8 to 10 minutes. Remove the skillet from the oven (careful—the handle of the skillet will be very hot), transfer the chicken to a plate, and let it rest, covered loosely with foil.

Meanwhile, place the skillet on the stovetop over medium heat and add the onion. Cook, stirring occasionally and scraping up any browned bits in the skillet, until the onion starts to soften, about 3 minutes. Lower the heat to low and cook until tender and wilted, about 7 minutes. Add salt to taste.

Arrange the chicken on plates or a platter and top with the onion. Serve hot, drizzled with any accumulated juices or pan drippings.

> **These chicken breasts would also be good cooked on the grill, topped with grilled** onion. Keeping the root end intact, cut the whole onion into wedges (so that each wedge has a bit of root holding it together) and grill them on both sides.

Lavender Roasted Chicken with Roasted Yams

ONCE YOU'VE BOUGHT YOURSELF A FULL-FLAVORED, FREE-RANGE chicken, it's nice to enjoy it in a way that let its natural goodness shine. Here, the chicken gets a pinch of fresh thyme and a sprinkle of lavender, then a basic roast. The yams are basted by the juices, giving them the flavor of that tasty chicken as well.

SERVES 4 TO 6

$^3/_4$ cup/180 mL organic reduced-sodium chicken or vegetable stock (see note on page 127)

$^1/_4$ cup/60 mL organic extra-virgin olive oil, divided

1 (3$^1/_2$- to 4-pound/1.6 to 1.8 kg) organic chicken

1$^1/_2$ teaspoons dried lavender flowers (see note)

1$^1/_2$ teaspoons chopped fresh thyme

Fine sea salt

Freshly ground black pepper

$^1/_2$ lemon, halved

1$^1/_2$ pounds/680 g yams or sweet potatoes, or a combination, cut into 1-inch/2.5 cm pieces

Preheat the oven to 425°F/220°C. Pour the stock into a 9 by 13-inch/25 by 35 cm baking pan.

Rub the chicken all over with 2 tablespoons of the oil. Sprinkle the outside of the chicken with the lavender and thyme, then sprinkle inside and out with salt and pepper. Place the lemon pieces inside the chicken, tie the legs together with kitchen string, and tuck in the wings. Set the chicken in the baking pan, breast side up, and roast for 30 minutes.

Meanwhile, in a large bowl, combine the yams and the remaining 2 tablespoons of oil. Set aside.

Baste the chicken with the pan juices. Add the yams to the baking pan, arranging them around the chicken. Continue roasting, basting both the chicken and the yams about every 15 minutes, until an internal thermometer inserted in the thickest part of the thigh reads 165°F/75°C and the yams are browned and tender, about 45 minutes. Let the chicken rest, covered loosely with foil, for 10 minutes.

Carve the chicken and arrange on a platter or plates with the yams on the side. Squeeze the lemon from the cavity over the chicken and yams, if you like. Drizzle with the pan juices and serve.

> **You can find culinary-grade dried lavender flowers at specialty food stores and in the** bulk dried herbs and flowers section at many natural food stores.

Turkey Chili Verde

HERE'S A NICE TWIST ON THE FAMILIAR, A CHILI MADE WITH PINTO beans, green peppers, mild green chiles, and generous chunks of turkey. It's a great way to enjoy leftover roast turkey, but if you haven't roasted a turkey recently—and don't plan to—you can substitute leftover roast chicken (page 240).

SERVES 6 TO 8

8 ounces/225 g tomatillos, papery hulls removed, cut into large chunks

6 garlic cloves

¹/₄ cup/6 g packed fresh oregano leaves

¹/₄ cup/8 g packed fresh sage leaves

2 tablespoons organic extra-virgin olive oil

2 green bell peppers, cored and cut into ¹/₂-inch/1.25 cm dice

2 medium-size mild green fresh chile peppers, such as pasilla, cored and cut into
  ¹/₂-inch/1.25 cm dice

1 medium-size yellow onion, cut into ¹/₂-inch/1.25 cm dice

12 to 16 ounces/340 to 455 g cooked organic turkey or chicken, torn into large shreds or cut into ¹/₂-inch/1.25 cm dice

2 teaspoons ground coriander

2 teaspoons ground cumin

6 cups/1.1 kg cooked, drained pinto beans, plus 3 cups/710 mL of the
cooking liquid (see page 277 for how to cook beans)

Fine sea salt to taste

Freshly ground black pepper to taste

2 cups/120 g crumbled *queso fresco* or shredded Jack cheese (optional)

1 cup/50 g finely chopped red onion

In the bowl of a food processor, combine the tomatillos, garlic, oregano, and sage and pulse to a coarse puree, scraping down the bowl as necessary. Set aside.

In a medium stockpot over medium-high heat, heat the oil. Add the bell peppers, chile peppers, and yellow onion and cook, stirring occasionally, until the vegetables are tender and starting to brown, 6 to 8 minutes. Add the turkey, coriander, and cumin and cook, stirring occasionally, for 2 minutes. Stir in the tomatillo mixture, beans, and bean cooking liquid. Bring to a boil over high heat, lower the heat to a simmer, and cook until the chili is heated through, about 5 minutes. Add salt and black pepper to taste.

Serve the chili hot, with the cheese (if using) and red onion sprinkled on top.

Glazed Spare Ribs

UNDER THE LEADERSHIP OF EXECUTIVE CHEF-PARTNER AND 2012 JAMES Beard Award–winner Michael Anthony, New York City's Gramercy Tavern has earned countless accolades and is considered one of the country's best restaurants. With a farm-to-table approach focusing on seasonal, sustainable ingredients and greenmarket produce, Michael's simple, straightforward cuisine inspires a connection between diners and their food. Bring his celebrated culinary style into your kitchen with this rustically elegant glazed pork entrée.

SERVES 2 TO 3

1 (3-pound/1.4 kg) rack organic pork spare ribs, at room temperature

Fine sea salt

Freshly ground black pepper

3 tablespoons organic extra-virgin olive oil

2 garlic cloves, minced

2 cups/475 mL raw apple cider

$^1/_4$ cup/60 mL unsulfured molasses

2 tablespoons raw apple cider vinegar

2 tablespoons red wine vinegar

$^1/_2$ jalapeño pepper, seeded and sliced thinly

$^1/_2$ star anise

$^1/_2$ teaspoon smoked paprika

1 teaspoon black sesame seeds, toasted (see note on page 122)

1 teaspoon white sesame seeds, toasted (see note on page 122)

1 teaspoon ground Aleppo pepper (see note)

Fleur de sel or other coarse sea salt

Preheat the oven to 250°F/120°C.

Generously sprinkle the ribs with salt and pepper. In a small bowl, combine the olive oil and garlic, then rub the mixture over all sides of the ribs. Place the ribs in a shallow roasting pan and cook until tender but not falling apart, 2 to 3 hours.

Meanwhile, in a medium, nonreactive saucepan over medium heat, bring the apple cider to a boil. Cook until reduced to 1⅓ cup/315 mL, 20 to 30 minutes.

In a small, nonreactive saucepan over medium heat, combine the molasses, cider vinegar, red wine vinegar, jalapeño, and star anise and bring to a simmer. Remove from the heat and set aside for 5 minutes.

Strain the molasses mixture through a medium-mesh sieve, then slowly add it to the reduced cider, stirring constantly. Stir in the smoked paprika and set the glaze aside.

When the ribs are done, remove them from the oven and brush all sides with the glaze. Return the ribs to the oven and cook until the glaze is warm, about 15 minutes.

Meanwhile, in a small bowl, combine the sesame seeds and Aleppo pepper.

Cut the ribs into two- to three-rib sections, sprinkle with the sesame seed mixture and fleur de sel, and serve. Pass the remaining glaze at the table.

Aleppo is a type of dried chile. You can find it at specialty food stores and at Middle Eastern markets.

Mustard-Maple Pork Tenderloin with Carrots, Onion, and Apples

A PORK TENDERLOIN IS THE PERFECT WEEKNIGHT ROAST: IT'S SO SMALL that it cooks relatively quickly. Here, it's slathered with a mustard-maple glaze and garnished with roasted carrots, onion, and apple—for a dinner that's sweet enough for kids, but sophisticated enough for grown-ups, too.

SERVES 6

¼ cup/60 mL organic extra-virgin olive oil, divided, plus more as needed

¼ cup/65 g whole-grain mustard

2 tablespoons pure maple syrup

2 (1-pound/455 g) organic pork tenderloins, trimmed

Fine sea salt

Freshly ground black pepper

1 pound/455 g carrots, cut into ³/₄-inch/2 cm dice

1 large sweet-crisp apple, such as Fuji, cored and cut into ³/₄-inch/2 cm dice

1 large yellow onion, cut into ³/₄-inch/2 cm dice

Preheat the oven to 450°F/230°C. Arrange a rack in the upper half of the oven and another in the lower half. Lightly coat a 9 by 13-inch/25 by 35 cm baking pan with oil.

In a small bowl, combine the mustard and maple syrup. Spread the mixture all over the pork. Place the pork in the prepared pan and pour any remaining mustard mixture over the top. Sprinkle all sides of the tenderloins with salt and pepper and set aside.

In a medium bowl, combine the carrots and 2 tablespoons of the oil, tossing to coat. Spread the carrots on a large, rimmed baking sheet. Place the pork on the upper rack and the carrots on the lower rack and roast for 20 minutes.

Meanwhile, in the same medium bowl, combine the apple, onion, and the remaining 2 tablespoons of oil, tossing to coat.

Remove the carrots from the oven and add the apple and onion (leaving the pork in the oven). Return the vegetables to the oven and continue cooking until an internal thermometer in the pork reads 140°F/60°C for medium rare, about 10 minutes. Transfer the pork to a cutting board and let it rest, covered loosely with foil, for 10 minutes.

Meanwhile, toss the carrot mixture and continue roasting until tender, about 10 minutes. Add salt and pepper to taste.

Slice the pork on an angle and arrange on plates or a platter. Spoon the carrot mixture on top or alongside. Drizzle with any accumulated juices and serve hot.

Spice-Rubbed Pork Chops with Smoky Cabbage and Collards

INSPIRED BY SOUTHERN COMFORT FOOD, THIS DISH IS FULL OF BOLD flavors and colors. A chili powder rub gives the pork chops oomph, while red cabbage mellows and sweetens the sometimes bitter nature of collard greens.

For dessert, keep the comfort vibe going with Chocolate Avocado Pudding (page 267)—or cool your taste buds with Honey Ice Cream (page 265).

SERVES 6

1 tablespoon chili powder

1¹⁄₂ teaspoons granulated garlic powder

1¹⁄₂ teaspoons granulated onion powder

4 teaspoons smoked paprika, divided

6 boneless or bone-in organic pork loin chops, about 1 inch/2.5 cm thick

Fine sea salt to taste

Freshly ground black pepper to taste

3 tablespoons organic extra-virgin olive oil, divided

¹⁄₂ medium-size red onion, sliced thinly

2 garlic cloves, minced

¹⁄₈ teaspoon cayenne pepper

¹⁄₂ medium-size red cabbage, cored and cut into ¹⁄₂-inch/1.25 cm shreds

1 pound/455 g collard greens, ribs removed, leaves cut crosswise into ¹⁄₂-inch/1.25 cm shreds

1 cup/240 mL organic reduced-sodium chicken or vegetable stock (see note on page 127) or water

Raw apple cider vinegar to taste

In a small bowl, combine the chili powder, garlic powder, onion powder, and 2 teaspoons of the paprika. Sprinkle both sides of the pork with the spice mixture, rubbing it evenly over the meat. Sprinkle with salt and pepper, cover, and chill in the refrigerator for 1 to 2 hours.

Return the pork to room temperature.

In a wide saucepan or large skillet over medium-high heat, heat 1 tablespoon of the oil. Add the onion and cook, stirring occasionally, until it's starting to soften, 1 to 2 minutes. Add the minced garlic, cayenne, and remaining 2 teaspoons of paprika and cook, stirring occasionally, until the garlic is fragrant, about 30 seconds. Working in batches, add the cabbage and collards, stirring until wilted before adding the next batch. Once all the cabbage and collards have been added, add the stock and bring to a boil. Lower the heat to a simmer, cover, and cook until the cabbage and collards are tender, about 20 minutes.

When the collards are about 10 minutes from being done, in a large skillet over medium heat, heat the remaining 2 tablespoons of oil. Add the pork chops and cook until well browned and cooked through, about 5 minutes per side. Transfer the pork to plates or a platter and let rest, covered loosely with foil, for 5 minutes.

Meanwhile, add salt, pepper, and vinegar to taste to the cabbage and collards. Arrange alongside the pork and drizzle with any pan juices. Serve hot.

Greek Lamburgers with Eggplant and Lemon "Aioli"

A LAMBURGER, OR A GROUND LAMB HAMBURGER, IS A REALLY NICE change of pace from a beef burger, especially because the deeply savory qualities of lamb make way for all kinds of out-of-the-ordinary burger add-ons. This Greek-inspired patty is served with a lemony sauce that's not really aioli—it's a cleaner version that uses yogurt instead of mayonnaise.

SERVES 4

1 lemon
²/₃ cup/160 mL grass-fed organic plain yogurt or kefir
2 teaspoons chopped fresh mint
1 garlic clove, minced
Fine sea salt to taste

Freshly ground black pepper to taste

1¼ pounds/565 g ground grass-fed lamb

¼ cup/15 g chopped fresh flat-leaf parsley

1 large shallot, diced finely

2 medium-size Asian-style eggplants, halved lengthwise

Organic extra-virgin olive oil, for brushing

2 pita breads (sprouted wheat, gluten-free, or your favorite variety),
  cut in half to make 4 pita pockets

3 cups/40 g loosely packed mixed salad greens

Zest half of the lemon. Juice the lemon to yield 2 teaspoons of juice. In a small bowl, combine the lemon zest, lemon juice, yogurt, mint, garlic, and salt and pepper to taste. Set aside.

In a large bowl, combine the lamb, parsley, and shallot and gently mix well. With dampened hands, shape the mixture into four oblong patties about 4 inches/10 cm long and ¾ inch/2 cm thick. Sprinkle both sides with salt and pepper and set aside.

Arrange the eggplant on a plate. Brush both sides with oil and sprinkle with salt and pepper.

Prepare the grill to medium-high heat and lightly oil the grate. Grill the patties to desired doneness, about 3½ minutes per side for medium. Grill the eggplant until tender and lightly charred, about 3 minutes per side. During the last minute, place the pitas on the grill and turn to lightly toast both sides.

To serve, cut each piece of eggplant in half crosswise and place two pieces in each pita pocket. Add the lamburgers, mixed greens, and some of the lemon aioli. Serve hot, passing the remaining lemon aioli at the table.

Lamb Tikka Masala

IN THIS BELOVED INDIAN DISH, *TIKKA* IS CHUNKS OF MEAT COOKED ON
a skewer and *masala* is the blend of spices that flavor the meat, along with adding
a nice load of antioxidants. Once the meat is cooked, it's served in a spicy tomato
sauce that's typically finished with cream—but this clean version replaces the
cream with yogurt, adding a nice tang, and probiotics, in the process. On the side,
try brown basmati or brown jasmine rice.

SERVES 4

LAMB

1 cup/240 mL grass-fed organic plain yogurt or kefir

1 tablespoon finely grated fresh ginger

2 garlic cloves, minced

1 1/2 teaspoons ground coriander

1 1/2 teaspoons ground cumin

1 teaspoon fine sea salt

1/2 teaspoon freshly ground black pepper

1/4 teaspoon ground cardamom

1/4 teaspoon ground turmeric

1/8 teaspoon cayenne pepper

1 1/2 pounds/680 g grass-fed lamb stew meat or boneless leg of lamb,
    cut into 1 1/2-inch/4 cm pieces

Organic high-heat cooking oil, such as grapeseed, as needed

SAUCE

2 tablespoons organic neutral-flavored oil, such as grapeseed

1 large yellow onion, cut into 1/4-inch/0.65 cm dice

2 garlic cloves, minced

1 teaspoon finely grated fresh ginger

4 1/2 teaspoons garam masala (see note)

1 1/2 teaspoons chili powder

1/8 teaspoon cayenne pepper

1¹/₂ pounds/680 g tomatoes, peeled (optional), seeded, and cut into
   ¹/₄-inch/0.65 cm dice

Fine sea salt to taste

²/₃ cup/160 mL grass-fed organic plain yogurt or kefir, at room temperature

Cilantro sprigs, for garnish

To make the lamb: In a medium bowl, combine the yogurt, ginger, garlic, coriander, cumin, salt, pepper, cardamom, turmeric, and cayenne. Transfer to a large resealable plastic bag and add the lamb, tossing to coat. Close the bag, squeezing out as much air as possible, and chill in the refrigerator for 4 to 8 hours.

Thread the lamb onto skewers, shaking off any excess marinade (discard the marinade).

Preheat a grill to high heat and lightly oil the grate; or preheat the broiler, lightly oil a rimmed baking sheet, and position a rack about 5 inches/13 cm from the heating element. Arrange the skewers on the grill or the baking sheet and grill or broil until just cooked through and browned in spots, 6 to 8 minutes per side. Set aside and let rest, covered loosely with foil.

To make the sauce: In a large skillet over medium heat, heat the oil. Add the onion, garlic, and ginger and cook, stirring occasionally, until the onion is tender and lightly browned, about 8 minutes. Add the garam masala, chili powder, and cayenne and cook, stirring, for 1 minute. Add the tomatoes and lamb, sliding the lamb off the skewers and into the skillet. Cook, stirring frequently, until the tomatoes release some of their juices, 1 to 2 minutes. Bring to a boil and lower the heat to a simmer. Cover partially and cook, stirring occasionally, until the tomatoes become saucelike, about 10 minutes.

Stir in the yogurt and salt and pepper to taste. Serve hot, garnished with cilantro sprigs.

> **Garam masala is an Indian spice blend. You can find it at Indian markets and in the spice** section of better supermarkets and specialty food stores.

Big Beef Burgers with Grilled Onions and (Sometimes) Blue Cheese Sauce

SOMETIMES ONLY A BIG, BEEFY BURGER WILL DO. FOR THOSE occasions, this burger delivers, with a 6-plus-ounce/170-plus-gram patty, grilled onions, and arugula. For special occasions, add the blue cheese sauce, which is also good on a portobello mushroom burger or drizzled over a grilled chicken breast. Because it's so rich, it's meant as a once-in-a-while indulgence.

SERVES 6

2¹/₂ pounds/1.1 kg lean grass-fed ground beef

Fine sea salt

Freshly ground black pepper

1 large yellow onion

1 tablespoon organic extra-virgin olive oil, plus more as needed

6 hamburger buns (sprouted wheat, gluten-free, or your favorite variety)

4 cups/55 g loosely packed arugula leaves

BLUE CHEESE SAUCE (OPTIONAL)

1¹/₄ cups/140 g crumbled blue cheese

¹/₃ cup/80 mL grass-fed organic plain yogurt or kefir

1 tablespoon whole-grain mustard

Fine sea salt to taste

Freshly ground black pepper to taste

With dampened hands, shape the beef into six patties, about 4¹/₂ inches/11 cm in diameter and ³/₄ inch/2 cm thick. Sprinkle both sides with salt and pepper.

Keeping the root end intact, cut the onion into twelve wedges (so that each wedge has a bit of root holding it together). In a large bowl, toss the onion with the oil, salt, and pepper.

Prepare the grill to medium-high heat and lightly oil the grate. Grill the patties to medium rare, about 2½ minutes per side. Grill the onion until it's softened and lightly charred, 4 to 5 minutes per side. During the last minute, place the buns on the grill, cut side down, to lightly toast.

Meanwhile, for the sauce (if using): In a medium bowl, combine the cheese, yogurt, mustard, and salt and pepper to taste.

Arrange the arugula on the buns. Top with the patties, onion, and blue cheese sauce (if using). Serve hot.

A TIP FOR COOKING GRASS-FED MEATS

Because grass-fed meats tend to be less fatty, they also tend to dry out if they're cooked for too long. So aim for rare, medium rare, or medium doneness for grass-fed steaks, chops, and burgers.

More-Veggies-Than-Beef Stew

CERTAINLY, ONE WAY TO EAT MORE SUSTAINABLY IS TO EAT LESS MEAT, and meaty soups and stews are great candidates for places to cut down. This stew is a great example—it has plenty of beefy taste and texture, but with only about two ounces/55 grams of beef per serving. But it's plenty hearty with an abundance of vegetables, including carrots, parsnips, mushrooms, and sweet potatoes.

SERVES 6 TO 8

¼ cup/30 g organic spelt flour or amaranth flour (see note on page 142)
Fine sea salt
Freshly ground black pepper
1½ teaspoons chopped fresh rosemary
1½ teaspoons chopped fresh sage
1½ teaspoons chopped fresh thyme

2 medium-size yellow onions

2 tablespoons organic extra-virgin olive oil

1 pound/455 g grass-fed beef stew meat, cut into 1- to 1¹/₂-inch/2.5 to 4 cm pieces

6 garlic cloves, sliced thinly

6 cups/1.4 L organic reduced-sodium beef stock (see note on page 127)

12 ounces/340 g carrots, cut into 1-inch/2.5 cm lengths

12 ounces/340 g parsnips, cut into 1-inch/2.5 cm lengths

8 ounces/225 g brown mushrooms, halved (larger ones quartered)

8 ounces/225 g yellow-fleshed sweet potatoes, cut into 1-inch/2.5 cm dice

4 ounces/115 g sugar snap peas, halved crosswise

In a large shallow bowl, combine the flour with a generous pinch of salt and pepper. In a small bowl, combine the rosemary, sage, and thyme. Keeping the root ends intact, cut the onions into six or eight wedges each (so that each wedge has a bit of root holding it together). Set the flour mixture, herb mixture, and onions aside separately.

In a medium stockpot over medium heat, heat the oil. Dredge the meat in the flour mixture a few pieces at a time, shaking off the excess, and add the meat to the pot. Cook well on all sides in batches without crowding the pan, about 5 minutes, and transfer the meat to a plate.

When all the meat is cooked, return the meat to the pot and add the garlic and half of the herb mixture. Cook, stirring occasionally, until the garlic is fragrant, about 2 minutes. Add the stock, increase the heat to high, and bring to a boil, scraping up any browned bits on the bottom of the pot. Lower the heat to a simmer and cook for 45 minutes.

Add the carrots and cook for 5 minutes. Add the parsnips and cook for 10 minutes. Add the onions and cook for 30 minutes. Add the mushrooms and potatoes and cook until the meat and vegetables are just shy of tender, 10 to 15 minutes. Add the peas and cook until the meat and vegetables are tender, about 10 minutes. The meat should be fork-tender but not completely falling apart.

Stir in the remaining herb mixture and salt and pepper to taste, and serve.

Mom's Meat Loaf with Quinoa

THIS MEAT LOAF IS COMFORTINGLY FAMILIAR, YET PLENTY FLAVORFUL. The quinoa is a secret of sorts, keeping every slice deliciously moist. Quinoa also adds lysine, an essential amino acid that aids in tissue growth and repair.

SERVES 8

Organic extra-virgin olive oil, for the pan

3 large organic, pasture-raised, or antibiotic-free eggs

1 tablespoon whole-grain mustard

2 teaspoons fine sea salt

1 teaspoon freshly ground black pepper

1 cup/160 g cooked quinoa (see page 275 for how to cook grains)

2 medium-size tomatoes, cut into ¼-inch/0.65 cm dice

1 small carrot, shredded coarsely

½ medium-size red onion, cut into ¼-inch/0.65 cm dice

¼ cup/15 g chopped fresh flat-leaf parsley

2 garlic cloves, minced

½ cup/60 g grated Parmesan cheese (optional)

1½ pounds/680 g lean grass-fed ground beef, organic pork, organic turkey, or a combination

Preheat the oven to 375°F/190°C. Oil a 9 by 5 by 3-inch/23 by 13 by 8 cm loaf pan.

In a large bowl, place the eggs, mustard, salt, and pepper, whisking to combine. Add the quinoa, tomatoes, carrot, onion, parsley, garlic, and cheese (if using). Add the meat, gently mixing and breaking up any clumps of quinoa until well combined.

Gently pack the mixture into the prepared loaf pan, without compressing the meat. Place the pan on a rimmed baking sheet and bake until an internal thermometer inserted into the center reads 165°F/75°C, about 1 hour and 20 minutes. Remove the meat loaf from the oven and let it rest, covered loosely with foil, 10 minutes. Slice the meat loaf and serve hot.

Spiced Braised Short Ribs with Red Cabbage

THERE'S NO HURRYING SHORT RIBS. IF YOU TRY TO COOK THEM QUICKLY, you'll end up with sinewy toughness. But if you cook them low and slow, you'll be rewarded with meltingly tender, deeply flavorful meat that falls off the bones. As a side benefit, you'll also get a household full of wonderful, warming smells.

This particular recipe is especially rich and aromatic, thanks to balsamic vinegar and Chinese five-spice blend. The cabbage adds beautiful color and texture, plus loads of vitamin C. It all goes particularly well with Mashed Celeriac (page 203).

SERVES 6

2 tablespoons organic extra-virgin olive oil

4 pounds/1.8 kg grass-fed beef short ribs, trimmed

1 tablespoon Chinese five-spice blend (see headnote on page 136)

Fine sea salt to taste

Freshly ground black pepper to taste

1 medium-size red onion, cut into ¼-inch/0.65 cm dice

6 garlic cloves, minced

3 cups/710 mL organic reduced-sodium beef stock (see note on page 127)

1 pound/455 g tomatoes, peeled (optional), seeded, and cut into
    ¼-inch/0.65 dice

½ cup/120 mL balsamic vinegar

¼ cup/60 mL raw cider vinegar

¼ cup/60 mL pure maple syrup

½ medium-size red cabbage, cored and cut into ¼-inch/0.65 cm shreds

1 teaspoon arrowroot powder dissolved in 1 tablespoon cold water

Preheat the oven to 300°F/150°C.

In a very large, ovenproof skillet or braising pan over medium-high heat, heat the oil. Sprinkle the ribs with the five-spice blend, salt, and pepper. Working in batches, add the ribs to the skillet and brown all the meaty sides, about 2 minutes per side. Transfer the browned ribs to a large bowl or platter.

Add the onion to the skillet and cook until lightly browned, 3 to 5 minutes. Add the garlic and cook, stirring occasionally, until fragrant, 30 to 60 seconds. Stir in the stock, scraping up any browned bits in the skillet. Add the tomatoes, vinegars, and maple syrup. Add the ribs, nestling them into the liquid, increase the heat to high, and bring to a boil. Cover and transfer the pan to the oven. Bake for $1\frac{1}{2}$ hours.

Remove the skillet from the oven and add the cabbage, nestling it into the liquid. Cover, return to the oven, and bake until the meat and cabbage are tender, about 30 minutes more.

Use a slotted spoon to transfer the ribs and cabbage to plates or a platter and cover loosely to keep warm. Skim any fat off the surface of the liquid, then return the skillet to the stovetop. Bring to a boil over high heat and cook until the liquid is reduced to $1\frac{1}{2}$ cups/355 mL, 8 to 10 minutes. Add the arrowroot mixture, stirring until the sauce thickens, about 30 seconds. Add salt and pepper to taste.

Arrange the cabbage on plates. Top with the ribs and drizzle with sauce. Serve hot, passing any remaining sauce at the table.

Grass-Fed Rib Eyes with Garlic-Chive Butter

JUICY, FLAVORFUL, AND TENDER, A GRASS-FED RIB EYE IS SIMPLY A great steak. And so you don't want to mess with it too much. This garlic-chive butter is just what a rib eye deserves—a flavorful bit of something that comes together quickly and easily, and that makes an already special steak even more so. (Choose grass-fed for extra conjugated linoleic acid, or CLA, which has anticancer properties and might also help with weight management.)

SERVES 6

8 fresh chives, cut into rough 1-inch/2.5 cm pieces, plus whole chives for garnish

2 tablespoons packed fresh flat-leaf parsley

4 garlic cloves

4 tablespoons/55 g unsalted grass-fed organic butter, at room temperature

Fine sea salt to taste

Freshly ground black pepper to taste

3 (10- to 12-ounce/285 to 340 g) grass-fed rib eye steaks, about 1 inch/2.5 cm thick, excess fat trimmed

2 tablespoons extra-virgin olive oil

In the bowl of a food processor, combine the cut chives, parsley, and garlic and pulse until chopped coarsely, scraping down the bowl as necessary. Add the butter and pulse to combine, scraping down the bowl as necessary. Add salt and pepper to taste. Transfer to a small bowl and set aside.

Sprinkle both sides of the steaks with salt and pepper.

In a large skillet over medium-high heat, heat the oil. Add the steaks and cook, without moving, to desired doneness, about 3½ minutes per side for medium-rare. Transfer the steaks to a cutting board and spread about half of the garlic-chive butter on top. Let the steaks rest, covered loosely with foil, for 5 minutes.

Cut the steaks on a diagonal into ½-inch/1.25 cm slices and arrange on plates or a platter. Dot with the remaining garlic-chive butter and drizzle with any accumulated juices. Serve hot, garnished with the whole chives.

> **For other flavored butters that'd also go with this steak, see page 282.**

DESSERTS

CHERRY ALMOND OATMEAL COOKIES

DOUBLE GINGER COOKIES

CACAO CHERRY BROWNIES

COCONUT ALMOND MACAROONS

CARAMEL APPLE SORBET

HONEY ICE CREAM

COCONUT-LIME "ICE CREAM"

CHOCOLATE AVOCADO PUDDING

GRILLED PEACHES KISSED WITH
CINNAMON AND CHOCOLATE

BUCKWHEAT CREPES WITH ORANGES
AND GINGERED AGAVE

OLIVE OIL CAKE WITH SYRUPY FRESH FRUIT

FLOURLESS CHOCOLATE HAZELNUT CAKE

Cherry Almond Oatmeal Cookies

JAM-PACKED WITH OATS, FRUIT, NUTS, CINNAMON, NUTMEG, AND CLOVES, these cookies are thoroughly satisfying and nicely spicy.

MAKES 2 DOZEN

$^{3}/_{4}$ cup/90 g spelt flour

1 teaspoon aluminum-free baking powder

1 teaspoon ground cinnamon

$^{1}/_{2}$ teaspoon fine sea salt

$^{1}/_{4}$ teaspoon ground nutmeg

$^{1}/_{8}$ teaspoon ground cloves

1 cup/150 g coconut palm sugar (see page 82)

6 tablespoons/90 mL organic neutral-flavored oil, such as grapeseed, plus more as needed

2 large organic, pasture-raised, or antibiotic-free eggs

$^{1}/_{4}$ cup/85 g unsweetened or homemade applesauce (see page 279 to make your own)

$^{1}/_{4}$ teaspoon pure almond extract

2 cups/190 g old-fashioned rolled oats

$^{1}/_{2}$ cup/50 g sliced raw almonds

$^{1}/_{2}$ cup/70 g unsweetened and unsulfured dried cherries

Preheat the oven to 375°F/190°C. Oil two baking sheets or line them with parchment paper.

In a medium bowl, whisk together the flour, baking powder, cinnamon, salt, nutmeg, and cloves.

In the bowl of an electric mixer, using the paddle attachment, combine the sugar, oil, eggs, applesauce, and extract and mix on medium-high speed to blend well. Add the flour mixture and mix on low speed until just short of combined. Add the oats, almonds, and cherries and mix until just combined.

Arrange 2 tablespoon–size balls of dough on the prepared baking sheets, about 1¹⁄₂ inches/4 cm apart. Bake until set and lightly browned, 12 to 14 minutes. Transfer to a wire rack to cool.

> **You can change the fruit and nuts in these cookies to make any combination you like—** cranberries and pecans, apricots and hazelnuts, raisins and walnuts. For those flavors, substitute vanilla extract for the almond extract.

Double Ginger Cookies

THESE COOKIES GET THEIR INTENSE FLAVOR FROM TWO SOURCES OF anti-inflammatory ginger, plus blackstrap molasses. And they bake up just as a ginger cookie should—chewy on the edges and soft in the middle.

MAKES 4 DOZEN

4 ounces/115 g unsalted grass-fed organic butter

¹⁄₄ cup/60 mL unsulfured blackstrap molasses

1 teaspoon pure vanilla extract

2¹⁄₄ cups/275 g spelt flour

1 tablespoon aluminum-free baking soda

1 tablespoon ground ginger

2 teaspoons ground cinnamon

¹⁄₂ teaspoon fine sea salt

¹⁄₄ teaspoon ground cloves

¹⁄₄ teaspoon ground nutmeg

1¹⁄₃ cups/200 g coconut palm sugar (see page 82), divided

1 large organic, pasture-raised, or antibiotic-free egg, lightly beaten

2 tablespoons finely grated fresh ginger

In a small saucepan over low heat, melt the butter. Remove from the heat and stir in the molasses and vanilla. Set aside to cool to warm room temperature.

Meanwhile, in a large bowl, whisk together the flour, baking soda, ground ginger, cinnamon, salt, cloves, nutmeg, and 1 cup/150 g of the sugar.

Add the egg and fresh ginger to the cooled butter mixture, whisking to combine. Add the butter mixture into the dry ingredients, stirring until just combined. Cover and refrigerate until the dough is firm, about 30 minutes.

Meanwhile, preheat the oven to 375°F/190°C. Oil two baking sheets or line them with parchment paper. Place the remaining ⅓ cup/50 g of sugar in a small bowl.

Roll the dough into 1-inch/2.5 cm balls and roll the balls in the sugar to coat. Arrange the balls on the prepared baking sheets, about 2 inches apart, and bake until set and slightly browned at the edges, 10 to 12 minutes. Transfer to a wire rack to cool.

Cacao Cherry Brownies

THESE BROWNIES DON'T DISAPPOINT. THEY'RE DEEPLY CHOCOLATY and nicely chewy, with brightness from the cherries and crunch from cacao nibs. They're even super easy to make.

MAKES ONE 8-INCH/20 CM SQUARE PAN

½ cup/70 g unsweetened and unsulfured dried cherries

Organic neutral-flavored oil, for the pan

1½ cups/225 g coconut palm sugar (see page 82)

1 cup/95 g unsweetened raw cacao powder

¾ cup/90 g organic spelt flour or amaranth flour (see note on page 142)

½ teaspoon fine sea salt

4 ounces/115 g unsalted grass-fed organic butter, melted

3 large organic, pasture-raised, or antibiotic-free eggs, lightly beaten

1 teaspoon pure vanilla extract

¼ cup/30 g raw cacao nibs

In a small saucepan, bring ½ cup/120 mL of water to a boil over high heat.

Remove from the heat and stir in the cherries. Set aside for at least 10 minutes, to plump the cherries.

Meanwhile, preheat the oven to 375F/190°C. Oil an 8-inch/20 cm square baking pan.

In a large bowl, whisk together the sugar, cacao powder, flour, and salt. Add the melted butter, stirring until thoroughly combined. Add the eggs and vanilla, stirring until just shy of combined.

Drain the cherries. Add the cherries and cacao nibs to the large bowl. Transfer the mixture to the prepared baking pan, spreading it out in an even layer, and bake until a cake tester or toothpick inserted into the center comes out almost entirely clean, about 25 minutes. Transfer to a wire rack to cool completely. Cut into squares and serve.

Coconut Almond Macaroons

THESE MACAROONS ARE NEITHER A TRADITIONAL VERSION MADE WITH almond paste nor a straight-ahead coconut version; rather, a hybrid of the two, using sliced almonds and shredded coconut. They have the best characteristic of all macaroons, however—a chewy-crunchy outside that gives way to a soft inside. Bet you can't eat just one.

MAKES ABOUT 30

2 cups/160 g unsweetened shredded coconut

1 cup/95 g sliced raw almonds, plus more as needed

2/3 cup/100 g coconut palm sugar (see page 82)

1/4 teaspoon fine sea salt

2 large organic, pasture-raised, or antibiotic-free egg whites

Preheat the oven to 350°F/160°F. Line two large baking sheets with parchment.

In the bowl of a food processor, combine the coconut, almonds, sugar, and salt and pulse until finely chopped. Add the egg whites and pulse until the mixture is evenly moistened and will hold together when you squeeze a handful of the dough. (If the mixture is too dry, add water 1 or 2 teaspoons at a time.)

With dampened hands, roll the mixture into 1-inch/2.5 cm balls and arrange about 1 inch apart on the prepared baking sheets. Slightly flatten each ball and garnish with an almond slice. Bake until the bottoms are lightly browned, 15 to 18 minutes. Transfer to a wire rack to cool completely.

WAYS TO VARY YOUR MACAROONS

Replace ¼ cup/25 g of the almonds with cacao nibs or coarsely chopped dried fruit, adding it to the food processor along with the rest of the almonds.

Caramel Apple Sorbet

COCONUT PALM SUGAR HAS A DISTINCTLY CARAMEL-LIKE SWEETNESS, which means that using it instead of white sugar in a basic apple sorbet recipe makes for a healthier, less processed dessert—but also one that has the color and flavor of a caramel apple. Sweet.

MAKES ABOUT 3½ CUPS/830 ML

1¼ cups/185 g coconut palm sugar (see page 82)

1¼ pounds/565 g sweet-crisp apples, such as Fuji, cored and
   cut into large bite-size chunks (see notes)

2 tablespoons freshly squeezed lemon juice (from 1 or 2 lemons),
   or more to taste

Fine sea salt to taste

In a medium saucepan over medium-high heat, combine the sugar with 1¼ cups/295 mL of water and bring to a boil, stirring to dissolve the sugar. Remove from the heat and set aside to cool to room temperature.

Meanwhile, in another medium saucepan over medium-high heat, combine the apples and $^1\!/_4$ cup/60 mL of water and bring to a boil. Lower the heat to a simmer, cover partially, and cook, stirring occasionally, until the apples are very tender, 15 to 20 minutes.

Transfer the apples, along with any accumulated juices, to a food processor and puree, scraping down the bowl as necessary. Strain the puree through a medium-mesh sieve into a mixing bowl, pressing the solids with the back of a spoon or ladle. Stir in the sugar mixture and lemon juice. Add more lemon juice and salt to taste.

Thoroughly chill the sorbet base in the refrigerator, then freeze in your ice-cream maker according to the manufacturer's directions (see notes).

If you don't have an ice-cream maker, pour your ice cream or sorbet base into a shallow baking pan and freeze, stirring and breaking it up with a fork every hour for 3 or 4 hours. Once solid, set the mixture aside at room temperature for about 10 minutes, then break it up and add it to a food processor. Pulse until smooth, then transfer the mixture to a container and refreeze.

This recipe is also good using pears instead of apples.

Honey Ice Cream

HERE'S A TWIST ON A TRADITIONAL VANILLA ICE CREAM, WITH coconut palm sugar helping to accentuate the unique sweetness that is honey. The ice cream is delicious on its own, but even better with Cherry Almond Oatmeal or Double Ginger Cookies (page 259 or 260) alongside.

MAKES ABOUT 5 CUPS/1.2 L

1 vanilla bean
3¹/₂ cups/830 mL grass-fed organic milk, divided
8 large organic, pasture-raised, or antibiotic-free egg yolks
²/₃ cup/100 g coconut palm sugar (see page 82)
²/₃ cup/160 mL raw honey, ideally dark (see note on page 106)
Fine sea salt to taste

Use the tip of a paring knife to split the vanilla bean lengthwise, then use the back of the knife to scrape the seeds from the inside of the bean. In a medium, heavy saucepan over medium-high heat, combine the vanilla seeds, vanilla pod, and 2 cups/475 mL of the milk and heat until the mixture is just beginning to bubble at the edges. Remove from the heat and set aside for 30 minutes.

In a medium bowl, whisk the yolks, sugar, and honey until smooth. Whisk about ¹/₂ cup/120 mL of the milk mixture into the egg mixture to temper it, then pour the whole egg mixture back into the milk. Cook over low heat, stirring and scraping the sides and bottom of the pot almost constantly, until the mixture reaches 170°F/75°C and it coats the back of a wooden spoon, 5 to 8 minutes depending on how warm the mixture got in the previous step. Strain through a medium-mesh sieve into a mixing bowl and stir in the remaining 1¹/₂ cups/355 mL of milk. Add salt to taste.

Thoroughly chill the ice-cream base in the refrigerator, then freeze according to your ice-cream maker's manufacturer's directions (if you don't have an ice-cream maker, see note on page 264).

Coconut-Lime "Ice Cream"

IF YOU CAN PRESS THE 'ON' BUTTON ON A FOOD PROCESSOR, YOU CAN make this refreshingly good ice-creamy treat. Just add all the ingredients, buzz, buzz, buzz, and your ice-cream base is done.

The finished dessert has a beautifully creamy texture—not too hard or soft, and not at all icy. You won't believe it's completely dairy-free. (And neither will your friends.)

MAKES ABOUT 3 CUPS/710 ML

3 to 4 limes

2 medium-size ripe avocados, quartered, peeled, and pitted

1 cup/240 mL coconut milk (see note on page 108)

$^1\!/_2$ cup/120 mL raw agave nectar

$^1\!/_2$ teaspoon pure vanilla extract

Fine sea salt to taste

Zest two of the limes. Set the zest aside.

Juice the zested limes, plus enough of the remaining limes, to yield $^1\!/_3$ cup/ 80 mL of juice. In the bowl of a food processor or the jar of a blender, combine the lime juice, avocados, coconut milk, agave, and vanilla and process until smooth, scraping down the bowl or jar as necessary. Stir in the lime zest and salt to taste.

Thoroughly chill the "ice cream" base in the refrigerator, then freeze according to your ice-cream maker's manufacturer's directions (if you don't have an ice-cream maker, see note on page 264).

> **If you want to accentuate the coconut flavor in this dessert, serve it sprinkled** with shredded coconut.

Chocolate Avocado Pudding

ALTHOUGH IT MIGHT BE UNUSUAL TO INCLUDE A TYPICALLY SAVORY ingredient—avocado—in a sweet setting, here it totally works. Not only does the subtle avocado flavor nicely complement the pudding's chocolate intensity, but it makes for a wonderfully creamy texture without eggs or dairy. The net result is a dessert that's dairy-free, vegan, and raw *plus* healthy and delicious. You're welcome.

SERVES 4

2 medium-size ripe avocados, quartered, peeled, and pitted

³/₄ cup/70 g unsweetened raw cacao powder

¹/₂ cup/120 mL unsweetened nut milk, or more as needed

6 tablespoons/90 mL raw agave nectar

¹/₄ teaspoon pure vanilla extract

Fine sea salt to taste

In the bowl of a food processor or the jar of a blender, combine the avocados, cacao powder, nut milk, agave, and vanilla and process until smooth, scraping down the bowl or jar as necessary. Add more nut milk as needed to reach the desired consistency. Add salt to taste.

Transfer the pudding to serving bowls and serve immediately or chill before serving.

> **If you like, serve the pudding with a splash of nut milk.**
>
> For another dessert that uses avocado to make a creamy, sweet treat, try Coconut-Lime "Ice Cream" (page 266).
>
> For more about why avocado is good for you, see page 49.

Grilled Peaches Kissed
with Cinnamon and Chocolate

SERVE THESE SIMPLY DELICIOUS PEACHES ON THEIR OWN OR, FOR a special occasion, alongside a scoop of Honey Ice Cream (page 265).

SERVES 6

2 tablespoons coconut palm sugar (see page 82)

1 teaspoon ground cinnamon

3 medium-size ripe peaches (freestone variety, if available), halved and pitted

Organic neutral-flavored oil, such as grapeseed, as needed

1 ounce/30g grain-sweetened semisweet or bittersweet chocolate, cut into 6 chunks, or 1 ounce/30 g grain-sweetened chocolate chips

Prepare a grill to medium-high and lightly oil the grate.

In a small bowl, combine the sugar and cinnamon. Slice a thin piece off the round side of each peach so that the finished peach will sit flat, pit side up. Brush all the cut sides of the peaches lightly with the oil, then sprinkle with the sugar mixture.

Grill the peaches, pit side down, until lightly charred, 2 to 3 minutes. Turn the peaches and place a chunk of chocolate or a few chocolate chips in the cavity. Cover and grill until the bottom is lightly charred and the chocolate is slightly melted, 2 to 3 minutes. Serve warm.

> **To make this recipe vegan and dairy-free, use vegan chocolate.**

Buckwheat Crepes with Oranges and Gingered Agave

THIS IS AN AMAZINGLY EASY YET IMPRESSIVE DESSERT THAT YOU CAN enjoy year round—just change out the fruit for whatever is in season. Use mixed berries in the spring and summer; persimmons or pears in the fall; and apples, oranges, or tangerines in the winter.

Perhaps even better, the buckwheat helps stabilize your blood sugar, so it's a nicely balanced dessert.

SERVES 4

$^1/_2$ teaspoon finely grated fresh ginger

5 tablespoons/75 mL raw agave nectar, divided (see note)

2 small seedless oranges

$^2/_3$ cup/160 mL grass-fed organic milk, unsweetened nut milk, or coconut milk (see note on page 108)

$^1/_3$ cup/40 g buckwheat flour

2 tablespoons arrowroot powder

2 large organic, pasture-raised, or antibiotic-free eggs

2 tablespoons organic neutral-flavored oil, such as grapeseed, plus more as needed

$^1/_2$ teaspoon pure vanilla extract

Pinch of fine sea salt

In a small saucepan over medium-high heat, combine the ginger and $^1/_4$ cup/60 mL of the agave. Bring to a boil, remove from the heat, and set aside for at least 10 minutes.

Meanwhile, use a knife to cut the peel from the oranges. Cut the remaining fruit into small bite-size pieces and set aside.

In a blender, combine the milk, flour, arrowroot, eggs, oil, vanilla, salt, and the remaining 1 tablespoon of agave and blend until smooth, scraping down the jar as necessary.

Warm a small, nonstick skillet over medium-low heat and lightly brush it with oil. Add 2 tablespoons of the crepe batter, tilting the skillet to spread the batter in a thin, even layer. Cook on one side only until the center is cooked through and the edges are browned, 1 to 1½ minutes. Loosen the crepe with a spatula and invert onto a parchment paper- or paper towel–lined plate. Stir the batter and repeat, brushing the skillet with more oil as needed and layering the finished crepes between parchment paper or paper towels (you should have at least twelve crepes).

To serve, fold the crepes into quarters, browned side out, and arrange them on plates or a platter. Arrange the fruit on top, drizzle with the gingered agave syrup, and serve.

> **If you like, you can replace the agave nectar with raw honey.**

Olive Oil Cake with Syrupy Fresh Fruit

MOIST, RICH, AND RUSTIC, THIS CAKE IS DEEPLY SATISFYING AND MAKES for a perfect end to a similarly rustic meal—try it after Rosemary-Stuffed Grilled Trout (page 233) or Moroccan-Marinated Chicken Breasts (page 238). Without the fruit, it also makes a nice tea cake, served as part of a breakfast or brunch, or as a snack.

MAKES ONE 9-INCH/25 CM CAKE

1 cup/240 mL organic extra-virgin olive oil, plus more as needed

1 lemon

¾ cup/180 mL grass-fed organic plain yogurt

1 teaspoon pure vanilla extract

1½ cups/200 g brown rice flour

¾ cup/120 g organic cornmeal

2¼ teaspoons aluminum-free baking powder

1 teaspoon fine sea salt

4 large organic, pasture-raised, or antibiotic-free eggs

1¹/₂ cups/225 g coconut palm sugar (see page 82), divided

1 medium-size peach, pitted and cut into ¹/₄-inch/0.65 cm slices

2 medium-size apricots, pitted and cut into ¹/₄-inch/0.65 cm slices

2 medium-size plums, pitted and cut into ¹/₄-inch/0.65 cm slices

Preheat the oven to 350°F/175°C. Brush a 9-inch/25 cm cake pan with oil. Line the bottom of the pan with parchment paper and brush the parchment with oil.

Zest the lemon. Juice the lemon to yield 1 tablespoon of juice. In a small bowl, combine the lemon zest, lemon juice, yogurt, and vanilla. In a medium bowl, combine the flour, cornmeal, baking powder, and salt. Set both bowls aside separately.

Using an electric mixer on high speed, beat the eggs and 1¹/₄ cups/185 g of the sugar until light and frothy, about 5 minutes. Add the oil, beating on medium speed until combined. With the mixer running, add the dry ingredients in three batches, alternating with the yogurt. Transfer the batter to the prepared pan and bake until a toothpick inserted into the center comes out clean, about 50 minutes.

Meanwhile, in a medium bowl, combine the peaches, apricots, and plums with the remaining ¹/₄ cup/35 g of sugar. Set aside for at least 1 hour at room temperature, stirring occasionally.

Let the cake cool in the pan on a wire rack 10 minutes, then unmold and return to the rack to cool completely.

Serve the cake with the fruit mixture spooned on top.

Flourless Chocolate Hazelnut Cake

HERE'S A SUPER SIMPLE CAKE THAT TAKES ONLY ABOUT TEN MINUTES to get into the oven, yet once baked, it's special enough to be company worthy. If you serve it room temperature, it'll have a puddinglike consistency. If you chill it before serving, it'll be fudgy. Either way, it's so rich, one thin slice is thoroughly satisfying.

MAKES ONE 9-INCH/25 CM CAKE

6 ounces/170 g unsalted grass-fed organic butter, cut into 12 or 16 pieces, plus more as needed

12 ounces/340 g grain-sweetened chocolate chips

6 large organic, pasture-raised, or antibiotic-free eggs

1 cup/150 g coconut palm sugar (see page 82)

¼ cup/60 mL grass-fed organic milk or unsweetened nut milk

1½ cups/125 g hazelnut meal or hazelnut flour (see note)

½ teaspoon fine sea salt

¼ cup/30 g chopped hazelnuts, toasted (see note on page 122)

Preheat the oven to 350°F/175°F. Butter a 9-inch/25 cm springform pan and line the bottom of the pan with parchment paper. Wrap the outside of the pan with foil, covering the bottom and up the sides with two layers so that it is watertight.

In a medium saucepan over high heat, bring 1 inch/2.5 cm of water to a boil. Lower the heat to a simmer. Set a bowl over the boiling water so that it fits tightly—the bottom of the bowl should not touch the water. Combine the chocolate and butter in the bowl and stir occasionally just until it melts. Remove the bowl from over the boiling water and set aside.

In a large bowl, whisk together the eggs, sugar, and milk. Add the melted chocolate and whisk until smooth. Whisk in the hazelnut meal and salt. Transfer the mixture to the prepared springform pan, place the pan in a larger roasting pan, and pour enough very hot tap water into the roasting pan to come halfway up the sides of the springform pan. Place the entire setup in the oven and bake until a tester comes out clean, about $1\frac{1}{2}$ hours.

Remove the springform pan from the roasting pan, transfer to a wire rack, and let cool to room temperature. Chill if desired.

Run a knife around the sides of the pan to loosen the cake, then unmold. Cut the cake into wedges and serve cold or room temperature, sprinkled with the chopped hazelnuts.

You can find hazelnut flour, sometimes called hazelnut meal, at some supermarkets and at most natural foods supermarkets. You can also make your own by using a food processor to finely grind toasted, skinned hazelnuts.

BASICS

HOW TO COOK GRAINS

HOW TO COOK RICE

HOW TO COOK BEANS

CLEAN CRANBERRY SAUCE

THREE-APPLE APPLESAUCE

DASHI

ROASTED GARLIC OIL

FOUR FLAVORED BUTTERS

How to Cook Grains

THE TRADITIONAL METHOD FOR COOKING GRAINS CAN SOMETIMES BE challenging because, as with cooking rice, the object of the game is to add enough water so that it's perfectly cooked off at the same time that the grains are perfectly tender. Making matters more complex is the fact that different grains need different cooking times and, therefore, different amounts of water. Bottom line—it's hard to use the traditional method and have grains turn out great every time.

So, instead of guessing, I prefer to cook grains the same way I cook pasta—using plenty of water, letting the grains boil in that water, and then draining off the water in a sieve or colander when the grains are done to my liking. No stress and perfectly cooked grains every time!

MAKES 2 TO 4 CUPS (WEIGHT DEPENDS ON THE TYPE OF GRAIN)

1 cup whole grains, such as amaranth, barley, bulgur, couscous, farro, groats, kamut, millet, quinoa, spelt, or wheat berries (weight depends on the type of grain)
Pinch of fine sea salt (optional)

Place the grains in a medium bowl or saucepan, cover with water by 1 to 2 inches, and soak in the refrigerator for at least an hour or up to 36 hours.

Drain the grains, transfer them to a medium saucepan, and add the salt (if using) and 3 cups/710 mL of fresh water. Bring to a boil over medium-high heat and lower the heat to a simmer. Cover partially and cook until the grains are tender, 5 to 20 minutes for smaller grains, such as quinoa and amaranth, and up to $1\frac{1}{2}$ hours for larger ones, such as barley and wheat berries. Drain well and serve as desired.

> **Soaking time, saucepan size, grain type, and other variables will affect the** cooking time. Use this recipe as a guide, experiment, and find what works for you.
>
> Some grains, such as quinoa and amaranth, don't soften completely with cooking, but instead have a delicate crunch that pops in your mouth.
>
> For more about the benefits of soaking grains before cooking, see page 52.

How to Cook Rice

IN CONTRAST TO MY PREFERRED GRAIN COOKING METHOD, I USE A traditional method to cook rice. Why do I like a traditional method for rice and a pasta method for grains? Because water and cooking times are variable for the different grains, whereas they're pretty much consistent for all types of brown and wild rice.

That said, the pasta method will work, too. If you want to go that route, see page 275 for details.

MAKES 2$\frac{1}{2}$ TO 3 CUPS (WEIGHT DEPENDS ON THE TYPE OF RICE)

1 cup brown rice, wild rice, or brown and wild rice blend
   (weight depends on the type of rice)
Pinch of fine sea salt (optional)

Place the rice in a medium bowl or saucepan, cover with water by 1 to 2 inches, and soak in the refrigerator for at least an hour or up to 36 hours.

Drain the rice, transfer it to a medium saucepan, and add the salt (if using) and 1$\frac{3}{4}$ cups/415 mL of fresh water. Bring to a boil over medium-high heat and lower the heat to a simmer. Cover and cook until the rice is tender and the liquid is absorbed, 30 to 35 minutes.

> **Soaking time, saucepan size, and other variables will affect how much** water is needed, as well the cooking time. Use this recipe as a guide, experiment, and find what works for you.
>
> For more about the benefits of soaking rice before cooking, see page 83.

How to Cook Beans

BEANS ARE COOKED BY FIRST SOAKING, THEN BOILING UNTIL THEY ARE tender. But don't drain off the cooking liquid as you would do for grains. That liquid is good for storing the beans, plus it can be useful in recipes. If you're making a bean soup, for example, using some or all of the bean cooking liquid instead of water is a great way to add extra flavor and texture to your soup.

MAKES 2$\frac{1}{4}$ TO 3 CUPS (DRAINED) (WEIGHT DEPENDS ON THE TYPE OF BEAN)

**1 cup dried beans, rinsed and picked over
(weight depends on the type of bean)
Pinch of fine sea salt (optional)**

Place the beans in a medium bowl or saucepan, cover with water by 1 to 2 inches, and soak in the refrigerator for at least 8 hours or up to 36 hours (see notes).

Drain the beans, transfer them to a medium saucepan, and add the salt (if using) and 3 cups/710 mL of fresh water. Bring to a boil over medium-high heat and lower the heat to a simmer. Partially cover and cook until the beans are tender but not falling apart, 20 to 50 minutes depending on the type of bean.

> **Adzuki beans, mung beans, and lentils don't need to be soaked.**
> Soaking time, saucepan size, bean type, and other variables will affect the cooking time. Use this recipe as a guide, experiment, and find what works for you.
> For more about the benefits of soaking beans before cooking, see page 58.

Clean Cranberry Sauce

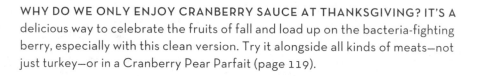

WHY DO WE ONLY ENJOY CRANBERRY SAUCE AT THANKSGIVING? IT'S A delicious way to celebrate the fruits of fall and load up on the bacteria-fighting berry, especially with this clean version. Try it alongside all kinds of meats—not just turkey—or in a Cranberry Pear Parfait (page 119).

MAKES ABOUT 2$\frac{1}{2}$ CUPS/590 ML

1 (12-ounce/340 g) bag fresh cranberries

1 cup/240 mL coconut nectar (see page 82)

1 teaspoon finely grated fresh ginger

Zest of 1 medium-size orange

$\frac{1}{4}$ teaspoon fine sea salt

In a medium saucepan over medium-high heat, combine the cranberries, coconut nectar, ginger, orange zest, salt, and $\frac{2}{3}$ cup/160 mL of water. Bring to a boil, lower the heat to a simmer, and cook, stirring occasionally, until most of the cranberries have popped, about 10 minutes.

Remove from the heat and let cool to room temperature, then refrigerate until thoroughly chilled.

Three-Apple Applesauce

WITH TART AND SWEET, SOFT AND CRISP APPLES, THIS SAUCE HAS a wonderful balance of taste and texture.

MAKES ABOUT 4$\frac{1}{4}$ CUPS/1.1 L

2 tablespoons freshly squeezed lemon juice (from 1 or 2 lemons)

2 medium-size sweet-crisp apples, such as Fuji

2 medium-size tart apples, such as Granny Smith

2 medium-size soft-textured apples, such as Jonathan

$\frac{1}{2}$ cup/120 mL coconut nectar (see page 82)

$\frac{1}{8}$ teaspoon ground cinnamon

$\frac{1}{8}$ teaspoon ground allspice

In a large saucepan or small stockpot, combine the lemon juice with 1 cup/240 mL of water. Peel, core, and cut the apples into $\frac{1}{2}$-inch/1.25 cm dice, stirring them into the lemon water as you go to prevent browning. Add the coconut nectar, cinnamon, and allspice and bring to a boil over medium-high heat. Lower the heat to a simmer, cover, and cook, stirring occasionally, until the apples are soft and mostly translucent, 10 to 15 minutes (doneness will vary depending on the type of apples).

Remove from the heat and use a potato masher or the back of a large spoon to gently mash the apples to the desired consistency. Set aside to cool to room temperature, then refrigerate until thoroughly chilled.

Dashi

DASHI IS A TRADITIONAL STOCK USED IN MANY JAPANESE SOUPS, including Morning Miso Soup (page 126), and using it in your cooking is a great way to get minerals and chlorophyll from sea vegetables.

The easiest way to make dashi is to buy it granulated or instant from an Asian market or well-stocked natural foods store. It's easy to make from scratch, though, and the ingredients can be found at those same stores.

MAKES 6 CUPS/1.4 L

2 3-inch/8 cm pieces kombu (dried kelp) (see note)
1 cup/5 g *katsuobushi* (dried bonito flakes) (see note)

In a medium saucepan over medium heat, combine 6 cups/1.4 L of cold water and the kombu. Bring to a boil, then remove from the heat and discard the kombu. Stir in the *katsuobushi,* cover and let steep 3 minutes.

Strain the mixture though a fine-mesh sieve. Use immediately or let cool to room temperature, then chill in the refrigerator.

> **You can find kombu and *katsuobushi* in the Asian or ethnic food sections** at some supermarkets and most natural foods supermarkets, and at Asian markets.

Roasted Garlic Oil

ROASTED GARLIC OIL IS SO EASY TO MAKE, AND SUCH A GOOD SOURCE of sulfur and polyphenols, that you'll never be tempted to buy a bottle again.

MAKES 1 CUP/240 ML

1 cup/240 mL organic neutral-flavored oil, such as grapeseed
20 garlic cloves

In a small saucepan over very low heat, combine the oil and garlic and cook until the garlic is dark golden brown, 45 to 50 minutes. Let cool to room temperature, then strain.

WAYS TO ENJOY ROASTED GARLIC OIL

- Drizzle it over soups (for example, Cauliflower Soup, page 155).
- Drizzle it on grilled or roasted meats, chicken, fish, or vegetables.
- Toss it with pasta and grated Parmesan cheese.
- Brush it onto flatbread or pizza.
- Serve it as a dip with crusty bread.

Four Flavored Butters

IF YOU'VE EVER MIXED TOGETHER BUTTER AND GARLIC TO MAKE GARLIC bread, you've made a flavored butter—also known as compound butter. Flavored butters are useful to have around because they can turn an otherwise ordinary chicken breast, fish fillet, steak, chop, or vegetable dish into something special. See below for more ideas.

For a fifth flavored butter, check out Grass-Fed Rib Eyes with Garlic-Chive Butter (page 256).

MAKES $^1/_2$ CUP/115 G

4 ounces/115 g unsalted grass-fed organic butter, at room temperature
Flavoring ingredients (see sidebar)
Fine sea salt to taste

In the bowl of a food processor, combine the butter and flavoring ingredients and pulse to combine, scraping down the bowl as necessary. Add fine sea salt to taste.

FLAVORING INGREDIENTS

Herb Butter
• Add 2 tablespoons of coarsely chopped fresh sage, 1 tablespoon of coarsely chopped fresh rosemary, and 1 tablespoon of fresh thyme leaves to the food processor with the butter.

Sun-Dried Tomato Butter
• Add 2 tablespoons of coarsely chopped sun-dried tomatoes plus 2 tablespoons of coarsely chopped fresh basil.

Lemon-Lime Butter
• Add the zest of 2 lemons and 4 limes.

Blue Cheese Butter
• Add ¼ cup/30 g of crumbled blue cheese and 1 small coarsely chopped shallot.

WAYS TO ENJOY FLAVORED BUTTERS

• Use them to make Grilled Corn with Flavored Grass-Fed Butter (page 185).
• Place a pat on a just-cooked, simply prepared chicken breast, fish fillet, steak, or chop—the butter will melt into the meat, flavoring it.
• Toss a pat or two with steamed or blanched vegetables.
• Off the heat, stir a pat into sautéed meats or vegetables.
• Toss them into just-cooked rice, grains, or beans.
• Spread them on bread, then toast—for a twist on garlic bread.

CHAPTER 10

Resources, Recommendations, and Sample Menus

This is a compendium of my favorite websites, books, films, apps, and other tools that can help support and further a clean-eating lifestyle. Some provide information, some provide access to useful ingredients and equipment, and some provide motivation and inspiration.

Clean-Eating
Ingredients and Equipment

FARMERS' MARKETS, FOOD CO-OPS, AND CSAS

Cooperative Grocer
http://www.cooperativegrocer.coop/coops—
A user-friendly website with a database of food
co-ops searchable by state.

Eat Well Guide
www.eatwellguide.org—Provides resources for
farmers' markets, CSAs, and food co-ops. You can
also search by zip code to find sustainable bak-
eries, coffee shops, butchers, and even food trucks.

Local Harvest
www.localharvest.org—A list of farmers'
markets, food co-ops, and CSAs all over
America.

National Sustainable Agriculture Information Service
https://attra.ncat.org/attra-pub/local_food/
search.php—A directory of sustainable food
organizations, farmers' markets, CSAs, and food
co-ops that's searchable by state.

ORGANICS

Shiloh Farms
www.shilohfarms.com—A one-stop shop for all
your organic needs, including whole and
sprouted flours, beans, dried fruits, and even
grass-fed meats.

Sun Organic Farms
www.sunorganicfarms.com—An all-organic
online market offering everything from raw
honey to salsa to pet food.

The Organic Pages
www.theorganicpages.com—Search by ingredient to find multiple retailers that sell what you're
looking for, online and in-store, and determine
the best way to get it.

SUSTAINABLE MEAT, DAIRY, AND SEAFOOD

Eat Wild
www.eatwild.com—A state-by-state database
and online retailer for finding local, grass-fed
meat, eggs, and dairy.

Real Milk
www.realmilk.com—A campaign of the Weston
A. Price foundation, this site provides information on where to buy unpasturized and pasture-
fed milk by state.

U.S. Wellness Meats
www.grasslandbeef.com—An online source for
grass-fed beef, bison, lamb, dairy, and even rab-
bit, along with wild-caught seafood. Raw and
organic ice cream is also available for order.

Vital Choice
www.vitalchoice.com—For sustainable and
wild seafood.

WHOLE AND SPROUTED GRAINS AND FLOURS

Arrowhead Mills

www.arrowheadmills.com—Organic grains and flours, including spelt flour, buckwheat flour, and many gluten-free options.

Bob's Red Mill

www.bobsredmill.com—High-quality stone-milled flours, oats, and grains, including almond meal, hazelnut meal, amaranth flour, flaxseeds, wheat bran, hulled barley, and polenta.

To Your Health Sprouted Flour Company

www.organicsproutedflour.net—Sprouted grains and flours, including amaranth, millet, quinoa, and lentils.

NUTS, SEEDS, AND OILS

Arrowhead Mills

www.arrowheadmills.com—Organic and all-natural nut and seed butters without added sugars.

La Tourangelle

www.latourangelle.com—High-quality, artisan oils, including expeller-pressed grapeseed oil.

Maranatha

www.maranathafoods.com—Nut and seed butters without trans fats, hydrogenated oils, or preservatives.

Raw Nuts and Seeds

www.rawnutsandseeds.com—Raw nuts and seeds.

Spectrum Organics

www.spectrumorganics.com—An extensive line of high-quality oils, including flax and coconut.

BEANS AND LEGUMES

Bulk Foods

www.bulkfoods.com—Dried beans and legumes in bulk.

Eden Foods

www.edenfoods.com—A great line of dried beans as well as BPA-free and very low-sodium organic canned beans.

ASIAN FOODS

Asian Food Grocer

www.asianfoodgrocer.com—Asian foods and condiments, including seaweed and other sea vegetables (*arame*, nori, wakame, etc.), along with miso, dashi, wasabi paste, and pickled ginger.

Eden Foods

www.edenfoods.com—Another source for miso, dashi, wakame, wasabi paste, pickled ginger, nori, dulse, and *arame*.

SPICES, TEAS, AND HONEY

Frontier Natural Products Co-op

www.frontiercoop.com—An extensive line of organic seasonings, spices, and herbs. Also bulk items and a nice selection of Fair Trade teas.

Numi Tea

www.numitea.com—An assortment of pure organic and Fair Trade teas and iced teas.

Really Raw Honey

www.reallyrawhoney.com—100 percent raw honey as well as fermented raw honey.

Rishi Tea

www.rishi-tea.com—Organic and fair-trade certified loose leaf teas.

The Spice Hunter
www.spicehunter.com—100 percent organic spices, sea salts, and spice blends.

SWEETENERS
Coconut Secret
www.coconutsecret.com—Coconut nectar.

Navitas Naturals
www.navitasnaturals.com—Organic coconut palm sugar.

CULTURED/ FERMENTED FOODS
Cultures for Health
www.culturesforhealth.com—A wide array of raw cultured vegetables, juices, and condiments as well as starters to make your own.

Kombucha Kamp
www.kombuchakamp.com—Make-your-own *kombucha* kits.

Lifeway
www.lifeway.net—Organic kefir.

Rejuvenative Foods
www.rejuvenative.com—Raw sauerkraut, live ketchup, salsa, and other fermented and cultured vegetables.

JUICES AND JUICE CLEANSES
All of these resources will deliver juices directly to your home or office.

Blueprint
www.blueprintcleanse.com

Cooler Cleanse
www.coolercleanse.com

Organic Avenue
www.organicavenue.com

RAW CACAO POWDER
My Natural Market
www.mynaturalmarket.com—Find raw cacao powder here, along with an assortment of other products.

SPROUTED TORTILLAS, BUNS, BREADS, PASTAS
Food For Life
www.foodforlife.com—A full product line of sprouted goods as well as a fair selection of gluten-free products.

WATER FILTRATION
Brita
www.brita.com—Although not as efficient as reverse osmosis, this is the most affordable way to get filtered water. Offers filtration systems for the sink, as well as water pitchers with replaceable filters.

H$_2$O Distributors
www.h2odistributors.com—Reverse osmosis water filtration systems for your counter, under the sink, and in your shower. They also have self-standing filters.

Information and Education

MOBILE AND ONLINE SHOPPING AND RESTAURANT GUIDES

Blue Ocean Institute

www.blueocean.org—A color-coded guide to sustainable seafood with information for more than ninety different species.

Clean Plates App

www.app.cleanplates.com—Plug in your destination or current location to find the healthiest and tastiest restaurants close by. Currently available in New York, Los Angeles, and Austin.

Dirty Dozen App

A free portable guide to the Environmental Working Group's list of which fruits and vegetables have the most pesticide exposure and therefore are the most important to buy organic.

FoodpH App

This reference guide provides acidity levels for any food to help make your day more alkaline.

Fooducate App

Scan barcodes into this free app to see how different products rate nutrition-wise, plus learn healthier alternatives. You can also compare health properties of different products against one another.

Good Guide App

This free app allows you to scan a product's bar code to reveal its nutrition value and whether the company is socially responsible. There are over 120,000 items in the database.

Great Health 24/7

www.greathealth247.com/ph-acid-alkaline-food-chart.html—An informative website on what it means for foods to be alkalizing or acidic. Acid/alkaline food charts can be found here as well.

Marine Stewardship Council App

www.msc.com—A global organization working with fisheries, seafood companies, scientists, conservation groups, and the public to identify and promote sustainable seafood, and an app that helps you find it.

Seafood Watch App

www.seafoodwatch.org—Learn which seafood is best to buy, and which is best to avoid to maintain a wild, diverse, and healthy ocean ecosystem. Track the names of restaurants and stores in the United States where you've found sustainable seafood and see where other users have tracked as well.

INFORMATIONAL AND CAUSE-BASED WEBSITES

Clean Plates

www.cleanplates.com—Find the healthiest, tastiest, and most sustainable restaurants in New York City, Los Angeles, and Austin as well as a whole host of interesting articles and recipes.

Coconut Oil

www.coconutoil.com—Research on the health benefits of coconut oil.

Cornucopia Institute

www.cornucopia.org—Promotes economic justice for family-scale farming.

The Environmental Working Group

www.ewg.org—A helpful resource for scientific data on topics ranging from mining, fishing, oil, and gas to toxins, chemicals, and safe cleaning tips for your home.

Farm Sanctuary

www.farmsanctuary.org—Farm Sanctuary was founded to combat and educate people on the abuses of factory farming. The sanctuary works to protect farm animals from cruelty and to inspire change in the way society views and treats farm animals.

Food and Water Watch

www.foodandwaterwatch.org—Works to ensure our food, water, and fish products are safe, accessible, and sustainably produced. A good resource for safety information on these products.

Fungi Perfecti

www.fungi.com—Learn all about medicinal and gourmet mushrooms at this site, including how to grow and culture them. Starter kits can be purchased from the site as well.

Jamie Oliver

www.jamieoliver.com—All about Jamie's food revolution.

The Organic Consumer's Association

www.organicconsumers.org—Provides articles that campaign for health, justice, and sustainability and deal with crucial issues of food safety, industrial agriculture, genetic engineering, children's health, corporate accountability, Fair Trade, environmental sustainability, and other topics.

The Organic Pages

www.theorganicpages.com—Find information on all things organic.

Slow Food

www.slowfood.com—This organization promotes the practice of small-scale and sustainable production of quality foods while defending biodiversity. Also includes a schedule of Slow Food events.

Take Part

www.takepart.com—Inspiring content on topics like education, food, animals, water, and the environment.

Wild Fermentation

www.wildfermentation.com—This website is dedicated to the benefits of fermented foods, including information on how to ferment at home.

The World's Healthiest Foods

www.whfoods.com—A great resource for specific nutritional information, such as what percentage of spinach is made of protein and what vitamins are most prominent in kale.

MEDICAL WEBSITES

The American Academy of Environmental Medicine

www.aaemonline.org—This group of physicians is interested in how our environment impacts our health.

The American Board of Integrative Holistic Medicine

www.holisticboard.org—Learn about holistic medicine and/or find a holistic practitioner near you, that is, a physician that focuses on healing the whole person, body, mind, and spirit.

American Holistic Medical Association

www.holisticmedicine.org—Another resource for finding a holistic physician.

The Institute for Functional Medicine

www.functionalmedicine.org—Functional medicine practitioners focus on a patient-centered approach rather than a disease-centered approach, so that they can address the needs of the person as a whole instead of simply focusing on individual symptoms.

FILMS

Big River
Travel down the Mississippi River in this documentary and discover how fertilizers and pesticides have changed our water systems.

Dirt: The Movie
This documentary showcases how various groups have come together to save our soil.

Fat, Sick, and Nearly Dead
After Joe Cross brought himself back to health with a sixty-day juice cleanse, he travels across the country to introduce others to the power of juicing.

Food Inc.
A documentary that explores how factory farms and the food industry have had damaging effects on our health and environment.

Forks over Knives
Based on the research of two food scientists, this documentary reveals how our dependency on modern processed foods as well as animal products has led to unprecedented rates of obesity, diabetes, and heart disease.

The Future of Food
This documentary reveals the unappetizing truth about genetically modified foods.

Killer at Large
Demonstrates why obesity is America's greatest threat.

King Corn
This documentary follows corn, America's number one field crop, from the ground to our food supply.

The Price of Sugar
A look into sugarcane plantations that raises an important question about where the products we consume originate and at what human cost they are produced.

Super Size Me
Follow director Morgan Spurlock as he eats only at McDonald's for thirty days and documents the effects on his well-being.

What's on Your Plate
A kid-friendly film that follows two eleven-year-olds as they learn how food systems work and they explore their place on the food chain.

BOOKS

Clean Plates Restaurant Guides by Jared Koch
A restaurant guidebook for the healthiest, tastiest, and most sustainable restaurants in Manhattan, Brooklyn, and Los Angeles.

Blood Sugar Solution by Dr. Mark Hyman
Dr. Hyman demonstrates that by controlling our insulin levels we can not only lose weight, but also combat a multitude of different illnesses and diseases.

The China Study: The Most Comprehensive Study of Nutrition Ever Conducted and the Startling Implications for Diet, Weight Loss, and Long-term Health by T. Colin Campbell and Thomas M. Campbell II
From extensive work in China and Taiwan, this study demonstrates the definitive link between nutrition and illness and shows that reducing animal-based foods is the first step for optimum health.

Diet for a Small Planet by Frances Moore Lappé
One of the first books to criticize our food system and emphasize a plant-based diet.

Fast Food Nation: The Dark Side of the All-American Meal by Eric Schlosser
An inside look at our country's fast-food operations.

Food Rules by Michael Pollan
A simple set of rules for wise eating.

Omnivore's Dilemma by Michael Pollan
Pollan examines our foods' origins by following three meals—from an industrial farm, from an organic farm, and from a hunting and foraging expedition.

Natural Health, Natural Medicine by Andrew Weil
This is Dr. Weil's guide for how to maintain overall wellness and treat common ailments, including simple recipes, home remedies, and practical tips.

The New Glucose Revolution: Low GI Eating Made Easy by Jennie Brand-Miller, Kaye Foster-Powell, and Philippa Sandall
This book examines how to choose low-GI foods so that we feel fuller longer and our energy levels are maintained.

Nourishing Traditions by Sally Fallon
Part of Weston A. Price's Foundation, Fallon argues that animal fats and cholesterol are actually necessary for good health as long as they are responsibly sourced. She provides tips for enjoying more healthy saturated fats and lots of recipes.

Nourishing Wisdom: A Mind-Body Approach to Nutrition and Well-Being by Marc David
David discusses the necessity of examining the emotional and spiritual aspects of our lives in order to be truly nourished.

Sugar Blues by William Duffy
Duffy shows how simply reducing sugar in our diet can possibly save our lives.

The 3 Season Diet by John Douillard
An easy-to-read guide on seasonal eating.

Your Body's Many Cries for Water: You Are Not Sick, You Are Thirsty! by Fereydoon Batmanghelidj
Explains how dehydration could be the cause of stress, chronic pains, and many other degenerative diseases.

What to Eat by Marion Nestle
Nestle takes us through the supermarket, explaining and investigating the issues surrounding food labels and health claims.

The Whole Soy Story by Kaayla T. Daniel, PhD
An exposé that reveals the not-so-healthy truth about soy.

Sample Menus

These menus are designed to help you make this book's clean recipes, and clean eating in general, part of your life. They include a weeklong menu for getting started, a weeklong menu for maintenance, a five-day menu for cleansing, and a menu for a weekend with guests. Follow them exactly, or use them as inspiration for a clean-eating lifestyle—it's up to you.

MENU 1/GETTING STARTED

This weeklong menu is designed to help you ease your way into clean eating. Remember to stay active and drink lots of water throughout the day. Tea and 100 percent fruit and vegetable juices are other good beverage choices.

DAY 1	DAY 2	DAY 3
BREAKFAST Two eggs, any style Avocado on sprouted toast	**BREAKFAST** Two eggs, any style Sautéed spinach	**BREAKFAST** Oatmeal with a scoop of almond butter
LUNCH Leafy green salad with salmon Brown rice Handful of berries	**LUNCH** Grilled organic chicken Sweet Potato Salad with Scallions and Seaweed (page 172)	**LUNCH** Trout fillet Leafy green salad Brown rice
SNACK Hummus (page 143) with handful of non-GMO tortilla chips	**SNACK** Homemade trail mix of raw nuts, dark cacao nibs, and dried fruit	**SNACK** Kale Chips (page 143)
DINNER Grass-fed steak Braised Greens with Nori (page 198)	**DINNER** Baked White Fish (page 236) Steamed asparagus	**DINNER** Chicken and Pepper Paprikash (page 237) Roasted cauliflower
DESSERT Organic ice cream (or nut or coconut milk ice cream)	**DESSERT** Fruit drizzled with coconut nectar or other natural sweetener	**DESSERT** Cherry Almond Oatmeal Cookies (page 259)

DAY 4	DAY 5	DAY 6	DAY 7
BREAKFAST	**BREAKFAST**	**BREAKFAST**	**BREAKFAST**
Comforting Quinoa Cereal (page 129)	Fruit with yogurt or kefir and Vanilla Pecan Granola with Steel-Cut Oats (page 117)	Glass of water with juice of $\frac{1}{2}$ lemon Two eggs, sunny-side up or poached Sautéed spinach	Glass of water with juice of $\frac{1}{2}$ lemon Oatmeal with berries
LUNCH	**LUNCH**	**LUNCH**	**LUNCH**
Organic turkey salad with lemon juice and olive oil Grapefruit	Mixed vegetables with beans and quinoa	Black Bean "Burgers" (page 227) Crisped Cucumbers with Cilantro (page 169)	Tuna salad with tahini dressing Carrot and celery sticks
SNACK	**SNACK**	**SNACK**	**SNACK**
Sliced apple with nut butter	Roasted Eggplant Dip (page 138) with carrot sticks	Handful tortilla chips with guacamole	Banana Almond Kefir Shake (page 112)
DINNER	**DINNER**	**DINNER**	**DINNER**
Lavender Roasted Chicken with Roasted Yams (page 240) Broccoli with Olive Oil and Lemon (page 190)	Grass-Fed Rib Eyes with Garlic-Chive Butter (page 256) Caramelized Roasted Endive (page 190)	Arugula with Chicken and Blueberries (page 183) Steamed carrots	Flank Steak and Chimichurri Salad (page 184)
DESSERT	**DESSERT**	**DESSERT**	**DESSERT**
Chocolate Avocado Pudding (page 267)	Sliced banana with cinnamon and coconut nectar	A couple of pieces of dark chocolate (at least 70% cacao)	Cherry Almond Oatmeal Cookies (page 259)

MENU 2/MAINTENANCE

This menu is designed to assist you in carrying on a clean lifestyle, focusing on whole, high-quality, full-flavored ingredients that will leave you satisfied. Remember, the aim isn't perfection and these menus don't need to be followed exactly—they're a guide to what a whole, balanced day of clean eating looks like.

Try to begin as many mornings as possible with an alkalizing glass of water with lemon juice. Continue to drink plenty of water throughout the day and drink tea as you please. One hundred percent juice is another good option, but try to enjoy juices that aren't just fruit—in other words, enjoy juices that include some vegetables in there as well. And notice how alcohol and caffeine make you feel. At some point, it might be a good idea to begin reducing them, or switching to decaf once in a while.

DAY 1	DAY 2	DAY 3
BREAKFAST	**BREAKFAST**	**BREAKFAST**
Glass of water with juice of $^1/_2$ lemon Oatmeal with kefir and berries	Glass of water with juice of $^1/_2$ lemon Morning Miso Soup (page 126)	Glass of water with juice of $^1/_2$ lemon Two eggs, any style Half an avocado
LUNCH	**LUNCH**	**LUNCH**
Salmon Brown rice Sautéed greens	Grass-fed steak Leafy green salad	Mixed vegetables and beans on brown rice, millet, or quinoa
SNACK	**SNACK**	**SNACK**
Basic Berry Smoothie (page 113)	Homemade trail mix of raw nuts and dried fruit	Chocolaty Superfoods Smoothie (page 115)
DINNER	**DINNER**	**DINNER**
Cauliflower Soup with Roasted Garlic Oil (page 113) Arugula with Chicken and Blueberries (page 183)	Roasted Eggplant and Peppers with Parmesan Polenta (page 221) Steamed asparagus	Miso-Glazed Halibut with Daikon and Carrots (page 231) Rainbow Chard and Radicchio Sauté (page 193)
	DESSERT	
	Coconut-Lime "Ice Cream" (page 226)	

DAY 4	DAY 5	DAY 6	DAY 7

BREAKFAST

Glass of water with juice of $1/2$ lemon
Oatmeal with scoop of almond butter

LUNCH

Grilled organic chicken
Quinoa Salad with Arugula and Grapes (page 173)

SNACK

Basic Berry Smoothie (page 113)

DINNER

Beans and Greens Soup (page 157)
Half a baked sweet potato

DESSERT

Chocolate Avocado Pudding (page 267)

BREAKFAST

Glass of water with juice of $1/2$ lemon
Kamut and Brown Rice Breakfast Bowl (page 127)

LUNCH

Cold Vegetable Salad with Almond Butter Sauce (page 179)

SNACK

White Bean Dip with Garlic and Parsley (page 139)
Sliced Cucumber

DINNER

Cauliflower Curry with Chard and Coconut Milk (page 208)
Brown rice

BREAKFAST

Glass of water with juice of $1/2$ lemon
Morning Miso Soup (page 126)

LUNCH

Organic chicken
Spring Slaw (page 167)
Apple

SNACK

Roasted Pecans with Rosemary, Olive Oil, and Sea Salt (page 135)

DINNER

Poached halibut
Sautéed Shaved Brussels Sprouts with Shallots and Almonds (page 192)

BREAKFAST

Glass of water with juice of $1/2$ lemon
Two eggs, sunny-side up or poached
Half an avocado

LUNCH

Kale Salad (page 178)
Tempeh and quinoa

SNACK

Apple slices with almond butter

DINNER

Big Beef Burgers with Grilled Onions and (Sometimes) Blue Cheese Sauce (page 251)
Sweet Potato Oven Fries (page 204)

DESSERT

Grilled Peaches Kissed with Cinnamon and Chocolate (page 268)

MENU 3/CLEANSING

Rejuvenation is important if you've been feeling under the weather, but also if you've been overdoing it physically or mentally or if you've not been eating well. This five-day menu is inspired by the Fifth Precept: To feel better immediately, simply reduce your intake of artificial, chemical-laden processed foods and sugar. It cuts out gluten, dairy, and meat and emphasizes fish, whole grains, vegetables, and fruits. To drink, stick to water, tea, and 100 percent fruit and vegetable juices.

DAY 1

BREAKFAST

Glass of water with juice of $^1/_2$ lemon
Millet oatmeal with citrus fruit

LUNCH

Mustard Greens Salad with Roasted Beets and Toasted Pistachios (page 176)
Simple Soup with Carrots, Parsnips, and Scallions (page 162)

SNACK

Hummus (page 140) with sliced cucumbers and bell peppers

DINNER

Grilled Salmon with Strawberry Avocado Salsa (page 234)
Brown rice

DAY 2

BREAKFAST

Glass of water with juice of $^1/_2$ lemon
Comforting Quinoa Cereal (page 129) (without sweetener or dairy) and berries

LUNCH

Green Bean Succotash with Collards and Black-Eyed Peas (page 186)
Sliced tomato and cucumber

SNACK

Apple with nut butter

DINNER

Thai-Style Mussels with Lemongrass (page 229)
Steamed bok choy

DAY 3

BREAKFAST

Glass of water with juice of $^1/_2$ lemon
Morning Miso Soup (page 126)

LUNCH

Salmon
Brown rice
Steamed spinach with lemon juice

SNACK

Kale Chips (page 143)

DINNER

Raw Pad Thai (page 214)
Quinoa

DAY 4

BREAKFAST
Glass of water with juice of $\frac{1}{2}$ lemon
Millet oatmeal with berries

LUNCH
Grilled fish with olive oil and lemon juice
Sautéed Shaved Brussels Sprouts with
Shallots and Almonds (page 192)

SNACK
Sliced apple with nut butter
or Hummus (page 140)

DINNER
Simple, Satisfying Rice with Tempeh,
Broccoli, and Kale (page 219)

DAY 5

BREAKFAST
Glass of water with juice of $\frac{1}{2}$ lemon
Oatmeal with scoop of almond butter

LUNCH
Beans and Greens Soup (page 157)
Leafy green salad
Handful of berries

SNACK
Half an avocado

DINNER
Millet-Stuffed Acorn Squash (page 218)
Broccoli with Olive Oil and Lemon (page 191)

MENU 4/GUESTS FOR THE WEEKEND

Eating clean doesn't mean sacrificing great meals with company. Here's a weekend's worth of impressing guests while still indulging in clean eating.

FRIDAY

DINNER
Mustard Greens Salad with Roasted Beets and Toasted Pistachios (page 176)
Mom's Meat Loaf with Quinoa (page 254)
Garlic Mashed Butternut Squash (page 202)

DESSERT
Cacao Cherry Brownies (page 261)

BREAKFAST

Apple-Cucumber-Lime Agua Fresca
(page 111)
Huevos Rancheros (page 130)
Citrus salad

LUNCH

Roasted Tomato Soup (page 166)
Green Salad

SNACK

Spiced Mixed Nuts with Dried Fruit
(page 136)

DINNER

Moroccan-Marinated Chicken Breasts with
Wilted Onions (page 238)
Quinoa Salad with Arugula and Grapes
(page 173)
Crisped Cucumbers with Cilantro (page 169)

DESSERT

Olive Oil Cake with Syrupy Fresh Fruit
(page 270)

BRUNCH

Orange, Herb, and Honey Iced Tea (page 0109)
Apple and Applesauce Bran Muffins (page 120)
Potato, Leek, and Spinach Frittata (page 0131)

SNACK

Ratatouille (page 200)
Black and White Sesame Seed Crackers
(page 141)
Kale Chips (page 143)

DINNER

Heirloom Tomatoes with Basil Vinaigrette
(page 170)
Grass-Fed Rib Eyes with Garlic-Chive Butter
(page 256)
Sweet Potato Oven Fries (page 204)

DESSERT

Flourless Chocolate Hazelnut Cake (page 272)

Index